Kerberos
The Definitive Guide

Other computer security resources from O'Reilly

Related titles

802.11 Security

Building Internet Firewalls

Computer Security Basics

Java Cryptography

Java Security

Linux Security Cookbook

Secure Programming Cookbook for C and C++

Network Security with OpenSSL

Practical Unix and Internet Security

Secure Coding: Principles & Practices

Securing Windows NT/2000 Servers for the Internet

SSH, The Secure Shell: The Definitive Guide

Web Security, Privacy, and Commerce

Database Nation

Building Secure Servers with Linux

Security Books Resource Center

security.oreilly.com is a complete catalog of O'Reilly's books on security and related technologies, including sample chapters and code examples.

oreillynet.com is the essential portal for developers interested in open and emerging technologies, including new platforms, programming languages, and operating systems.

Conferences

O'Reilly & Associates bring diverse innovators together to nurture the ideas that spark revolutionary industries. We specialize in documenting the latest tools and systems, translating the innovator's knowledge into useful skills for those in the trenches. Visit *conferences.oreilly.com* for our upcoming events.

O'REILLY NETWORK Safari Bookshelf.

Safari Bookshelf (*safari.oreilly.com*) is the premier online reference library for programmers and IT professionals. Conduct searches across more than 1,000 books. Subscribers can zero in on answers to time-critical questions in a matter of seconds. Read the books on your Bookshelf from cover to cover or simply flip to the page you need. Try it today with a free trial.

Kerberos
The Definitive Guide

Jason Garman

O'REILLY®

Beijing · Cambridge · Farnham · Köln · Sebastopol · Taipei · Tokyo

Kerberos: The Definitive Guide
by Jason Garman

Copyright © 2003 O'Reilly & Associates, Inc. All rights reserved.
Printed in the United States of America.

Published by O'Reilly & Associates, Inc., 1005 Gravenstein Highway North, Sebastopol, CA 95472.

O'Reilly & Associates books may be purchased for educational, business, or sales promotional use. Online editions are also available for most titles (*safari.oreilly.com*). For more information, contact our corporate/institutional sales department: (800) 998-9938 or *corporate@oreilly.com*.

Editor:	Mike Loukides
Production Editor:	Colleen Gorman
Cover Designer:	Ellie Volckhausen
Interior Designer:	David Futato

Printing History:

August 2003:	First Edition.

ISBN: 978-0-596-00403-3
[LSI]

*Dedicated in loving memory
to my grandfather, Harry Stumpff.*

—Jason Garman

Table of Contents

Preface

Kerberos is a sophisticated network authentication system—one that has been publicly available since 1989 and provides that eternal holy grail of network administrators, single-sign-on. Yet, in that intervening decade, documentation on Kerberos has been notably lacking. While many large organizations and academic institutions have enjoyed the benefits of using Kerberos in their networks, the deployment of Kerberos in smaller networks has been severely hampered by a lack of documentation.

I decided to write this book precisely because of this lack of useful documentation. My own experiences with Kerberos are those of extreme frustration as I attempted to decipher the documentation. I found that I had to keep copious notes to keep everything straight. Those notes eventually became the outline of this book.

Today, Microsoft, through its adoption of the latest Kerberos protocol as the preferred authentication mechanism in its Active Directory, has single-handedly driven the use of Kerberos into the majority of the operating-system market that it controls. Thanks to the openness of Kerberos, organizations now can establish cross-platform, single sign-on network environments, giving an end-user one set of credentials that will provide him access to all network resources, regardless of platform or operating system. Yet the workings and benefits of Kerberos remain a mystery to most network administrators. This book aims to pull away the curtain and reveal the magician working behind the scenes.

This book is geared toward the system administrator who wants to establish a single sign-on network using Kerberos. This book is also useful for anyone interested in how Kerberos performs its magic: the first three chapters will be most helpful to these people.

Organization of This Book

Here's a breakdown of how this book is organized:

Chapter 1, *Introduction*
> Provides a gentle introduction to Kerberos, and provides an overview of its history and features. It provides a gentle prologue by bringing you from the reasons for the development of Kerberos at MIT through to the latest versions of the protocol.

Chapter 2, *Pieces of the Puzzle*
> Continues where Chapter 1 left off, presenting an introduction to the concepts and terminology that permeate the use and administration of Kerberos. The knowledge of these concepts is essential to the understanding of how Kerberos works as well as how to use and administer it.

Chapter 3, *Protocols*
> Speaking of how Kerberos works, Chapter 3 reviews the Kerberos protocol via a historical perspective that takes you through the evolution of Kerberos from an academic paper published in 1978 to the modern Kerberos 5 protocol used today. Chapter 3 provides a detailed yet easy-to-follow description of how the Kerberos protocol works and describes the numerous encrypted messages that are sent back and forth.

Chapter 4, *Implementation*
> Takes you from the realm of the theoretical and conceptual into the practical aspects involved in administering a Kerberos system. Here, the Kerberos implementations that will be discussed throughout the book are introduced, and the basics of the installation and administration of a Kerberos authentication system are described.

Chapter 5, *Troubleshooting*
> When things go wrong with your Kerberos implementation, Chapter 5 will come in handy. Chapter 5 provides a methodology for diagnosing Kerberos-related problems and demonstrates some of the more common errors that can occur.

Chapter 6, *Security*
> Provides a detailed look at the practical security concerns related to running Kerberos.

Chapter 7, *Applications*
> Reviews some common software that can be configured to use Kerberos authentication.

Chapter 8, *Advanced Topics*
> Provides information about more advanced topics in running a Kerberos authentication system, including how to interoperate between Unix and Windows Kerberos implementations. This chapter also reviews how multiple Kerberos realms can cooperate and share resources through cross-realm authentication.

Chapter 9, *Case Study*

Presents a sample case study that demonstrates the implementation tasks presented earlier in a practical example.

Chapter 10, *Kerberos Futures*

Finishes off the book with a description of the future directions Kerberos is taking. We'll examine new protocol enhancements that will enable Kerberos to take advantage of new security and encryption technologies.

Appendix, *Administration Reference*

Provides an in-depth reference on the various commands avialable to Kerberos administrators.

Conventions Used in This Book

The following conventions are used in this book.

Italic

Used for file and directory names and for URLs. It is also used to emphasize new terms and concepts when they are introduced.

Constant Width

Used for code examples, commands, options, variables, and parameters.

Constant Width Italic

Indicates a replaceable term in code.

 Indicates a tip, suggestion, or general note.

 Indicates a warning.

Comments and Questions

We have tested and verified all of the information in this book to the best of our ability, but you may find that features have changed, that typos have crept in, or that we have made a mistake. Please let us know about what you find, as well as your suggestions for future editions, by contacting:

O'Reilly & Associates, Inc.
1005 Gravenstein Highway North
Sebastopol, CA 95472
(800)998-9938 (in the U.S. or Canada)
(707)829-0515 (international/local)
(707)829-0104 (fax)

You can also send us messages electronically. To be put on the mailing list or request a catalog, send email to:

info@oreilly.com

To ask technical questions or comment on the book, send email to:

bookquestions@oreilly.com

We have a web site for the book, where we'll list examples, errata, and any plans for future editions. You can access this page at:

http://www.oreilly.com/catalog/kerberos/

For more information about this book and others, see the O'Reilly web site:

http://www.oreilly.com

Thanks...

First, I'd like to thank my editor at O'Reilly, Michael Loukides, without whom this book would not exist. His encouragement and direction (along with his seemingly infinite patience) allowed me to finish this book while sustaining only minor injuries.

There were many people who took the time to review this text and suggest valuable changes. These people, in no particular order, include Mike Lonergan, Ken Hornstein, Frank Balluffi, Robbie Allen, Mohammad Haque, and Marcus Miller. Their constructive criticism of my early drafts helped to make this book as complete and technically accurate as possible.

I'd also like to thank the friends and co-workers who have provided support and entertainment during this process. Brian Dykstra, Brad Johnson, Mark Yu, Nan Ting, Keith Jones, and many others helped me finish this project through their encouragement over this past year.

And last but not least, I'd like to thank my parents, Arthur and Mary Garman, who encouraged me to explore my interest in computers and provided me with the Commodore 64 that sparked my imagination.

## CHAPTER 1

Introduction

Who are you? It's a question with an obvious response, at least for people. Humans have the ability to distinguish one another through several senses; most commonly, we use our sense of vision to recognize people we have met before. We also can tell one another apart through other means, such as body language, speech patterns and accents, and shared secrets between people. It has even been shown that newborn babies can discern between their mother and other females solely through their scent. Our ability to recognize patterns in our surroundings provides us with this ability to determine the identity of, or *authenticate*, people we know.

However, when you bring a computer into the picture, the situation changes dramatically. Computers (at least today's computers) don't have eyes, ears, or noses. Even if they did, the current state-of-the-art in pattern recognition is still woefully inaccurate for widespread use. While there is a lot of research in this area, the most common method by far for authenticating people to computers is through passwords. A password, also known as a *shared secret*, is the one critical piece of information that determines whether the person behind the keyboard really is whom they claim to be. While humans sometimes use this shared secret method—for example, a secret handshake, or perhaps the knowledge of obscure trivia—computers almost exclusively use shared secrets to authenticate people.

There are two issues with passwords as used today for authentication. The first is a human problem. We don't like to remember a long, complex string of numbers, letters, and maybe even symbols that make up a secure password. If left to our own devices, we use simple dictionary words or maybe even our spouses' name or birthdate as passwords. Unfortunately, a "shared secret" that really isn't a secret (such as your spouse's name) is easily guessable by an attacker who wishes to impersonate you to the computer. This problem is exacerbated by the fact that, even within a company network, there are literally dozens of machines a person has access to, each of which requires its own password. As a general rule, as the number of passwords goes up, the quality of each password decreases.

The second issue is a technical problem. While the computer gives you the illusion of security by printing stars, or nothing at all, on the screen while you type your password, somehow that information must travel some communications network to a computer on the other end. The most common method that computers use to send passwords over the network is by sending the password in "clear text," that is, unmodified. While this wouldn't be a problem if each computer had a completely separate, dedicated connection to every other computer it wishes to communicate with, in reality, computer networks are a shared resource. Sending passwords over the network in the clear is analogous to standing in a crowded room shouting across the room to a friend standing on the other side.

Kerberos is a network authentication system that can help solve those two issues. It reduces the number of passwords each user has to memorize to use an entire network to one—the Kerberos password. In addition, Kerberos incorporates encryption and message integrity to solve the second issue, ensuring that sensitive authentication data is never sent over the network in the clear. By providing a secure authentication mechanism, Kerberos is an essential part of a total network security plan, providing clear benefits for both end users and administrators.

But before we go further, let's take a step back and explore the history of Kerberos.

Origins

The word *Kerberos* originates from Greek mythology, which contains the legend of Cerberus. Cerberus guarded the realm of the underworld, ruled by Hades and his wife, Persephone. What Cerberus looked like depends on whom you ask; Hesiod claims that Cerberus has fifty heads, while Apollodorus describes him as a strange mixture of creatures with three dog-shaped heads, a serpent as a tail, and heads of snakes over his back. Cerberus is most often pictured as a creature with three heads. Either way, Cerberus was a vicious creature that few dared to challenge.

The Greeks believed that when a person dies, his soul is sent to Hades to spend eternity. While all souls were sent to Hades, those people who had led a good life would be spared the eternal punishment that those who had not would have to endure. Cerberus, as the gatekeeper to Hades, ensured that only the souls of the dead entered Hades, and he ensured that souls could not escape once inside.

As the gatekeeper to Hades, Cerberus authenticated those who attempted to enter (to determine whether they were dead or alive) and used that authentication to determine whether to allow access or not. Just like the ancient Cerberus, the modern Kerberos authenticates those users who attempt to access network resources.

Like every other great figure in mythology, Cerberus had a fatal flaw that enabled some clever people to pass through Cerberus to Hades. We'll revisit the legend and discuss one such story and its modern counterparts in Chapter 6.

Finally, if the ancient mythological character was named Cerberus, why is the modern authentication system called Kerberos? Simply put, they are just different spellings of the same word. In order to provide a distinction between the ancient mythology and the present-day software system, we will refer to the mythological character as Cerberus and the modern software system as Kerberos.

Modern History

The modern-day origins of the Kerberos network authentication system are a bit more mundane than the ancient mythology of Cerberus. Kerberos began as a research project at the Massachusetts Institute for Technology (MIT) in the early 1980s. The MIT faculty at the time recognized that the explosion of widely available, inexpensive computers would transform the computing industry.

The time-sharing model

Traditionally, computers were a large, expensive, and centralized resource that end users accessed through dumb terminals connected via serial lines. This is called the *time-sharing model* (Figure 1-1).

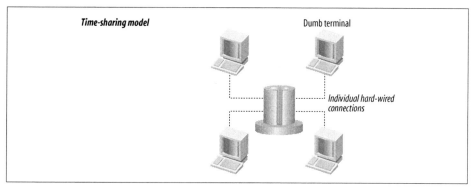

Figure 1-1. Time-sharing model

The time-sharing model had some distinct administrative advantages. Since there was only one (albeit large) computer, maintaining user accounts and privileges was easy. To add a user account, the administrator simply created an entry in the machine's password file and the user immediately had access. Deleting accounts or changing passwords was similarly easy; there was a single point of administration by definition, since there was only one machine involved.

In addition, the time-sharing model had no need for encryption of passwords during transit. Users connected to the machine via dedicated serial lines, and each user had their own dumb terminal connected to their own serial line. Since the communication medium was not shared, one user could not listen into the communications of another user without physically tapping their serial wire.

The client-server model

The advent of the packet-switched computer network dramatically changed how users interfaced with computers. With the computer network, users all had an inexpensive computer on their desk, connected to all of the other computers in the organization through the network. Since the desktop computers still were not very powerful, specialized, more powerful server computers were used to provide services such as file storage, printing, and electronic mail to users.

This new computing model, widely referred to as *client-server*, provided some distinct advantages to both users and administrators (Figure 1-2). End users enjoyed increased usability since the desktop computers, while not very powerful, were powerful enough to present menu-driven interfaces to the resources of the server machines; a marked improvement over typing cryptic commands on a dumb terminal or line printer.

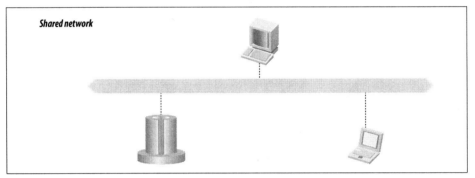

Figure 1-2. Client-server model

However, the faculty at MIT recognized that this new model required a dramatic new software architecture and a new way of thinking about computing: a way of thinking that recognized that computing power, rather than being centralized, was now distributed throughout the entire campus.

A major problem that the advent of personal computers and the network presented was that the end-user clients could no longer be trusted. In the traditional time-sharing model, end users only had a dumb terminal, which had no processing power at all. Since the computer all of the users shared was under the total control of the system administrators, it could be trusted.

Now, with inexpensive personal computers on all of the end-users desks, the system administrators no longer had total control over all of the computing power; indeed, end users could modify any part of the software on their personal machine they wanted, going as far as replacing the operating system itself. Since the end users now controlled their own computer, they could spoof messages to other machines, listen in on connections between other machines on the network, and impersonate the identities of other users.

Project Athena

Enter Project Athena. Project Athena was established with support from a consortium of computer vendors in May 1983 with a five-year timeline. Athena's focus was to develop strategies and software for integrating computers into MIT's curriculum. In particular, Athena was designed from the start as a networked, client-server system. While Project Athena had a decidedly educational focus, the end result included several software packages that are still in wide use today.

As mentioned earlier, passing passwords over a network in clear text is akin to shouting in a crowded room. However, that is exactly how software of the day functioned: the standard remote login protocols such as Telnet and rlogin sent user credentials over the network in clear text. Even worse, other server software, such as rlogin, blindly believed the identity that the client computer sent to it. Thus, unscrupulous users could (trivially) write fake rlogin clients that would be able to impersonate anyone else on the network. This was unacceptable in an academic environment, where dishonest users could listen to network messages for other users' passwords or steal others' work.

In addition, the now decentralized nature of the computing resources presented the problem that every user had access to several computers on the network, each requiring its own username and password. This model contrasted with the older timesharing model, in which end-user machines were connected to one centralized computer via a dedicated serial line, and only one login was required.

To solve these problems, Project Athena developed the Kerberos protocol for network authentication. The Project Athena Technical Plan outlined the major goals of the new service; namely, to extend the services of authentication typically found in large time-sharing systems to a distributed network consisting of servers and untrusted end-user client machines. The new authentication system had to centralize the trust into machines that were tightly controlled and monitored, and encrypt any sensitive transactions between these authentication servers and other machines on the network.

Many other packages also came out of the efforts of Project Athena. Project Athena developed the X Window System, which is now used as the basis for every Unix system's Graphical User Interface. Other packages that relate to distributed computing include the Hesiod distributed name service, and the Moira distributed network administration system.

The combination of Project Athena and similar projects at other large universities across the U.S. and the world provided these institutions with advanced single-sign-on network infrastructure across all major network protocols, including electronic mail, file sharing, and even instant messaging. By using Kerberos and applications that support Kerberos authentication in your own network, you can achieve this goal as well.

What Is Kerberos?

The full definition of what Kerberos provides is a secure, single-sign-on, trusted, third-party mutual authentication service. What does that mean? Let's break that definition down into its parts and quickly describe each one.

Secure
> Kerberos is *secure* since it never transmits passwords over the network in the clear. Kerberos is unique in its use of *tickets*, time-limited cryptographic messages that prove a user's identity to a given server without sending passwords over the network or caching passwords on the local user's hard disk.

Single-sign-on
> *Single-sign-on* means that end users only need to log in once to access all network resources that support Kerberos. Once a user has authenticated to Kerberos at the start of her login session, her credentials are transparently passed to every other resource she accesses during the day.

Trusted third-party
> *Trusted third-party* refers to the fact that Kerberos works through a centralized authentication server that all systems in the network inherently trust. All authentication requests are routed through the centralized Kerberos server.

Mutual authentication
> *Mutual authentication* ensures that not only is the person behind the keyboard who he claims to be, but also proves that the server he is communicating with is who it claims to be. Mutual authentication protects the confidentiality of sensitive information by ensuring that the service the user is communicating with is genuine.

These three concepts describe the basis of the Kerberos network authentication service. We'll take a closer look at these concepts and the surrounding terminology in the following chapter.

Goals

The Kerberos system has several goals. It strives to improve security and convenience at the same time. First is the goal of centralizing authentication into one server (or set of servers). The Kerberos system operates through a set of centralized *Key Distribution Centers*, or KDCs. Each KDC on your network contains a database of usernames and passwords for both users and Kerberos-enabled services. Centralizing this information eases the burden on administrators, as they now only need to maintain this single username/password database. In addition, it provides an advantage to security administrators, who now only have a small set of machines on which usernames and passwords are stored, and can specially harden and protect these machines accordingly.

Kerberos provides a secure means of authentication over insecure networks. Instead of sending plain-text passwords over the network in the clear, Kerberos uses encrypted *tickets* to prove the identity of both end users and network servers. These tickets are generated by the centralized Key Distribution Centers on behalf of users who wish to authenticate to the network. When using Kerberos, user passwords are never sent over the network in the clear.

In addition, implementing the other two elements of the "three A's" (authorization and auditing—authentication, of course, is the third A) are made easier using Kerberos. While Kerberos does not directly provide authorization or auditing services, Kerberos' ability to accurately identify both users and services allows programmers and administrators to provide authorization and auditing to further enhance the security of their network. We'll talk more about what exactly authorization and auditing are in the next chapter.

Evolution

The modern Kerberos protocol has gone through several major revisions since it was first conceived as part of Project Athena. During each revision, major improvements have been made in usability, extensibility, and security.

Early Kerberos (v1, v2, v3)

The early versions of Kerberos (pre-Version 4) were created and used internally at MIT for testing purposes. These implementations contained significant limitations and were only useful to examine new ideas and observe the practical issues that arose during development and testing.

Kerberos 4

The first version of Kerberos distributed outside of MIT was Kerberos 4. First released to the public on January 24, 1989, Kerberos 4 was adopted by several vendors, who included it in their operating systems. In addition, other, large distributed software projects such as the Andrew File System adopted the concepts behind Kerberos 4 for their own authentication mechanisms.

The basics of what was to become the Kerberos 4 protocol are documented in the Athena Technical Plan. Ultimately, the details of the protocol were documented through the source code in the reference implementation published by MIT.

However, due to export control restrictions on encryption software imposed by the U.S. government, Kerberos 4 could not be exported outside of the United States. Since Kerberos 4 uses DES encryption, organizations outside of the U.S. could not legally download the Kerberos 4 software as-is from MIT. In response, the MIT development team stripped all of the encryption code from Kerberos 4 to create a specialized, exportable version. Eric Young, at Bond University of Australia, took this stripped version of Kerberos 4 and added his own implementation of DES to create "eBones." Since eBones contained encryption software developed outside of the United States, it was unencumbered by the U.S. encryption export controls, and could be legally used anywhere in the world.

Today, several implementations of Kerberos 4 still exist. The original MIT Kerberos 4 implementation is now in a maintenance mode and officially considered "dead." The kth-krb distribution, developed in Sweden, is still actively developed but it is highly recommended that new installations use the superior Kerberos 5 instead. In this book, coverage of Kerberos 4 is restricted to a discussion of the protocol in Chapter 3. Most of the book covers the next version of Kerberos, Kerberos 5.

Kerberos 5

Kerberos 5 was developed to add features and security enhancements that were not present in Version 4 of the protocol. Kerberos 5 is the latest version of the Kerberos protocol and is documented in RFC 1510.

To correct the deficiencies in the Kerberos 4 protocol, several new features were added. They include:

- A better wire protocol, based on ASN.1
- Credential forwarding and delegation
- Replay cache
- More flexible cross-realm authentication
- Extensible encryption types
- Pre-authentication

(Don't worry, we'll discuss these features in more detail later on, in Chapter 3, Chapter 6, and Chapter 8.)

In addition to the reference implementation by MIT, many other implementations of Kerberos 5 have been developed, some commercial and some open source. The implementations covered in this book include MIT, Heimdal, Microsoft (Windows 2000 and above), and Apple (Mac OS X and above).

Unfortunately, while the rules surrounding encryption export out of the United States have been relaxed on open source software as of January 2000, the MIT distribution is still available to U.S. residents only. Because of the overly cautious actions of the MIT lawyers, a group in Sweden is developing and distributing the Heimdal Kerberos 5 distribution, which is unencumbered by any export control laws.

New Directions

The Kerberos protocol is constantly changing and evolving to incorporate the latest technologies and lessons learned from practical implementation experience, as well as to face new challenges presented by adversaries with ever-increasing computing power available at little cost. Currently, a new set of specifications are being developed by a set of developers who are part of the Internet Engineering Task Force's (IETF) Kerberos working group. As of this writing, the Kerberos working group is in the final stages of writing a document named the Kerberos Clarifications, which will supercede RFC 1510 and become the new Kerberos 5 standard document. The Kerberos Clarifications also includes several new features that will extend the Kerberos protocol, providing for future growth and interoperability with current Kerberos 5 implementations.

In addition to the Kerberos Clarifications, the Kerberos working group is also working on several additional extensions to the Kerberos protocol, published as separate Internet draft documents. Some of these extensions have already been implemented based on earlier versions of the draft, such as the Public Key extensions that Microsoft includes with Windows 2000, XP, and 2003. We will discuss these future directions of Kerberos and some of the new extensions that are being proposed as Internet standards in Chapter 10.

These additional features and refinements to the Kerberos protocol ensure its continued success as the most widely implemented single-sign-on authentication protocol. In addition, through the adoption of Kerberos in the latest versions of Microsoft Windows, Kerberos is now enjoying more widespread popularity in small- and medium-sized networks.

Other Products

Many other products have been developed that either directly implement the Kerberos protocols or borrow concepts from Kerberos to implement similar authentication systems. We'll take a brief look at these alternative systems, and discuss the relationship between these systems and Kerberos.

DCE

The *Distributed Computing Environment*, or DCE, is a set of libraries and services that enable organizations to build cross-platform, integrated computing environments. It includes components that enable applications to communicate across a diverse set of platforms and securely locate and access information, whether it's in the same room on a local network or across the globe over the Internet. DCE provides many services to make this possible, including directory services, remote procedure calls, and time-synchronization. Most notable to our discussion, it provides a security service, which just happens to be based on Kerberos 5.

Work on DCE began in 1989, and was developed through a committee of vendors who have submitted various bits and pieces. The work was coordinated by The Open Group, an organization that is most widely known for the Motif widget set. Unfortunately, while the concepts that underlie DCE were revolutionary and ahead of their time, DCE was difficult to install and administer, and early versions were riddled with bugs. Today, DCE itself is not in wide use, but the concepts behind it have been integrated in most modern operating systems today, including Windows 2000 and above.

In 1997, The Open Group released the source code to the latest version of DCE, 1.2.2, to download for free from their web site. More information on DCE, including information on how to download Free DCE, can be found at *http://www.opengroup.org/dce/*.

Globus Security Infrastructure

The Globus Security Infrastructure is part of a larger project, the Globus Toolkit. The goal of the Globus Toolkit is to develop services that enable *grid computing*, also known as *High Performance Computing* (HPC) or *compute clusters*. Globus includes services to locate people and resources on the network, as well as submit and control compute jobs running on machines in the network. In order to perform its tasks securely, however, it needed a secure authentication and privacy mechanism. The Globus Security Infrastructure, or GSI, is the Globus Toolkit's implementation of a secure authentication system.

While the GSI operates under different principles than Kerberos, most notably through its use of public key encryption and infrastructure, it provides the same single-sign-on user experience that Kerberos does. In addition, the developers of Globus recognized the need for interoperability with existing Kerberos installations, so the Globus team has developed several tools that allow interoperability between Kerberos tickets and Globus certificates.

More information is available about the Globus Toolkit at *http://www.globus.org/*.

SESAME

The Secure European System for Applications in a Multivendor Environment, or SESAME, is a research and development project funded by the European Commission. SESAME implements a single-sign-on protocol that is similar to and compatible with Kerberos, but includes some enhancements. Most notably, SESAME includes the concept of limited delegation—that is, the ability to delegate only some privileges to another machine or user. This allows users to exercise fine-grained control over how their credentials are used by servers. For example, an end user can delegate her credentials to a mail server, but limit the mail server from using her credentials to delete her files.

Unfortunately, there is little information available on SESAME, and the installed user base is small, mostly consisting of developers using the system for further research. The software has few sample applications, and the ones that are available are difficult to compile due to the need to change hardcoded values in the source code in order to build. Information about SESAME can be found at its home page at *https://www.cosic.esat.kuleuven.ac.be/sesame/*.

## CHAPTER 2

Pieces of the Puzzle

In the previous chapter, we examined the ideas and history behind the Kerberos network authentication system. Now we'll begin to discover how Kerberos works. Instead of introducing these concepts as they're needed in the next chapter, I feel that it is easier to understand the nitty-gritty details of Kerberos when you have a working background in the surrounding terminology. To emphasize the importance of a solid understanding in these concepts, I have set aside this chapter to introduce you to the essential concepts and terminology that surround the use and administration of a Kerberos authentication system. While you may be familiar with some of these concepts, we're going to examine each one in turn and describe how it relates to Kerberos.

Kerberos is a complex system, with many parts. It requires the proper functioning of many separate software components, and with each comes a set of terms and concepts that underlie the entire system. A complete introduction to all of these concepts is critical to the understanding of the whole.

After all of these terms have been introduced, we'll finish off by putting all of the pieces together and set the stage for the detailed description of the Kerberos protocols in Chapter 3. For those who simply wish to implement a Kerberos realm and not worry about the low-level details of the protocol, this chapter will prepare you to skip directly to Chapter 4.

The Three As

We'll start out our discussion with a topic that many network professionals deal with on a daily basis, the three As. *Authentication, authorization,* and *auditing* are a crucial part of any network security scheme, yet the distinction between them is often unclear. Each one of these components serves a separate, distinct purpose in a network security scheme. In particular, we will focus on authentication and authorization, and how they relate to each other.

Authentication

Simply put, *authentication* is the process of verifying the identity of a particular user. To authenticate a user, the user is asked for information that would prove his identity. This information can fall into one or more of three categories: what he knows, what he has, or what he is. These categories are referred to as *factors*.

The first factor, what he knows, is the most common factor used in authentication today. A secret password is generated when the user is granted access to a machine or network. That secret can either be generated by the user himself, by choosing his own password and giving it to the system administrator when he grants the user access, or automatically through some process that generates random passwords.

The second factor, what he has, is a less common but more secure alternative. An example of this type of authentication is the widely deployed RSA SecurID token. The SecurID token is a small electronic device that has an embedded encryption key and an LCD display. Every minute, an algorithm runs inside the device and updates the LCD display with a new six-digit combination. Only the person who possesses the device can tell what the correct password is. Other systems, such as smart card systems, operate on similar principles.

The third factor, what he is, enters into the realm of biometrics. Since all humans have distinguishing characteristics, biometrics measures the physical properties of some portion of our body and uses that information to authenticate users. Current biometric systems include fingerprint scanning, retina scanning, voiceprint recognition, and face recognition. Biometrics does not yet enjoy a wide market for several reasons: products are still immature for widespread use, some are very expensive (such as retina scanning), and, perhaps the most important reason of all, there is currently little software support for these devices.

Of course, an authentication system can combine these factors. For example, the RSA SecurID login process involves not only the SecurID token but also a numeric PIN. Therefore, SecurID combines the first two factors, what you have and what you know. Obviously, a system that combines more than one factor is more secure than a system which depends on only one.

The Kerberos protocol itself does not specify which authentication factors must be used. Although most implementations use a password-based system, there are implementations, such as the one present in Microsoft's Windows 2000 and above, which allow Kerberos login tied to the use smart cards. Smart cards, which we'll cover further in Chapter 10, avoid the use of passwords as the sole factor of authentication. Therefore, they make the login process easier on users, as well as providing a more secure authentication mechanism.

Once the server receives the information from the user that proves his identity, the server determines whether that information is correct. Does the password that the user entered match the one listed in the password database? If so, then the user is authenticated. If not, then the request is denied.

Attacks against authentication systems are typically performed in a brute-force manner, where an attacker utilizes a computer that tries combination after combination until the user's password is found. Different policies can be employed during authentication to prevent an attacker from continuously trying a large list of passwords, and we'll discuss those in Chapter 6.

Authorization

Authorization refers to granting or denying access to specific resources based on the requesting user's identity. This step is performed after a user is identified through authentication. Authorization is usually performed through access control lists, which associate user identities with specific rights. Authorization includes information such as a user's group membership, user policies, and other information that determines what level of access that user has to computer or network resources.

It is important to note that the ability to make correct authorization decisions rests solely on a solid authentication mechanism. The only way that a correct authorization decision can be made is if the user has already been correctly authenticated. Authorization ceases to work if the authentication method can't be trusted. If the authentication mechanism returns a false identity to the authorization mechanism, then there is no way for the authorization mechanism to correct this, and it can allow an attacker to masquerade as a legitimate user.

As a result, solid authorization mechanisms depend on an effective authentication system. Systems that depend on weak authentication will fail, no matter how sophisticated the authorization may be. An example is the standard NFS protocol. NFS requires servers to trust the clients, since users are "authenticated" by a plaintext UID sent by the client. Clearly, this mechanism makes it trivial to spoof any username on an NFS server. The ease of bypassing authentication negates any sophisticated Access Control List authorization mechanism that may be employed on the server, since an attacker can easily masquerade as any other user ID given control of a client machine.

Auditing

The final A in the three As is *auditing*. Auditing takes the results from authentication and authorization and records these results into an audit log. The audit log records all actions taken by the authentication and authorization steps for future review by an administrator. While authentication and authorization are preventative systems in which unauthorized access is prevented, auditing is a reactive system. Auditing will not prevent an attacker from gaining access to your network; instead, it will give you a detailed log of when, where, and how the attacker penetrated your systems.

All Kerberos implementations we will cover have the ability to log events that take place during authentication requests. We'll take a very close look at auditing in

Chapter 6, where we'll review what logging can be enabled in the various Kerberos implementations and how to view those logs.

Directories

A common misconception surrounding Kerberos and other authentication technologies is that they somehow replace directories, such as the Unix /etc/passwd file, NIS, NetInfo, or LDAP. Along the same lines, another common misconception is that directories make good authentication systems by themselves. Therefore, a distinction needs to be made between authentication, authorization, and directories. For a real-life analogy of what roles each of these components play, see the sidebar "Confusing Authentication, Authorization, and Directories."

Directories contain data describing resources, such as computers, printers, and user accounts that are contained within a particular network. Directories can be as simple as a text file, such as the /etc/passwd and /etc/group files on traditional Unix systems, which list the active user accounts and their group permissions. Or a directory can be a complex LDAP directory structure, such as Microsoft's Active Directory.

Directories can contain authentication data. Authenticating "against" a directory takes two forms: a client machine can contact a directory, obtain the hashed version of the user's password, hash the password given by the user, and compare the two. This method is used by NIS, for example. The other form, employed by most LDAP authentication mechanisms, is to attempt to bind to the LDAP directory using the credentials that the user provided. If the user is granted access to the directory, the authentication is successful. The pam_ldap PAM module uses this latter method to authenticate against an LDAP directory.

Using Kerberos to handle authentication is superior to these methods for several reasons:

- Using Kerberos tickets, users can be granted single-sign-on access to all network resources without requiring the client machine to cache the user's password. Kerberos tickets are cryptographic messages that are only valid for a relatively short period of time, typically 8–24 hours. The compromise of a user's password, on the other hand, provides an attacker the ability to masquerade as the legitimate user for a much longer period of time—specifically, until the password is changed or expires.

- With Kerberos, the user's password is never sent in the clear over the network during the login process.

- Kerberos defines a widely adopted and standardized protocol that is suited for authentication.

Therefore, while a directory may contain authentication information (for example, Microsoft's Active Directory stores the Kerberos database in its LDAP store), it is preferable to use Kerberos to perform authentication rather than using the directory for authentication directly.

Confusing Authentication, Authorization, and Directories

Many authentication systems also include authorization functions, so these concepts can be easily confused with each other. For example, the traditional Unix /etc/passwd file contains both authentication and authorization data. To make matters worse, it also functions as a directory! So it is very easy to get confused when reading about the differences between all of these concepts when the distinction has never been made in the past.

To help make the distinction clear, let's say that you want to get in to the hottest local nightclub. We'll examine what steps you have to take in order to gain access to the bar.

First, you are authenticated. By issuing a driver's license from the Department of Motor Vehicles (analogous to the Kerberos Key Distribution Center), the state confirms your identity and generates a license, which includes data about you. That data includes information such as your name, your birthdate, your picture, and so on. In Kerberos parlance, this *ticket* that you've been issued proves your identity. Anyone possessing your ticket can masquerade as you, provided that the ticket is still valid (Kerberos tickets have limited lifetimes, as we'll discuss later; usually, the lifetime is one day).

Next, you make your way to the club, license in hand. Once you arrive, the bouncer obtains your name from your license and makes an authorization decision: is your name on the guest list? The guest list acts as a primitive directory, which simply lists the people who are authorized to enter. If your name appears, then you are allowed access into the club.

In this (rather simplified) analogy, there is a clear separation between the entity that performs authentication (the state government), and the entity that performs authorization (the club bouncer). This crude analogy is intended to demonstrate that just because a user possesses a valid Kerberos ticket, he is not necessarily authorized to use any network resources.

Privacy and Integrity

Next, we'll review some concepts that are integral to keeping communications on computer networks secure. In particular, we will discuss the roles of encryption and message-integrity algorithms. The distinction between encryption and message-integrity is important, as we'll see later in the discussion of Kerberos encryption types. Those familiar with encryption and message integrity can skip to the next section, which describes the Kerberos-specific terminology.

Encryption

The modern word *cryptography* is derived from two ancient Greek words, *cryptos*, which means hidden or secret, and *graphein*, or writing. Kerberos uses cryptography to provide encryption and decryption of its messages over the network. Therefore, encryption refers to the process of converting a message, or plaintext, into gibberish, which if intercepted, does not reveal the contents of the original message. Governments and corporations have long employed encryption to keep their information secure from prying eyes. The emergence of the Internet, where any network administrator can monitor and read traffic on her network and any traffic passing through her network, has forced software makers to build encryption into every day software programs. Kerberos uses encryption not only to protect the authentication exchanges it sends and receives from snoopers, but also to prevent hackers from creating fake messages.

There are many different ways of encrypting data. These methods are referred to as encryption algorithms, or in Kerberos-speak, encryption types. There are several different encryption types that are supported in Kerberos 5 implementations. The most widely supported encryption type is DES, but work is underway to replace it with Triple DES and the new Advanced Encryption Standard (AES). Another widely used encryption type is the RC4 algorithm, which is used primarily in Microsoft's implementation of Kerberos.

The advantage of moving to stronger encryption algorithms is protection against brute-force cryptanalysis. We'll take a look in more detail about brute-force attacks against the encryption algorithms in Kerberos in Chapter 6.

Message Integrity

While encryption provides privacy, message integrity ensures the recipient that the message was not tampered with during transit. While encryption as it is used in Kerberos gives you message integrity for "free," since only the two end points have the required key to encrypt and decrypt messages, there are specialized message-integrity algorithms that can ensure message integrity without the overhead of encryption. You will see message-integrity algorithms referred to as one-way hashes, or just hashes.

Hashes work as mathematical one-way functions. They take an input message that is arbitrarily long, run it through a mathematical algorithm, and output a fixed size (typically 64–256 bits) message that represents the input. The idea behind the hash function is that while it is easy to calculate the hash output for a given input, it is mathematically hard to go the opposite way and derive an input that produces the same output, hence their "one-way" nature.

A trivial example of a hash function is to add all of the byte values of a message together, and take the sum modulus a maximum number—say, 1024. It is not possible to reconstruct the original input stream from this sum. Another property of a hash algorithm is its cryptographic strength, or the ability for attackers to craft input designed to produce a given hash value. Since the hash value (in this case, the sum of the bytes of the message mod 1024) contains less data than the input stream (this simple example only provides 1025 possible hash values), there are many inputs that will produce a given hash value. These are called collisions, and cryptographically-secure hash algorithms aim to reduce the chance that an attacker can find two inputs that hash to the same value.

Just like there are different encryption algorithms, there are several different message-integrity algorithms commonly used in Kerberos. Ranging from weaker to stronger, the message-integrity algorithms included in the MIT Kerberos distribution include CRC-32, MD5, and the Secure Hash Algorithm (SHA1).

Kerberos Terminology and Concepts

Now we'll begin to examine terminology that is specific to the Kerberos authentication system. There are many parts to Kerberos, and each has a name that will be defined here and used throughout the rest of the book. The descriptions that follow suffice for implementing a Kerberos realm, but the details of how these work are covered in the next chapter, where we will examine the protocols in detail.

Realms, Principals, and Instances

Every entity contained within a Kerberos installation, including individual users, computers, and services running on servers, has a *principal* associated with it. Each principal is associated with a long-term key. This key can be, for example, a password or passphrase. Principals are globally unique names. To accomplish this, the principal is divided into a hierarchical structure.

Every principal starts with a username or service name. The username or service name is then followed by an optional instance. The instance is used in two situations: for service principals (which we'll discuss later), and in order to create special principals for administrative use. For example, administrators can have two principals: one for day-to-day usage, and another (an "admin" principal) to use only when the administrator needs elevated privileges.

The username and optional instance, taken together, form a unique identity within a given *realm*. Each Kerberos installation defines an administrative realm of control that is distinct from every other Kerberos installation. Kerberos defines this as the *realm name*. By convention, the Kerberos realm for a given DNS domain is the domain converted to uppercase. So, for example, Wedgie International, which owns the domain name *wedgie.org*, would create a Kerberos realm for its users named WEDGIE.ORG.

While it is the convention to make the realm name equivalent to the DNS domain name, it is not necessary to do so. It certainly makes configuration easier, as we'll see later on, but it is perfectly legal to have a realm name of, say, MYREALM.BOGUS when your domain name is *wedgie.org*. Also note that realms are case-sensitive (unlike domain names), so the realm MyRealm.BOGUS is different from MYREALM.BOGUS.

Now let's examine a Kerberos principal that has been assigned to John Doe, who works in the IT department of Wedgie International:

```
jdoe@IT.WEDGIE.ORG
```

This is the simplest form a principal can take, and is a valid principal under both Kerberos 4 and Kerberos 5. This principal represents the username jdoe, with no instance, and a realm of IT.WEDGIE.ORG.

Service and host principals

Users aren't the only ones assigned principals in a Kerberos realm; hosts and servers offering Kerberos services also have principals. Since, in Kerberos, each endpoint of a connection can request mutual authentication, both endpoints require an identity and a key. Therefore, every service and host that a user can connect to through Kerberos authentication requires a service principal.

Services principals are slightly different than user principals. The username component in a service principal is the name of the service that the principal represents. In the case of a host principal, the username is "host." To distinguish service principals for the same service but on different hostnames, the instance component contains the hostname of the machine the service principal is located on. Services that use Kerberos authentication are said to be *Kerberized*.

In addition to host and service principals, the Kerberos system itself contains several principals. The most important of these "special" principals is the krbtgt principal. We'll see examples of service and host principals in the next two sections, which discuss what Kerberos 4 and 5 principals look like. While the syntax is similar, there are some notable differences. We'll take a look at the Kerberos 4 principal format first.

Kerberos 4 principals

Kerberos 4 principals are made up of three components: the username, an optional instance, and the realm. The username and instance are separated by a period, and the username and instance are separated from the realm by an at symbol (@). Let's take a look at an example Kerberos 4 principal:

```
jdoe.admin@IT.WEDGIE.ORG
```

This example is similar to the one above, with the exception that this principal contains an instance—in this case, admin.

Kerberos 4 service principals contain only the hostname of the server the principal is assigned to. There is no domain component, since the separator for domain names is the same as the separator between username and instance (the dot). So an example host principal for the host *unixsvr.it.doesystems.com* in the IT.WEDGIE.ORG realm would be:

```
host.unixsvr@IT.WEDGIE.ORG
```

This is one of the shortfalls of Kerberos 4, as it dictates that you cannot have more than one machine with the same hostname in your realm, even if they have different domain names. A hostname of *unixsvr.it.wedgie.org* that is also a member of the IT.WEDGIE.ORG Kerberos realm would map to the same service principal as the example hostname above, *unixsvr.it.doesystems.com*.

In general, the forms that a Kerberos 4 principal can take are:

```
user[.instance]@REALM
service.hostname@REALM
```

Kerberos 5 principals

Kerberos 5 principals contain the same basic components as a Kerberos 4 principal. Instead of a single instance component, however, Kerberos 5 principals can contain several sub-instance components. Also, instead of using a dot to separate the username and instance components, Kerberos 5 uses a forward slash.

Let's take a look at an example Kerberos 5 user principal:

```
jdoe/admin@IT.WEDGIE.ORG
```

This example is equivalent to the first Kerberos 4 example, showing the format of John Doe's principal with an admin instance.

Kerberos 5 host and service principals include the fully qualified domain name (FQDN) of the host that the service is installed on. By embedding the FQDN in the principal, Kerberos 5 allows administrators to have more than one host with the same hostname, but with different domain components located in the same realm. Here is an example of a Kerberos 5 host principal:

```
host/unixsvr.it.wedgie.org@IT.WEDGIE.ORG
```

Generically, Kerberos 5 principals have the following format:

```
component[/component][/component]...@REALM
```

In this format, there is one required component, followed by any number of optional components, separated by forward slashes. Following the components is the realm name, which is separated from the components with an at sign (@), just as in Kerberos 4. Practically speaking, there are two types of Kerberos 5 principals that you'll see in use, just as in Kerberos 4, shown below:

```
username[/instance]@REALM
service/fully-qualified-domain-name@REALM
```

Keys, Salts, and Passwords

Many different terms are used to discuss encryption in Kerberos. They are all related to each other, but there are a few important Kerberos-specific concepts that require discussion.

First, all secret keys are shared between at least two parties, the end user or service and the Key Distribution Center. However, a method is needed to change an alphanumeric password that people can remember into a binary encryption key that the computer can use to encrypt and decrypt messages. A function called *string2key* is used to convert a user's password into an encryption key. This function applies several transformations to each user's password to turn a character-based password into a series of numbers that make up an encryption key.

The most important part of this transformation is known as the *salt*. Generally speaking, salt is a sequence of characters that is added to a password before hashing it to make it more unique. For Kerberos 5, the default salt is the realm name. By adding the realm name to the username, two different encryption keys are generated if a user uses the same password in two different realms. This means that if a user uses the same password in two realms, and his key is compromised in one of them, it does not automatically compromise his key in the other.

The Key Distribution Center

The Kerberos *Key Distribution Center*, or KDC for short, is an integral part of the Kerberos system. The KDC consists of three logical components: a database of all principals and their associated encryption keys, the *Authentication Server*, and the *Ticket Granting Server*. While each of these components are logically separate, they are usually implemented in a single program and run together in a single process space.

In a given Kerberos realm, there must be at least one KDC. While the resources required to run a KDC on a machine are small, it is strongly recommended that each KDC be a separate physical machine. Since all of the crucial data, including the secrets for every principal in your realm, is located on every KDC in the network, it is critical that those servers be as secure as possible. In addition, in order for users to successfully authenticate to Kerberos-enabled services, at least one KDC must be functioning at all times.

Each Key Distribution Center contains a database of all of the principals contained in the realm, as well as their associated secrets. Most KDC software also stores additional information for each principal in this database, such as password lifetimes, last password change, and more. Windows 2000 and 2003 keep this database in the Active Directory, its LDAP store. Open source implementations, including MIT and Heimdal, keep this database in a specialized, lightweight database file on the KDC's filesystem.

Since a Kerberos realm can contain multiple KDC machines, the database on each KDC must be kept in synchronization to ensure unified authentication. If a server has stale data, then legitimate attempts to authenticate against that server may fail, since it does not have an up-to-date copy of the Kerberos database. No standard method of synchronization is specified by the Kerberos protocol, so vendors have created their own replication protocols.

The Authentication Server

The Authentication Server (AS) issues an encrypted *Ticket Granting Ticket* (also known as a TGT) to clients who wish to "log in" to the Kerberos realm. The client does not have to prove its identity to the KDC; instead, the TGT that is sent back to the client is encrypted in the user's password. Since only the user and the KDC know the user's password, when the login process attempts to decrypt the ticket using the password supplied by the user, only the correct password will correctly decrypt the ticket. If an incorrect password is used, the ticket will decrypt into garbage, and the user is prompted to try again.

The TGT returned by the Authentication Server can then be used, once decrypted by the client, to request individual service tickets. The TGT is the crucial piece that eliminates the requirement for a user to retype their password for each subsequent service they contact.

The Ticket Granting Server

Not to be confused with the Ticket Granting Ticket that we briefly discussed in the last section, the Ticket Granting Server (TGS) issues individual service tickets to clients as they request them. The Ticket Granting Server takes in two pieces of data from the client: a ticket request that includes the principal name representing the service the client wishes to contact, and a Ticket Granting Ticket that has been issued by the Authentication Server. The TGS verifies the TGT is valid by checking to ensure that it is encrypted with the Kerberos server's TGT key, and then issues the user the service ticket he requested.

Tickets

Kerberos introduces the concept of *tickets*. Conceptually, a Kerberos ticket is an encrypted data structure issued by the Key Distribution Center that includes a shared encryption key that is unique for each session, and ticket flags that indicate, for example, if the ticket can be forwarded to another service, along with other fields. Tickets serve two purposes: to confirm identity of the end participants and to establish a short-lived encryption key that both parties can share for secure communication (called the *session* key).

The best way to think about tickets is as a license (issued by the KDC) that confirms your identity. Just like a license in the real world, each ticket issued by Kerberos includes data about you, how long the license (or ticket) is valid, and restrictions on its use. The major fields that Kerberos includes in every ticket are:

- The requesting principal name (the user's principal)
- The service's principal name
- When the ticket becomes valid, and when the ticket expires

- A list of IP addresses the ticket can be used from
- A shared secret encryption key ("session" key) for user/application communication

Some of these fields are filled in by the KDC; for example, the KDC enforces a maximum ticket lifetime, and the KDC generates a unique session key each time it issues a ticket. The other fields are filled in by the client and passed to the KDC when it makes a ticket request. When a ticket is generated by the KDC, it is encrypted to ensure that attackers cannot take a valid ticket and modify it; for example, to increase its lifetime or the validated client principal name.

Tickets are relatively short-lived. A typical maximum lifetime for a Kerberos ticket is 10–24 hours. This relatively short lifetime balances the convenience of single-sign-on with the security threat of an attacker stealing credentials and using them for a long period of time. By limiting the lifetime of Kerberos tickets, the damage of a stolen ticket is minimized, while the user still enjoys the convenience of single-sign-on during the working day.

The ticket (or credential) cache

Now that we have all of these tickets, where do we put them? Well, unfortunately, the answer is: it depends. The original Kerberos implementation written by MIT uses a file-based credential cache. That is, when you log into Kerberos, and as you are issued tickets for Kerberized services, all of the tickets are stored in a file. This method was chosen because it is the most portable; every platform has a filesystem, and it is easy to read and write to files. However, this method is inflexible and insecure. Therefore, other ports of the MIT Kerberos code, as well as independent implementations from other vendors, include other methods of storing tickets. Both the Microsoft and Apple implementations of Kerberos include a memory-based credential cache that ensures that credentials are kept in memory and destroyed upon the termination of the login session.

Since the default credential cache is a file-based credential cache, we'll take a look at what one looks like. No matter where the credential cache is stored, it still contains the same information: a user principal, and a set of service tickets that the user has obtained throughout their login session. A sample credential cache is shown below:

```
$ klist
Ticket cache: FILE:/tmp/krb5cc_502_auJKaJ
Default principal: jgarman@WEDGIE.ORG

Valid starting     Expires            Service principal
09/10/02 01:48:12  09/10/02 11:48:12  krbtgt/WEDGIE.ORG@WEDGIE.ORG
09/10/02 01:48:14  09/10/02 11:48:12  host/cfs.wedgie.org@WEDGIE.ORG
09/10/02 04:20:42  09/10/02 11:48:12  host/web.wedgie.org@WEDGIE.ORG
```

In this example, the credential cache for the user principal of *jgarman@WEDGIE.ORG* is stored in the file */tmp/krb5cc_502_auJKaJ*. Credential caches can only be associated with one user principal at a time; if I wanted to access services with a principal of *jgarman/admin@WEDGIE.ORG* instead, I would have to destroy my current tickets and re-login to Kerberos as *jgarman/admin@WEDGIE.ORG*.

Putting the Pieces Together

Now that we've covered the basic topics that you'll need to understand Kerberos, let's begin to put all of these pieces together by examining the credential cache above.

Inside the credential cache, I have obtained an initial Ticket Granting Ticket through the Authentication Server (this is the first ticket out of three). By logging into this system, the system created this credential cache and obtained a TGT for me. During my log in session, I also logged into a host called *cfs.wedgie.org*, which has a Kerberized telnet daemon running on it. Because I was using Kerberos authentication, I was able to log into cfs without typing a password; instead, my telnet client obtained a service principal from the Ticket Granting Server, and used that ticket to contact the Kerberized telnet on cfs. Later, I did the same, except this time I logged into *web.wedgie.org*.

During this time, after logging in to three machines (including my initial authentication to Kerberos), I have only typed in my password once. The Kerberos software requested, generated, and sent tickets on my behalf as necessary to transparently authenticate me to the other machines as I accessed them. As a user, all of this happens behind the scenes. Now we'll peel back the curtain, and uncover the magic that occurs behind the scenes.

CHAPTER 3

Protocols

The previous two chapters introduced the major concepts that underlie the Kerberos authentication system, and presented a short, high-level discussion of how Kerberos performs its magic. This chapter continues that discussion by drilling down into the nitty-gritty of the Kerberos protocol and presenting it on a fundamental level.

Creating a protocol that verifies the identity of two endpoints on a network given an underlying network that provides no security is a daunting task. Kerberos was designed under the assumption that attackers can read, copy, and create network traffic at will.

As you now know, there are two versions of Kerberos that are currently in wide usage: Kerberos 4 and Kerberos 5. This chapter covers the protocol details of both. While the concepts and protocol design of both Kerberos 4 and 5 are very similar, there are major differences between their byte-level protocol and implementation.

The original Kerberos 4 protocol was never published apart from the Kerberos 4 source distribution. As such, the Kerberos 4 source code from MIT is the only official documentation of the Kerberos 4 protocol. On the other hand, the newer Kerberos 5 protocol is extensively documented in RFC 1510, and also through a series of documents that are collectively known as the Kerberos Clarifications.

The basic operation of Kerberos is based on a paper published in 1978 by Needham and Schroeder. Since the Needham-Schroeder protocol is the basis upon which Kerberos is built, we will begin our discussion there.

The Needham-Schroeder Protocol

Roger Needham and Michael Schroeder of the Xerox Palo Alto Research Center published a paper in December of 1978 describing their framework for designing a secure network authentication system. The paper, entitled "Using Encryption for Authentication in Large Networks of Computers," described two different protocols that could be implemented to provide a reliable, secure authentication service for a distributed network of computers. The first protocol described in the paper uses private key encryption, and it is this protocol that forms the basis of the Kerberos network authentication protocol.

Needham and Schroeder outlined several assumptions around which they designed their protocol. One assumption, the ability for a malicious attacker to capture packets in-transit on the network, modify them, and send packets of his own design, was described by the authors as an "extreme view," yet now is regarded as a routine requirement for any secure network protocol. Designing a protocol that is resistant to these types of attacks is difficult, and I'll point out the specific design decisions that were made to thwart them as I discuss the protocol.

Other assumptions made by the authors, however, did not hold up as well in practice as they did on paper. The assumption that users' secret keys are not readily available through an exhaustive search has not held up in the hostile environments in which Kerberos operates. No matter how much education you provide users, users will continue to choose poor passwords. The Needham-Schroeder protocol, and consequently the basic Kerberos protocol, provides no protection against an offline brute force or dictionary attack against a user's secret key, as we'll see in Chapter 6.

The Needham-Schroeder protocol defines three participants in the protocol exchange: a client machine, a server that the client wishes to access, and an authentication server. The client is any machine that requests authentication; usually, it's a user's personal desktop. The server is any application server, say a mail server, which provides a service the client wishes to contact. Finally, the authentication server is a dedicated server that holds a copy of the encryption keys for all users and servers on the network (the "trusted third-party"). This should sound familiar; these are the same three players involved with the Kerberos protocol.

The concept behind the Needham-Schroeder protocol is not to authenticate the user directly by sending a password or password equivalent (such as a hash of the password) to the authentication server. Instead, the Needham-Schroeder protocol provides a mechanism to securely distribute a short-lived encryption key to two parties (a client and a server) so their communication can be secured with the encryption key. The verification of each endpoint's identity happens to be a side effect of this key exchange process. We'll see what this means as we discuss how the protocol works.

The protocol begins with the client contacting the authentication server. The client sends the authentication server a message containing its own identity and the identity of the application server that it wishes to contact. In addition, the client includes a nonce, or a random value, with its request. We'll see why this random value is important in a moment. Figure 3-1 illustrates the information sent by the client to the authentication server.

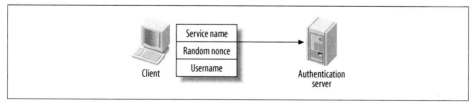

Figure 3-1. Needham-Schroeder authentication request

The authentication server receives this information and locates the secret encryption keys it has stored for both the client and application server. It also creates a third key, the *session key*, which can be used to enable secure communication between the client and application server. This new key is a random key generated by the authentication server, is completely unrelated to the long-term keys of both the client and server, and is never reused.

Next comes the tricky part. In the Needham-Schroeder protocol, the authentication server never communicates directly with the application server, only the client. Therefore, the authentication server sends a reply back to the client that includes the session key and the verified identities of both parties. But how can this message be kept secure from an observer who is watching network traffic to snag these session keys as they pass through the wire? And furthermore, when the client transmits the session key and its identity to the application server, how does the application server know that the client is not lying, and that the message is authentic?

The answer involves several layers of encryption. First, a message is constructed that is intended to be viewed only by the application server. This message includes the name of the requesting client and the session key. To keep this message secure from eavesdropping and tampering by a malicious client, it is encrypted with the long-term key of the application server. Since only the application server and the authentication server know this key, an attacker cannot decrypt this message to alter the contents or steal the session key. In Kerberos terminology, this encrypted message is also known as a *ticket*.

The message is wrapped inside of another message, this one intended for the client. The client message also includes the name of the application server, a copy of the session key, and a copy of the nonce originally sent in the first message. The whole message is then encrypted with the client's long-term key. Once all the information has been assembled and encrypted, the authentication server sends it to the client (Figure 3-2).

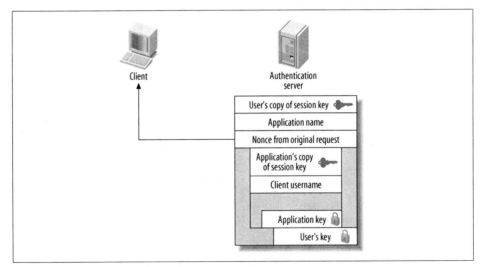

Figure 3-2. Needham-Schroeder authentication reply

Needham-Schroeder, Kerberos, and Locked Boxes

It's easy to get confused by all of the encryption that's happening in the Needham-Schroeder protocol (and, consequently, the Kerberos protocol). Since there are often multiple layers of encryption at work, it's useful to have a real-world analogy to relate to when discussing these protocol exchanges.

A good analogy in this case is a set of locked boxes, nested inside each other. The encryption keys can be thought of as real-life keys that can open these boxes. So, in this analogy, the user's password can be translated into a physical key. Two copies of that key exist: the user has one copy, and the authentication server has another copy. The same situation exists for service keys: each application server has two identical keys, one held by the server itself, and the other held by the authentication servers. Boxes locked with the user's key can be unlocked with a copy of the user's key, and the same with the service key.

Figure 3-3 shows the authentication server's reply to a client's authentication request. The first box (the *ticket* box) contains a copy of the session key and a piece of paper containing the name of the client; it is locked with the service's key. The second box (the *reply* box) contains the other copy of the session key and is locked with the user's key. In addition, the first box, locked with the service's key, is placed inside the second box. By placing the ticket box inside of the reply box, the authentication server ensures that only the legitimate user can unlock the reply in order to get the ticket, since only the user has a key that can open the reply.

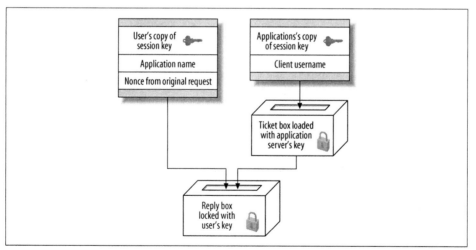

Figure 3-3. Needham-Schroeder authentication reply represented as locked boxes

Note that the authentication server does not know whether the requesting client is actually who she claims to be. The authentication server will return this encrypted message to anyone who requests it, granted of course that the client's name exists in the authentication server's database of encryption keys. This seems to indicate that any user could masquerade as any other user when requesting authentication to an arbitrary service. However, since the message is encrypted with the client's key, it cannot be decrypted by anyone but the legitimate client.

Therefore, when the client receives this reply from the authentication server, it first decrypts the "outer" layer with its key (the client's password). The user is prompted for her password. If the password fails to decrypt the message, then the authentication request has failed.

Now all that's left is for the client to send the session key back to the application server (Figure 3-4). This is where the inner contents of the last message come into play. Now that the client has removed the first "layer" of encryption, the client can send the application server the inner portion of the message (the ticket), which consists of a copy of the session key and the client's name. Since this message is still encrypted with the application server's key, only the application server can read it, and attackers are unable to modify it.

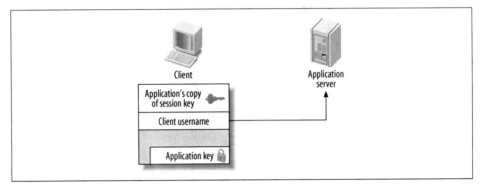

Figure 3-4. Client sends session key to application server

At this point, it would seem that we're done; any communication that occurs henceforth that is encrypted with the session key should only be understood by the client and application server. The client knows that the application server is legitimate since only the legitimate application server can decrypt the message containing the session key (as it is encrypted with the long-term key of the application server). The application server knows that the client is legitimate because only the legitimate client could decrypt the message that contains the session key and identity of the client that was forwarded to the application server.

There is, however, one more attack that can be undertaken against this scheme, and this is where the nonce that we mentioned earlier comes into play.

Let's take a look at the situation that is presented to an attacker who wishes to impersonate a client, so that the attacker can communicate with an application server under the guise of the victim's identity. We'll assume that the attacker has the ability to read all network messages and send messages of his own crafting, but does not have knowledge of the long-term key of the client or the service (which would, obviously, allow him to impersonate the victim without any trickery).

Since all of the protocol exchanges above are simply electronic messages sent over an insecure network, the attacker manages to acquire the authentication message sent from a victim to the application server (the message that contains the session key and the identity of the client, both encrypted with the application server's key). The attacker can simply resend that message at a later time to the application server. Since the message can be decrypted by the application server, generating a valid session key and identity (of the victim), then it is accepted as legitimate and the session is authenticated. While the attacker does not know the session key, if the application server only uses the protocol to ensure authentication and does not use the session key to encipher its communications to clients, then the attacker can completely impersonate the victim.

These attacks are known as *replay attacks*, and the Needham-Schroeder protocol supplies a rather obvious solution to thwart these attacks: force the client to prove to the application server that it really does know the session key. To do this, the application server generates another random number, encrypts it with the session key, and sends it to the client. Then the client decrypts the number, performs an operation on it (for example, adding one to it), encrypts the new number with the session key, and sends the message back to the application server. Through this process, only authentic clients that have knowledge of the session key can send back the correct number, and observers who replay previous messages cannot (Figure 3-5).

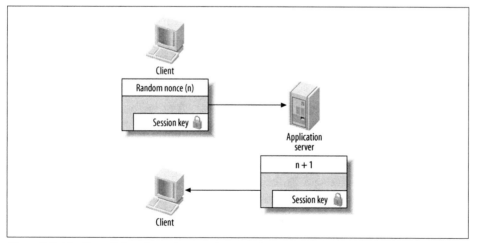

Figure 3-5. Needham-Schroeder replay attack prevention

Here we see one of the many practical problems presented when attackers are assumed to have the ability to both read all network traffic as well as send arbitrary messages on the network. The Needham-Schroeder protocol uses an interactive challenge-response system that requires the client to prove that it knows the session key.

The Kerberos protocol uses a slightly different approach—based on synchronized clocks—to thwart replay, as we'll see in the next section. We'll also discuss replay attacks in Chapter 6, with more replay attack scenarios that present themselves in some Kerberos software.

Kerberos 4

The Kerberos 4 protocol is largely based on the Needham-Schroeder protocol, with two major changes.

The hosts involved in the Kerberos 4 protocol exchanges map directly to the principals involved in the Needham-Schroeder protocol. The authentication client is a Kerberos 4 user workstation, and the authentication server maps to a Kerberos 4 Key Distribution Center.

The first change to the Needham-Schroeder protocol reduced the amount of network messages sent between the client and the authentication server. The original Needham-Schroeder protocol did not have a dependence on a network time source, but the cost was an extra two message exchanges. The last two message exchanges in the Needham-Schroeder protocol establish that there is no man in the middle posing as the authentication server, and that the session key is not a replay. In the Kerberos 4 protocol, replay is thwarted through an authenticator message that is constructed of the local time of the client encrypted with the newly-negotiated session key of the connection. While this requires time synchronization between all hosts involved, it does reduce the number of network messages required per authentication exchange.

The second, more significant, change to the basic protocol creates the concept of a Ticket Granting Ticket, which allows users to authenticate to multiple application servers while entering their authentication secret only once. If the original Needham-Schroeder protocol were implemented as-is, a user would need to enter her password every time that she wishes to log into an application server. One of the major design goals for Kerberos was to create a single-sign-on system in which users only need to enter their credentials once per day, and all future authentication requests are handled transparently, without user intervention.

As a result, the Kerberos 4 protocol is split into two logical components: the Authentication Server and the Ticket Granting Server. Note that there is an unfortunate clash in terminology here. The Kerberos Authentication Server should not be confused with the Needham-Schroeder authentication server; the former performs a subset of the services of the latter, as we'll see in a bit. To keep the distinction clear, references to the Kerberos Authentication Server and Ticket Granting Server will be capitalized or abbreviated as AS or TGS, respectively. While these components are usually implemented as a single program that runs on the KDC, they are logically separate processes.

Still other changes reflect the realities of the security of today's computer networks. The original Needham-Schroeder protocol assumed that all secrets involved, including the user's long term key, the application server's long term key, and the session key that is randomly generated by the KDC, are always kept secret. In reality, machines are compromised and people give away their passwords. In addition, the single-sign-on capability provided in Kerberos 4 means that users' workstations will have cached credentials that, if left unguarded, can be used by an attacker to impersonate the user. Therefore, Kerberos 4 introduces limited lifetimes for credentials, enforced by the Kerberos KDC and Kerberos libraries. Without ticket expiration, a user could log in once, and never have to log in again (provided that their credentials are never removed from the workstation). Lifetimes ensure that users must verify their identity periodically—say, once a day—by entering their password again. They also close the window of vulnerability in the case of stolen credentials.

The Authentication Server and the Ticket Granting Server

The Authentication Server performs one function: receive a request containing the username of the client requesting authentication, and return an encrypted Ticket Granting Ticket for that user. Then, the client can use this Ticket Granting Ticket (the TGT) to request further tickets for other services.

When a client has no Kerberos tickets cached, or tickets that have expired, then the client must communicate with the Authentication Server to get an initial ticket to the Ticket Granting Server. This typically happens at the beginning of each day, as most Kerberos implementations default to 8–10 hour ticket lifetimes.

The first message sent to the Kerberos KDC from the client is the Authentication Server Request message, also known as an AS_REQ message. This message is sent in plain text, containing the identity of the client, the client's local time, and the Ticket Granting Server's principal name. By convention, in Kerberos 4, the Ticket Granting Server's principal name is *krbtgt*. In addition, the Ticket Granting Server's principal always has an instance component. The instance component is the realm for which the ticket granting server can issue further tickets. Every realm contains at least one Ticket Granting Server, a TGS with an instance of the realm itself. For example, the Ticket Granting Server for the WEDGIE.ORG realm is *krbtgt.WEDGIE.ORG@WEDGIE.ORG*.

A special case occurs when two or more realms trust each other's users and services. This relationship, known as a *cross-realm trust*, requires special TGS principals to be set up in all participating realms, with different instance components representing the different realms. We won't talk more about cross-realm here; instead, we'll come back and explore the implementation of cross-realm authentication in Chapter 8.

Once the KDC receives the AS_REQ message, it verifies that the requesting principal exists, and that the client's timestamp is close to the KDC's local time (usually this means within five minutes). This check is made not to detect replay; after all, the AS_REQ message is sent entirely in clear text. Instead, it performs the timestamp check so that clients can provide users a message early in the authentication process in the event of a time mismatch between the client and the KDC. If either of these checks fails, an error message is sent back to the client and the client is not authenticated.

Next, the Authentication Server generates a random session key. This session key will be shared between the client and the Ticket Granting Server. This key secures the ticket requests that the client makes to the Ticket Granting Server later on for specific Kerberized services. The KDC makes two copies of this session key: one for the client, and one for the Ticket Granting Server.

The KDC responds with an Authentication Server Reply message, or AS_REP message. This message includes the information above—most importantly, a copy of the session key and verified identity of the client encrypted with the Ticket Granting Server's key, and another copy of the session key encrypted with the user's long-term key. As long as the client has knowledge of the user's long-term key, then the client can decrypt the message encrypted with the user's key, and acquire the session key now shared between the client and the Ticket Granting Server. The knowledge of this session key and the possession of the Ticket Granting Ticket (the other copy of the session key, encrypted with the Ticket Granting Server's key) allow the client to obtain tickets for further Kerberos services without requiring the user to re-enter their password.

This implies that the security of your Kerberos system is highly dependent on the passwords your users choose. Since the Authentication Server will happily return an encrypted Ticket Granting Ticket valid for any principal to any client, the only line of defense against attackers is a strong password. A further discussion of this issue can be found in Chapter 6. The AS_REQ and AS_REP exchange is summarized in Figure 3-6.

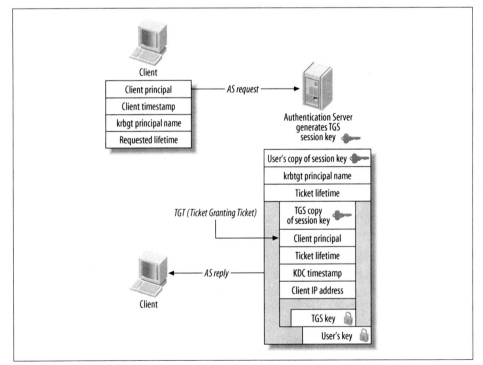

Figure 3-6. Authentication Server request-and-reply exchange

Once the Authentication Server transaction has completed, the client possesses a session key, encrypted with the user's long-term key, as well as a Ticket Granting Ticket, encrypted first with the Ticket Granting Server's key. The client attempts to decrypt the message with the user's long-term key (password). If this decryption is successful, then the password is correct and the client stores the Ticket Granting Ticket as well as its copy of the session key in a credential cache. Remember that even though the client has removed the outer layer of encryption of the Ticket Granting Ticket, it is still encrypted with the Ticket Granting Server's key. Therefore, the client cannot read the contents of the Ticket Granting Ticket; instead, it simply stores the encrypted contents in the credential cache.

When the user wishes to authenticate to a Kerberized service later, there is a separate protocol exchange with the Ticket Granting Server. The client prepares a message to the Ticket Granting Server consisting of three parts: a TGS request, a copy of the Ticket Granting Ticket acquired earlier, and an *authenticator* that serves to thwart replay.

The authenticator consists of a timestamp, encrypted with the session key acquired from the Authentication Server exchange. The authenticator ensures that every ticket request packet is unique, and also proves that the client has knowledge of the shared session key established during the Authentication Server exchange. Without the authenticator, an attacker could simply listen on the network for a ticket sent by the KDC to a legitimate client, make a copy of the ticket, and replay that ticket to either the KDC (in the case of a Ticket Granting Ticket) or an application server (in the case of a service ticket).

Upon receipt of the ticket request from the client, the KDC formulates a reply message that includes a new set of session keys, shared between the client and the application server. The client's copy of the new session key is encrypted with the older session key, established during the Authentication Server exchange. This ensures that only the valid client can read the new session key for use with the application server. The service's copy of the new session key is embedded inside of a *service ticket*, encrypted with the service's long-term key. The client appends this service ticket and the new session key to its credential cache for later retrieval. When the client contacts the application server, the knowledge of this service ticket and the session key will prove to the service that the client is authentic. Figure 3-7 depicts the protocol messages involved in the Ticket Granting Server exchange.

The three major cryptographic messages that are passed back and forth in both the Authentication Server and Ticket Granting Server exchange are the service ticket, the Ticket Granting Ticket, and the authenticator. Figure 3-8 depicts the contents of these cryptographic messages.

Note that in the Kerberos system, the KDC does not specify policy on what principals are authorized to access a given service. The KDC will, after ensuring the validity of the Ticket Granting Ticket sent by the client, happily issue a ticket for any

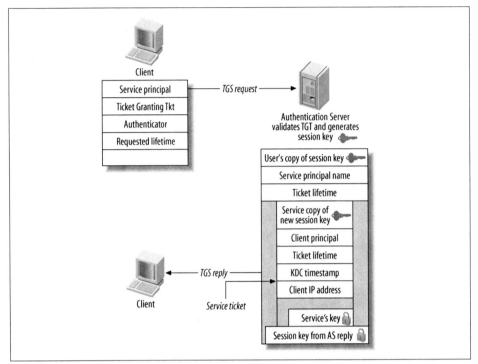

Figure 3-7. Ticket Granting Server message exchange

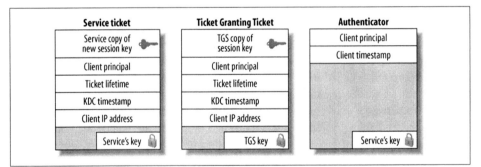

Figure 3-8. Service ticket, Ticket Granting Ticket, and authenticator

service that it knows about. Kerberos leaves the authorization decisions to the individual application servers. The possession of a valid service ticket for a given service does not imply that the user should be granted access to that service; instead, it assures the end service of the authenticity of the end user's credentials. Figure 3-9 summarizes the network exchanges between the Authentication Server and the Ticket Granting Server.

The details of the final step in authentication—how the client sends the service ticket to an application server—are different for every application server. Kerberos does not

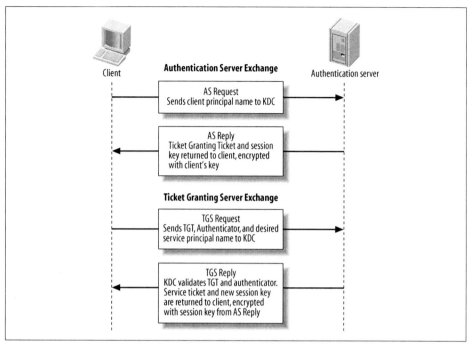

Figure 3-9. Authentication Server and Ticket Granting Server protocol exchanges

define a standard for doing this; instead, it is up to each application to define a method for the client to send its service ticket and an authenticator for authentication. While Kerberos provides function libraries that can formulate and read messages to perform these tasks, the actual transmission and reception of the messages is wholly application-dependent.

String-to-Key Transformation

Kerberos 4 requires a transformation between the textual passwords that people remember and the 56-bit DES key that is actually used for encryption and decryption of the messages passed back and forth between client, KDC, and application server. This transformation is referred to as a *string-to-key* function, usually shortened to simply *string2key*. The transformation is very similar to the functions used to "encrypt" passwords in the standard Unix */etc/passwd* file. It is a one-way hash function that, in the case of Kerberos 4, uses the principal's password as input, and outputs a 56-bit hexadecimal DES key. Since the function is one way, it is mathematically very hard (read as impossible) to reverse the algorithm to deduce the password from the generated DES key. However, since this algorithm is public (and, indeed, must be widely known in order for different Kerberos implementations to interoperate), a brute-force or dictionary attack can be used to try passwords to find a matching DES key for a particular message.

The details of the string2key function are not particularly important to this discussion. If you're interested in exactly how the transformation is performed, the string2key function is included in both the MIT and kth-krb Kerberos 4 distributions. In addition, kth-krb includes a kstring2key program that, given a password as input, outputs the hexadecimal DES key resulting from the string2key transformation.

The Key Version Number

The *key version number*, commonly abbreviated as kvno, distinguishes between different encryption keys that are stored for a given principal. For example, if a user changes his password, then his principal has a new encryption key associated with it. When the Kerberos KDC stores his new encryption key in the Kerberos database, it increments the key version number. Similarly, if a service's long-term key is changed, the key version number also changes.

Key version numbers are not important when dealing with user principals. However, they do become important when working with Kerberized services. In order for Kerberized services to be able to read the ticket contents sent by clients for authentication, both the encryption key and the key version number that is stored in the service's keytab must match the encryption key and key version number that is stored in the Kerberos database. A mismatch in either the encryption key or key version number will cause the decryption process to fail.

Password Changing

The original Kerberos specifications had no provisions to allow users to change their own passwords. However, the ability for users to change their passwords is a requirement for any practical authentication scheme, so Kerberos 4 implementations grafted on password-changing protocols. As a result, most Kerberos 4 packages implement password changing through a separate administrative protocol, the same protocol that is used to remotely administer the Kerberos database.

Both MIT and kth-krb run the password through the string2key function on the client side to avoid sending even the encrypted text password over the network. This has the advantage of not exposing a plain text password over the network, but has the down side that all password quality checks must be implemented on the client side, so a rogue password-changing client could bypass all quality checks.

The administrative protocols for MIT and kth-krb differ, so there is no interoperability between the password-changing services in either. The kpasswd program from one will not connect to the password-changing service provided by the other.

Kerberos 5

If you look strictly at the feature set, Kerberos 5 is an evolution of Kerberos 4. The Kerberos 5 protocol contains all of the functionality present in the Kerberos 4 protocol, but with many extensions. However, from an implementation perspective,

Kerberos 5 is a completely new protocol, and looks nothing like Kerberos 4 on the inside. In this section, we'll examine the new features present in Kerberos 5 as well as the new infrastructure provided by the protocol to make these features work.

The Kerberos 4 protocol had its share of shortcomings: it had a rather obtuse structure (for example, instead of standardizing on one byte order, it had a flag to specify which byte order was used to send a particular message) and it wasn't expandable, since many of its fields had fixed sizes. This limitation led to other problems, most notably the dependence on single-DES encryption keys. At the time that Kerberos 4 was developed, a brute-force attack against DES was still prohibitively expensive in terms of both resources and time. As computer speed continues to grow exponentially, it is now within the realm of well-funded adversaries to mount a brute-force attack against DES. Therefore, a more secure encryption algorithm with a longer encryption key size is needed. Unfortunately, since all of the fields in Kerberos 4 are fixed size, there is no way to retrofit Kerberos 4 with another encryption algorithm.

Another feature that users and administrators alike demanded from a new version of Kerberos was support for credential forwarding and delegation. Credential forwarding enables users to transfer their tickets to a remote server once they are authenticated to it. For example, take a user who has just logged in remotely to an application server via Kerberized telnet. Using Kerberos 4, if the user wishes to authenticate to, say, a file server, from the application server, she's essentially stuck. She must re-login to Kerberos from the remote server through kinit to acquire a new Ticket Granting Ticket on the remote server. This introduces security problems, since in order to re-authenticate to Kerberos, the user must retype her password, which in the case of telnet, is probably being sent in clear text over the network. In addition, the system no longer provides single-sign-on.

Kerberos 5 introduces support for credential forwarding so that in the previous example, when the user logs into the remote application server, her Ticket Granting Ticket is securely transmitted to the remote server and can be used by applications on that remote server to transparently authenticate her to further Kerberos services.

However, with these enhancements and extensibility comes complexity. In order to create an extensible protocol that can be implemented on multiple platforms by multiple vendors, and ensure that all these implementations can interoperate, the Kerberos development team chose to use a technology known as ASN.1 to describe their new Kerberos 5 protocol. ASN.1 allows protocol designers to create protocols with an abstract language, automating implementation details and allowing for future extensions. We'll talk more about ASN.1 and how ASN.1 is used to define the Kerberos 5 protocol messages in a bit.

Kerberos 5 strives to be as compatible with older clients and application servers as possible. In order to ensure compatibility with old Kerberos 4 software, Kerberos 5 provides the Kerberos 5-to-Kerberos 4 ticket translator service (commonly known as krb524). This service takes a valid Kerberos 5 ticket as input (the only requirement is that the ticket and session key encryption types be single-DES, as that is the only encryption type supported in Kerberos 4) and creates a valid Kerberos 4 ticket as output. By using the krb524 daemon, an organization can incorporate older Kerberos 4 services into a more modern Kerberos 5 infrastructure.

The Kerberos 5 protocol is under constant revision and development. The Kerberos home page at *http://www.kerberos.isi.edu* is the official home of the Kerberos Clarifications, a new set of documents being drafted to supersede the current RFC 1510. The Kerberos Clarifications documents are considered the definitive source for information on the Kerberos protocol.

The World's Shortest ASN.1 Tutorial

ASN.1 is an acronym for Abstract Syntax Notation One. It defines a methodology for describing protocol definitions in an abstract notation, and then provides several methods to convert those abstract definitions into a stream of bytes for transmission over a communications network. Several protocols use ASN.1 to define their protocols; along with Kerberos 5, SNMP and LDAP are popular protocols that use ASN.1.

As we saw earlier with the Kerberos 4 protocol definition, extensibility is an important attribute when designing protocols. No protocol remains static; it is much more efficient for both the implementer and users if a protocol has forward and backward compatibility built in from the start. A manually designed and coded protocol design such as that in Kerberos 4 is very difficult to add onto later, unless extreme care is undertaken during the design of the initial protocol. In addition, manual coding of the network encoding and decoding modules leads to bugs that then lead to trouble with interoperability when new implementations must work around or conform to bugs in the initial implementation. ASN.1 can help with both of these problems.

ASN.1 provides a grammar with which protocol designers can describe an application's protocol. ASN.1 also provides several built-in types such as INTEGER, representing an arbitrary integer number, and OCTET STRING, representing a string of characters. By chaining together these basic types to build more complex types, implementers can design what is referred to as the *abstract syntax* of their protocol, that is, a textual description of the protocol in an easily parseable form. The grammar used to describe this abstract syntax is similar to the BNF (Backus-Naur Form) commonly used to describe computer languages. Here's a sample ASN.1 definition:

```
Realm ::=           GeneralString
PrincipalName ::=   SEQUENCE {
                    name-type[0]     INTEGER,
                    name-string[1]   SEQUENCE OF GeneralString
}
```

These are the two ASN.1 definitions in Kerberos 5 that define the parts of a Kerberos 5 principal. The Realm definition is fairly straightforward; a realm can be defined as a string of characters. The PrincipalName consists of a type (which indicates a style of name—Kerberos 5 defines several, including the traditional Internet-style names in the form of user@REALM and X.500) and an ordered sequence of strings, representing the components of the Kerberos principal. With Realm and PrincipalName defined, future ASN.1 definitions can use these types in more complex structures, such as a ticket structure or authenticator structure.

Now that we have this abstract syntax in place, we need some way to transmit and receive data that conforms to our syntax. For example, if we want to send and receive a set of PrincipalNames over the network, we need some sort of rule that specifies how to encode strings, integers, and sequences of strings (we want to ensure we get things in the right order, too!). As it turns out, there are several different standards related to encoding ASN.1 data for transmission, but the one that Kerberos uses is the Distinguished Encoding Rule, or DER. DER takes an ASN.1 data structure—say, a PrincipalName with its fields filled in by an application—and converts it into *transfer syntax*, or a series of bytes that can be sent to another application that speaks the same ASN.1-based protocol.

I won't bore you with details of how DER does its dirty work, but it works on a simple principal: the so-called TLV rule. TLV refers to *type*, *length*, *value*—the three pieces of information that are sent for every data field in an ASN.1 structure. The type refers to the ASN.1 type that the data represents: a byte constant is assigned to GeneralStrings to mark them as such, another byte represents INTEGER data, and so on. In addition, labels can be added to the types of each field, as indicated by the square brackets above. The labels ensure that the ordering of the data is preserved, and that the recipient can identify any optional or missing data. The length of the encoded data is sent next, and finally the data itself. By sending all of this information, a receiving host can reconstruct the original data structure from the transfer syntax.

With an ASN.1 abstract syntax in place, a specialized ASN.1 compiler can read the abstract syntax and generate program code that converts a given data structure that matches the abstract syntax into transfer syntax, and vice versa. The ASN.1 compiler automates the troublesome process of creating code to send and receive encoded protocol messages, giving the protocol implementer more time to write the program logic dedicated to their protocol.

Readers with an interest in learning more about ASN.1 can read the Layman's Guide to ASN.1, BER, and DER, which is available in several formats from the RSA Laboratories web site at *http://www.rsasecurity.com/rsalabs/pkcs/index.html*. In addition, a freely downloadable book documenting ASN.1 is available in PDF format from *http://www.oss.com/asn1/dubuisson.html* for those interested in more technical details.

The Authentication Server and the Ticket Granting Server

The idea behind the AS and TGS exchanges are unchanged in Kerberos 5. The name of the Ticket Granting Server changes slightly, thanks to the different principal naming conventions in Kerberos 5. For example, the Ticket Granting Server principal name in Kerberos 5 for the WEDGIE.ORG realm is *krbtgt/WEDGIE.ORG@WEDGIE.ORG*.

There are some protocol level details that have been changed in Kerberos 5, however. We've already discussed the most important one, namely, the use of ASN.1 to formally describe and encode the new protocol. In addition, the other protocol-level change that was made during the development of Kerberos 5 was to eliminate the double encryption that occurs during the Authentication Server and Ticket Granting server KDC replies. Recall from the discussion of the Kerberos 4 protocol above that there were essentially two layers of encryption in either an AS or TGS reply; the ticket, encrypted with the service's key, is contained within a reply message encrypted with the user's key.

This double encryption proves to be unnecessary, so Kerberos 5 concatenates the two encrypted messages one after the other instead of nesting the ticket inside of the reply message. This step improves efficiency and performance, and does not reduce the security of the messages. As the messages are still both encrypted with their respective keys, they are unreadable to attackers who do not have the relevant encryption keys to decrypt the messages.

New Encryption Options

The new multiple encryption type support in Kerberos 5 also means that there can be more than one encryption type used in a given Kerberos protocol transaction. A separate encryption type can be used in each of the following messages:

Ticket
> The encryption type associated with the ticket is the encryption type used to encrypt the service ticket in the TGS or AS reply. Since the ticket can only be decrypted by the service, as it is encrypted with the service's encryption key, the ticket encryption type is determined by the highest strength encryption supported by the service for which the ticket is issued.

Reply
> The encryption type of the reply from the KDC to the client refers to the part of the reply encrypted with the user's encryption key. Since the client must decrypt the reply, the reply encryption type is determined by the highest strength encryption the client supports.

Session key
> Since the session key is shared between the client and the application server, the encryption type of the session key is the maximum-strength encryption algorithm that is supported by both the service and the client. For example, if the client supports single and triple DES but the service only supports single DES, then the KDC will issue single DES session keys for this service.

A diagram showing where each encryption key comes into play in a typical TGS reply is shown in Figure 3-10.

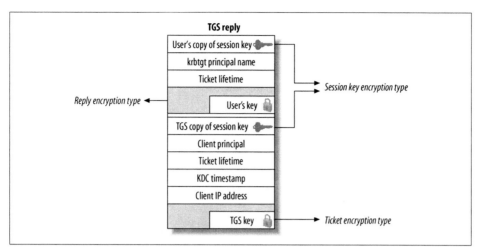

Figure 3-10. Encryption types in a typical TGS reply

Why the separation? Namely, to support interoperation between different Kerberos 5 implementations, older Kerberos 4 based applications, and interoperability between Kerberos 5 implementations that support different encryption types.

This fine-grained control enables any combination of encryption type support to interoperate on a Kerberos network, as long as all three parties involved (the application server, the client, and the KDC) all support at least one encryption type in common. When a principal is created on a KDC, it typically stores a copy of its encryption key using all of the different encryption types that it supports. Therefore, the KDC can respond to requests using the most secure encryption type supported by each participating party.

Unfortunately, while this scheme is rather flexible, it can also lead to problems that are difficult to track down. We'll look more into encryption-type mismatch issues in Chapter 5.

Ticket Options

Kerberos 5 includes advanced features that allow users more control over their Kerberos tickets. The following flags have been added to Kerberos 5:

Forwardable tickets

A user can request a *forwardable* ticket. A forwardable ticket can be forwarded to another host later—hence the name—and the ticket is valid for use on the new host. A common special case is the forwardable Ticket Granting Ticket. A forwardable TGT can be forwarded to another host, and the original TGT can be used to acquire a new TGT on the target host, without requiring the user to enter his password in again. For example, if a user logs into one host using Kerberos authentication, the user now has to acquire a new TGT before using

Kerberos software on the target host. If, instead, the user has a forwardable ticket and forwards his TGT to the target host as part of the login process, the user now has a copy of his TGT valid for any further Kerberos ticket requests from the new host. By requesting a forwardable TGT, users can enjoy the benefits of single sign on, even when arbitrarily nesting credential delegations.

Proxiable tickets

You can also set the *proxiable* flag on a ticket. Proxiable tickets are similar to forwardable tickets in that they can be transferred to another host. However, a proxiable TGT can only be used to acquire further service tickets; it cannot be used to acquire a new TGT on the target host. In this sense, proxiable tickets are less powerful than their forwardable counterparts, and are not used often in practice.

Renewable tickets

In Kerberos 4, ticket lifetimes were limited to reduce the window of vulnerability in case a user's credentials were stolen. Kerberos 5 introduces a two-tiered lifetime scheme that combines the benefits of longer lifetimes with the security of shorter lifetimes. When a user requests a renewable ticket, he is issued a ticket with a standard lifetime and a renewable lifetime. The ticket is valid only for the duration of the standard lifetime, but can be submitted back to the KDC for renewal any time before the ticket expires (at the end of the standard lifetime). The KDC can refuse to validate the ticket, if, for example, it has been reported compromised in the mean time. Otherwise, the KDC validates the ticket and returns another ticket. This process can be repeated until the ticket's renewable lifetime finally expires.

Postdated tickets

A postdated ticket is one which is not valid until some specified date in the future. If a postdated ticket is presented for validation before the start date embedded in the ticket, it will be refused. Postdated tickets are useful for jobs scheduled to be run some time in the future that require Kerberos authentication, such as batch or cluster jobs. This option is not commonly used in practice, and in fact some implementations, such as Microsoft's, do not support the issuing of postdated tickets.

Kerberos 5-to-4 Ticket Translation

To provide compatibility with older Kerberos 4 services, Kerberos 5 specifies a Kerberos 5-to-4 ticket translation service. This service, known as krb524, provides a way that Kerberos 5 clients can communicate with older Kerberos 4 services. It does not provide a way for Kerberos 4 clients to communicate with Kerberos 5 services or KDCs.

When a Kerberos 5 client wishes to contact a service that only understands Kerberos 4 tickets, the Kerberos libraries contact a machine running the krb524 daemon to provide Kerberos 4 compatible credentials to present to the service. When the krb524 daemon receives a request from a client, it decrypts the service ticket with the service's key, extracts the session key contained inside, and creates a new Kerberos 4 ticket for the same service and client, pasting in the session key from the original Kerberos 5 ticket.

Note that in this process, the session key contained inside of the original Kerberos 5 ticket must be a single DES key. The krb524 daemon will not create a new session key; instead, it only copies the session key from the current ticket to a new Kerberos 4 ticket. Since Kerberos 4 can only handle single DES key types, this session key must be a single DES key.

Also, the machine that runs the krb524 daemon does not necessarily have to be a Kerberos KDC. The krb524 daemon does, however, need access to the secret key of the Kerberos 4 services involved. This can be accomplished if the krb524 daemon is running on the same machine as one of the Kerberos KDCs. However, if this is not possible, for example, if your KDC is a Windows domain controller that does not support Kerberos 5-to-4 ticket translation, then the krb524 daemon can be run on a separate machine. The service keys for any Kerberos 4 services can be extracted to a keytab located on the machine running the krb524 daemon, so that it can decrypt the Kerberos 5 tickets and create a new Kerberos 4 ticket for the service.

Pre-Authentication

The original Kerberos 4 protocol was susceptible to offline dictionary and brute-force attacks, as we'll see in Chapter 6. This vulnerability stems from the fact that the KDC issues an encrypted TGT to any client for any principal (given that the requested principal exists in the Kerberos database). Since the KDC happily provides a ticket encrypted with the principals' secret key to any requestor, an offline attack can be mounted to determine the principal's secret key. This vulnerability is exacerbated by the fact that users typically choose poor passwords.

To make this attack more difficult, Kerberos 5 introduces *pre-authentication* (see Figure 3-11). Pre-authentication requires that requestors prove their identity before the KDC will issue a ticket for a particular principal. There are several types of pre-authentication defined by the Kerberos Clarifications document. However, only the encrypted timestamp (PA-ENC-TIMESTAMP) pre-authentication method is commonly implemented.

Pre-authentication is controlled by KDC policy. If a user attempts to acquire initial tickets through the AS exchange, but the KDC requires pre-authentication, then the KDC will send a KRB_ERROR message instead of an AS_REP in reply to the client's AS request. This KRB_ERROR message tells the client that pre-authentication is required. The client generates the requisite pre-authentication data, and resends its AS_REQ message with the pre-authentication data appended. If the pre-authentication data is accepted by the KDC, it responds with an AS reply that includes the client's initial ticket. Otherwise, the KDC will return another KRB_ERROR message that indicates pre-authentication failed, and the client will not receive an initial Ticket Granting Ticket.

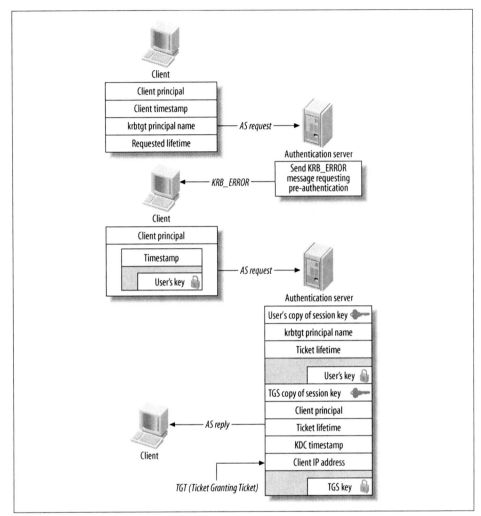

Figure 3-11. AS exchange with pre-authentication

We'll explore the practical security aspects of pre-authentication in more detail in Chapter 6.

Other Protocol Features and Extensions

There are also several useful extensions that are currently on the standards track to enhance Kerberos. Two such proposals, so-called PKINIT and PKCROSS, introduce public-key encryption to strengthen the initial authentication of the user to the KDC, and cross-realm authentication, respectively. These proposals are not standardized yet, but some early implementations are already available. We'll see what benefits

PKINIT and PKCROSS give over the standard initial authentication and cross realm capabilities built into the current Kerberos standard in Chapter 10.

String-to-Key Transformation

Just like Kerberos 4, Kerberos 5 requires a function that serves to transform a human-readable string password into an encryption key for internal use. However, Kerberos 5 makes several changes to this process, the most important resulting from the fact that Kerberos 5 supports any number of encryption algorithms with arbitrary key sizes. In addition, Kerberos 5 enforces the use of a *salt*, a piece of data added to the user's password in order to make it more resistant to brute force. Typically, this salt is the complete principal name—but other salts can be specified by the KDC.

Password Changing

The current status of password-changing protocols in Kerberos 5 is similar to that of Kerberos 4; unfortunately, as in Kerberos 4, password changing has been treated as an afterthought. The original Kerberos 5 specifications, as defined by RFC 1510, do not define a means by which clients can change their own passwords. Older implementations of MIT Kerberos 5 used the administrative protocol to perform password changes, but this is not interoperable between implementations as every implementation uses a different administrative protocol. A standard protocol for Kerberos 5 password changing was proposed as an Internet draft in 1998, referred to as the Horowitz password-changing protocol. The newer versions of MIT (1.2 and above) and Heimdal Kerberos, as well as the Windows 2000 and 2003 based Active Directory, support the Horowitz password-changing protocol. Other implementations, such as Solaris' SEAM, do not support this protocol and therefore are not interoperable with any other implementation for password changes.

A new draft proposal is now being discussed to replace the Horowitz password-changing protocol. This proposal, the Kerberos Set/Change Password Version 2, is the current Internet Draft proposal for Kerberos password changing. This new proposal has several advantages over the Horowitz password-changing protocol. First, it provides the capability for administrators to reset other users' passwords, as well as allowing users to change their own passwords. Additionally, this proposal allows for more fine-grained information to be returned to the client in the case of a rejected password. Since this proposal is still in development, readers interested in the details of the new Kerberos Set/Change Password Version 2 protocol can find more information at *http://www.kerberos.isi.edu*.

The Alphabet Soup of Kerberos-Related Protocols

Finally, there are several protocols that, while strictly speaking are not directly related to Kerberos, will be encountered when implementing a Kerberos authentication system.

The Generic Security Services API (GSSAPI)

The Generic Security Services API, as the name implies, is not specific to any authentication technique. Therefore, its mention in a book on Kerberos may seem a bit out of place. However, GSSAPI is widely used by protocol implementers as a means to implement Kerberos 5 support in their applications. By using GSSAPI, a protocol gains the ability to use other strong authentication methods "for free," and the GSSAPI layer also shields implementers from the complexities of the raw Kerberos 5 API.

GSSAPI is geared toward developers of client/server applications who wish to add strong authentication support to their protocols. It provides a generic interface and message format that can encapsulate authentication exchanges from any authentication method that has a GSSAPI-compliant library. GSSAPI insulates application programmers from the specific programming interface for particular authentication methods. GSSAPI also provides a standard message format so that protocols can support many different authentication methods without changing the protocol itself. GSSAPI does not define a protocol, authentication, or security mechanism itself; it instead makes it easier for application programmers to support multiple authentication mechanisms by providing a uniform, generic API for security services.

Most Kerberos 5 implementations also include a GSSAPI library. This means that all applications that support GSSAPI also support Kerberos 5. The notable exception is the Windows Kerberos implementation, which does not include GSSAPI support but instead includes a Microsoft-specific API, the Security Support Provider Interface (SSPI). SSPI is not API-compatible with GSSAPI; that is, programs written for GSSAPI will not compile with SSPI. Instead, applications written for SSPI can be made to be wire-compatible with GSSAPI applications. Therefore, an SSPI client can communicate with a GSSAPI server. Microsoft provides some example code that demonstrates how to achieve this network message-level interoperability.

While GSSAPI is mostly standardized, there are still some differences between the C language bindings of the available implementations, particularly the MIT and Heimdal implementations of GSSAPI. During the configuration stage, most open source software will detect which GSSAPI implementation you have and compile the appropriate code to work with it, but some software may only work with one or the other. Work to unify these APIs is ongoing.

The relevant standards documents defining GSSAPI include RFC 2743, which documents the basic GSSAPI message types, RFC 1509, which defines the C language bindings and API, and RFC 1964, which defines the Kerberos 5 GSSAPI mechanism.

The Simple and Protected GSSAPI Negotiation Mechanism (SPNEGO)

GSSAPI solves the problem of providing a single API to different authentication mechanisms. However, it does not solve the problem of negotiating which mechanism to use. Indeed, for GSSAPI to work, the two applications communicating with each other must know and agree ahead of time what authentication mechanism they plan to use. Since most GSSAPI implementations only support one mechanism anyway (namely, Kerberos 5), this is usually not a problem. However, if there are multiple mechanisms to choose from, a method is needed to securely negotiate an authentication mechanism that is mutually supported between both client and server. SPNEGO, documented in RFC 2478, performs this function.

Microsoft includes an implementation of SPNEGO in its Kerberos and SSPI implementation in Windows 2000 and above. Currently there is no widely accepted open source SPNEGO implementation for Unix, but work is ongoing to produce one. In addition, Microsoft has some sample code on its web site that provides a simple way to parse SPNEGO messages as part of its three-part article on HTTP authentication through the Negotiate protocol, available at *http://msdn.microsoft.com/library/default.asp?url=/library/en-us/dnsecure/html/http-sso-1.asp*. Many Microsoft-based products, including Exchange SMTP, file services through SMB, and web authentication with IE and IIS, use SPNEGO to negotiate an authentication mechanism.

## CHAPTER 4

Implementation

The previous chapters discussed the concepts and theory that form the basis of the Kerberos authentication system. Now, armed with a solid background, we're ready to tackle the actual implementation of a Kerberos authentication system from start to finish. This chapter prepares you to install the Kerberos KDCs in your network and also the Kerberos libraries on servers and client machines. We will continue the process in Chapter 7 by detailing installation processes for Kerberized application software.

The Basic Steps

We'll begin by outlining the steps for establishing a Kerberos realm. During this chapter, we'll follow these steps to create a sample Kerberos realm:

1. Plan your installation.
2. Install the KDC software.
3. Establish the Kerberos realm and create an administrative user principal.
4. Add user principals to your realm.
5. Install Kerberized server software, and install service principals for the server software as necessary.

Planning Your Installation

Your Kerberos implementation will be an important part of your network. As such, the Kerberos service needs to be always available, responsive, and in the event of failure, easily restored from backup. Therefore, integrating Kerberos authentication into your network calls for some planning.

The first consideration is what exactly you'll be using Kerberos for. The answer to this question depends on whether you'll need compatibility with Kerberos 4 clients/ services or not. We'll handle the simple case where you have no need to service Kerberos 4 clients or services first.

In this case, you'll be able to implement a Kerberos 5–based solution with no need for backwards compatibility with Kerberos 4–based systems. All of the KDCs we'll cover here will be able to handle Kerberos 5 clients, and there will be no need to enable any optional Kerberos 4 compatibility.

On the other hand, if you have to support Kerberos 4 services or clients, you'll need to plan a bit more carefully to integrate those legacy components into your Kerberos implementation. Typically, in this situation, you'll want to stick with a Unix-based KDC, since these have built-in support for the older Kerberos 4 protocol.

Your only option when dealing with Kerberos 4 client machines (machines which will be authenticating end users) is to use a KDC with direct support for Kerberos 4. This limits you to Unix-based KDCs. However, if you are supporting a Kerberos 4–based service (such as AFS), you can get away with a mixture of a Windows domain controller (or another KDC that supports only Kerberos 5 directly) and a machine that is running the Kerberos 5-to-4 ticket translator daemon (known as krb524) that is included with both MIT and Heimdal. We'll talk about this option in more detail in Chapter 8.

You'll want to determine the number of KDCs you'll deploy in your network. Since authentication requests to the KDC can be easily handled with today's overpowered processors, a single or dual processor machine should suffice for thousands of clients. Note that this applies to Unix-based system running only a KDC; Windows domain controllers function as much more than just a Kerberos KDC and therefore may have a higher server-to-client ratio than a dedicated Unix KDC. I won't go into detail about Active Directory planning here; readers interested in more detailed discussion about Active Directory should refer to *Active Directory* by Robbie Allen and Alistair G. Lowe-Norris (O'Reilly).

You should take into consideration not only how many authentication clients you'll be serving, but also where these clients are located. While the bandwidth requirements for Kerberos authentication are miniscule, the important metric for Kerberos performance is the network latency between clients and the Kerberos KDCs. Each authentication exchange requires time for at least one full round trip between client and KDC, and if this latency is long—for example, traveling through a satellite uplink or across congested Internet backbones—then users' authentication requests will become noticeably slow. Consequently, you want to position your KDCs so that they are as close to the clients network-wise as possible.

Of course, when rolling out a system as complex as Kerberos, you'll want to do a test run first, to become familiar with the system before performing a more substantial roll out to a larger user population.

Choose the Platform and Operating System

The choice of platform and operating system is made for you if you're using a Windows domain controller as your KDC; however, if you're using a Unix-based KDC, you'll have to consider what platform you'll run the KDCs on. Any reasonably modern machine will be able to handle the load of running the KDC software; the real concern when choosing a platform to run your Kerberos KDCs is reliability.

As a general rule, when your Kerberos KDC is unavailable, your users cannot acquire Kerberos tickets to authenticate to Kerberized services. Note that any tickets that clients may have in their credential caches will continue to work, but any attempts to acquire new service tickets during a KDC outage will fail. Mirrored RAID for your Kerberos database is a good idea, as well as stable hardware from a vendor with good support and spare parts.

Finally, consider disk layout issues when installing the operating system on your KDCs. We strongly recommend that a separate disk (or better yet, a RAID set of disks) be used to hold the Kerberos database, and a separate partition used to hold all log files. Keeping log files in a separate partition prevents either inadvertent or intentional log file overflows from affecting the system or Kerberos database partitions.

Choose a KDC Package

If you are establishing a new Kerberos realm, you'll need to start by choosing a Kerberos implementation for your KDC. There are many different KDCs available from different vendors, both commercial and open source. Each KDC implementation is different, with advantages and disadvantages over the others. Let's start by reviewing each KDC package we'll cover in detail.

Don't ignore your existing infrastructure. If you're a large organization or you've got an existing Windows domain, chances are that you already have a Kerberos KDC available. By the same token, if you're a predominantly Windows-based shop, you should strongly consider a Windows 2000 or 2003–based KDC, and vice versa for a Unix shop. The different implementations have enough of the essential features in common that the choice comes down to familiarity and comfort with the platform required to run the software.

Unlike Kerberos clients, you can't mix Kerberos KDC implementations. An MIT Kerberos KDC, for example, cannot replicate against a Windows domain controller (yet). In addition, each Kerberos implementation uses a different administration protocol. That is, the administrative interface contained with the MIT KDC cannot be used, for example, to add users to a Heimdal KDC, and vice versa.

MIT

We'll begin with MIT since it's the first, and still the reference implementation for both Kerberos 4 and Kerberos 5. Many large institutions, mostly universities, use MIT KDCs to handle authentication. There's a large support base for MIT Kerberos and it is used in many environments, which helps to exercise bugs out of the system.

MIT Kerberos contains support for the standard Kerberos encryption types, notably single and triple DES. In addition, the latest version of MIT Kerberos, 1.3, includes support for the RC4 encryption type used by the Microsoft Active Directory Kerberos service as well as the new Advanced Encryption Standard (AES). MIT is a great choice because of its wide support and appliction compatibility.

Heimdal

Heimdal is a slightly newer player to the game, and like MIT, contains full support for Kerberos 5, Kerberos 4, and the ticket translator. Since it is developed overseas and, as such, is unencumbered by any export restrictions, Heimdal enjoys considerable support outside the U.S.

There are several improvements that come out of the box with Heimdal over MIT Kerberos. First, Heimdal supports incremental database propagation, which allows Heimdal KDCs to send only the changed portions of the Kerberos database to slave servers when it is updated, instead of transmitting the entire database every time an update is made. Also, Heimdal includes integrated support for AFS-Kerberos 5 interoperability. However, Heimdal's Kerberos 5 API and GSSAPI differ slightly from MIT's, such that most Kerberos applications do not compile out of the box with the Heimdal Kerberos 5 libraries.

Recent versions of Heimdal Kerberos also contain support for the same encryption types supported by MIT Kerberos; namely, single and triple DES, AES, and RC4.

Heimdal is integrated with several free operating systems, including the BSDs: OpenBSD, NetBSD, and FreeBSD. Its popularity among these distributions can be attributed to the fact that it is unencumbered by export regulations, and so no special exceptions have to be made when distributing software outside of the U.S. Because of its integration with various free Unixes, Heimdal makes a good choice if you are planning on using one of those Unix varieties to host your KDC.

Windows domain controllers

The Kerberos implementation contained in Windows 2000 and above is the newest of the bunch. The Windows implementation only supports Kerberos 5 and does not support any of the backwards-compatibility features that MIT and Heimdal include for Kerberos 4 clients. This becomes a problem if you have Kerberos 4–only clients. If you have Kerberos 4–only services, such as AFS, you can still run a Windows domain controller, but you will also need a Unix machine to run the MIT krb524d daemon.

The Windows domain controller supports only the RC4 encryption type as well as the older DES encryption type. It does not support the newer Triple DES that MIT and Heimdal support. There are also several other peculiarities in the Windows KDC that need to be kept in mind; we'll cover these later in the chapter.

Before You Begin

Kerberos requires the proper functioning of several external services. Notably, the clocks on all machines participating in your realm must be synchronized to within a few minutes, and a working DNS domain should be established with forward and reverse mappings to at least the Kerberos KDC and application servers you intend to Kerberize.

First, NTP (the Network Time Protocol, official home page at *http:/www.ntp.org/*) should be installed on every server and KDC in your network. NTP will synchronize the clocks of these machines to a central source, which can be either a local time source (such as a GPS unit receiving time signals from the GPS satellites, or a Cesium time source, if you happen to have an atomic clock available at your site) or a remote Internet-accessible time server. While it is possible to set up all of your machines to synchronize over the network to an external, publicly available time server, site administrators are strongly encouraged to set up a centralized time source for their network, and set up other machines on the network to synchronize to that server. The time server machine can then synchronize to an accurate time source, such as a public time server.

The details of setting up NTP are beyond the scope of this book, and online references and software are readily available from the above URL. Clients will need to be synchronized also, but hand synchronization is sufficient unless you have enough control over the client systems to install NTP on them as well. While Kerberos does require synchronized clocks, Kerberos implementations typically provide for a plus-or-minus five-minute error when comparing times. Even with this built in time slack, poorly synchronized clocks are the root of many problems that are encountered when using Kerberos. Therefore, investing time up front to ensure accurate clocks on all machines on your network is time well spent.

Windows machines that are part of an Active Directory domain automatically synchronize their clocks to the domain controller's clock through the Windows Time Service. Unix systems typically do not have NTP installed and configured out of the box, so manual configuration is required to keep these systems' clocks in sync.

The proper functioning of your DNS server and client DNS resolver libraries are also important, and some time should be spent ensuring that they are functioning properly before installation. Every Unix system has different semantics for what it thinks its own hostname is: some use the fully qualified domain name (hostname plus domain name); others use just the hostname component. And to make matters worse, some Unix systems map their own hostname to 127.0.0.1 (the loopback IP address). Observe the following guidelines to avoid most DNS-related problems when implementing and maintaining your Kerberos system:

Ensure valid forward and reverse DNS mappings for machines in your domain

All machines in your domain that will participate in your Kerberos realm need to have working DNS entries, both forward and reverse. This means that, for every machine, a DNS entry exists that maps the hostname to an IP address, and a reverse entry exists for that IP address mapping it back to the original hostname.

Set all system hostnames to the fully qualified domain names

What a system considers its own hostname to be is important as well. When Kerberos needs to create the name of the host principal, it uses the output from the system's gethostname( ) call to generate the principal name. If this generated principal name doesn't match the host principal that is listed in the KDC's database, then the application will fail with a cryptic error message saying that it can't find the principal. For example, if a host thinks that its hostname is *bigserver* yet its host principal is *host/bigserver.wedgie.org@WEDGIE.ORG*, it will attempt to find a host principal of *host/bigserver@WEDGIE.ORG* and fail.

Ensure that local systems' /etc/hosts file, if used, map the hostname to a valid IP address
Some systems install an */etc/hosts* file with an entry such as this:

```
127.0.0.1                    bigserver.wedgie.org   bigserver
```

This line, which maps the system's hostname to the loopback interface, will most likely cause problems at some point. You should ensure that if an */etc/hosts* file is used, that all machine names point to real, network-accessible IP addresses. For example, if *bigserver.wedgie.org*'s IP address is 192.168.1.1, then the */etc/hosts* file should contain the following entries:

```
127.0.0.1           localhost  bigserver
192.168.1.1         bigserver.wedgie.org  bigserver
```

KDC Installation

With the boring planning out of the way, we're ready to get down to the nitty-gritty of installing a KDC. We'll cover each implementation in turn, and I'll take you through building the software, all the way to setting up test users and distributing the Kerberos database among a network of slave KDCs.

This section covers the topics required to set up the KDC software. It does not cover related topics, such as security of the underlying operating system; these security-related topics can be found in Chapter 6.

MIT

Since the MIT Kerberos distribution is available as open source, there are two ways to install it: building it from source, or obtaining a binary distribution from your Unix vendor. As for Linux, many of the popular Linux distributions have pre-built binary packages of MIT Kerberos 5.

We'll cover building MIT Kerberos from source for several reasons. One, many people feel more comfortable building security-sensitive applications directly from source. Also, some Unix distributions do not offer a pre-built MIT Kerberos distribution. Finally, by building from scratch, we can establish a common path structure and feature set that's independent of any tweaks individual vendors have decided to include in their pre-built versions. If you prefer to install from pre-built packages, such as RedHat RPMS, feel free to skip over this section and continue on to the next section, "Creating your realm."

The MIT distribution is available for users in the U.S. and Canada at the MIT Kerberos home page, located at *http://web.mit.edu/network/kerberos-form.html*. Users in other countries should visit the Cryptography Publishing Project's MIT Kerberos download page at *http://www.crypto-publish.org/mit-kerberos5/index.html*. The MIT Kerberos 5 source distribution is available at both sites, and the source code tarball available at both are bit-by-bit identical.

The source code distribution is signed with the PGP key of Tom Yu, a member of the MIT Kerberos development team. It is recommended that you verify the distribution you've downloaded against this signature, to ensure that the file has not been tampered with. If you obtained the source distribution from MIT, the signature is located within the *tar* file. If you obtained the source distribution from the Cryptography Publishing Project, the signature is located on the download web page. To verify the signature using the GNU Privacy Guard (a freely available implementation of PGP), ensure that the signature and the *.tar.gz* source tarball are in the same directory, and type:

```
% gpg --verify krb5-1.3.tar.gz.asc
```

where 1.3 is replaced with the latest version of the Kerberos distribution. Next, you'll unpack the source distribution tarball:

```
% gzcat krb5-1.3.tar.gz | tar xfv -
```

This creates a *krb5-1.3* directory, under which all of the files in the Kerberos source distribution are placed. Inside of the *krb5-1.3* directory, there is a *src* and a *doc* directory. Since we want to build the distribution, switch to the *krb5-1.3/src* directory.

Building the distribution

The Kerberos 5 distribution builds much like many other Unix software packages, using the GNU autoconf configure process. Table 4-1 contains some configure options that you may want to change during the configure process. A list of all the options are available by using the standard --help option to the configure script.

Table 4-1. Configure options

Option	Description
--prefix=<dir>	Sets the directory prefix where the Kerberos binaries, libraries, documentation, and KDC databases are located. By default, everything will be installed under */usr/local*; however, some sites may want to change this to something else that fits their naming scheme.
-localstatedir=<dir>	Sets the directory prefix where the KDC databases will be located. Some sites may want to place the databases on a separate disk for performance and reliability reasons. By default, the KDC database is located underneath <prefix>/var
-without-krb4	By default, the MIT Kerberos 5 distribution builds a small Kerberos 4 compatibility layer, so that the KDC can respond to Kerberos 4 requests and also to build a Kerberos 5-to-4 ticket conversion client library. This option disables the Kerberos 4 compatibility.
--enable-dns --enable-dns-for-realm --enable-dns-for-kdc	These options (and the corresponding --disable-dns.. options) determine whether the client libraries can use DNS to automatically determine Kerberos configuration. In particular, dns-for-realm switches the ability for clients to use DNS to find the realm name that they are a member of, and dns-for-kdc switches the ability for clients to use DNS to find the KDC for a given realm. The --enable-dns or --disable-dns options either enables or disables both of these options, respectively. By default, MIT Kerberos will use DNS for KDC lookups if information is not present in the Kerberos configuration file, */etc/krb5. conf*. More information can be found in the section, DNS and Kerberos, later in this chapter
--enable-shared	Enables the building of shared client libraries. By default, the client libraries are static. Note that shared libraries have not been thoroughly tested on most operating systems.

The defaults are sufficient in almost all cases, so we'll go ahead and execute the configure script, then compile the distribution:

```
% ./configure && make
```

 If you have trouble building the Kerberos distribution and get an error message such as cd: can't cd to obj, try using GNU Make instead of your vendor's Make utility.

Once the make completes, install the software:

```
# make install
```

The install step establishes the directory structure under your prefix (*/usr/local* by default) and places the binaries, include files, and libraries in their appropriate places under the prefix directory.

Note, however, that the install process does not create the *localstatedir* (*/usr/local/var* by default). You'll need to create this directory, as well as a *krb5kdc* directory underneath it, by yourself. In addition, you'll want to set permissions on the *krb5kdc* directory to ensure that unauthorized users cannot access sensitive KDC data. An example for the default directory structure would be:

```
# mkdir /usr/local/var
# mkdir /usr/local/var/krb5kdc
# chown root /usr/local/var/krb5kdc
# chmod 700 /usr/local/var/krb5kdc
```

Creating your realm

Now we'll use our new Kerberos installation to create our Kerberos realm. This step will only be performed on your master KDC. It creates the necessary database files and populates the KDC database with the necessary principals. First, we need to create some configuration files.

Strictly, the only configuration file that you need to create is a skeletal *krb5.conf*. The *krb5.conf* file lives in */etc*, and contains parameters that are used by the Kerberos libraries. The *krb5.conf* file looks similar to a Windows-style ini file, with stanzas (or groups) in brackets, and key-value pairs separated by an equals sign. At this point, all you'll need in this file is:

```
[libdefaults]
    default_realm = WEDGIE.ORG

[realms]
    WEDGIE.ORG = {
        kdc = freebsd.wedgie.org:88
        admin_server = freebsd.wedgie.org:749
        default_domain = wedgie.org
    }
```

```
[domain_realm]
    wedgie.org = WEDGIE.ORG
    .wedgie.org = WEDGIE.ORG

[logging]
    kdc = FILE:/var/log/krb5kdc.log
    admin_server = FILE:/var/log/kadmin.log
    default = FILE:/var/log/krb5lib.log
```

Of course, replace all instances of *WEDGIE.ORG* and *wedgie.org* with your realm name and DNS domain name, respectively. Also, replace *freebsd.wedgie.org* with the fully qualified DNS name of the KDC you're setting up. The log files specified in the logging stanza can go anywhere; however, we highly recommend that you include the logging section, as the logs will be useful for debugging as you implement Kerberos.

Kerberos is very picky when it comes to system hostnames and host lookups. Make sure that the hostname you place in the *krb5.conf* file actually resolves to the local machine. If you are just testing, an IP can be put in the *krb5.conf* file instead, in order to avoid any issues with host lookups.

Another configuration file that we'll create is the KDC configuration file, *kdc.conf*.

The MIT Kerberos 5 distribution contains a program that can be used to test whether your hostnames and DNS resolver settings are set correctly. In the *src/tests/resolve* directory, the resolve program will output the system hostname, followed by the results obtained by a gethostbyname, followed by a gethostbyaddr on the returned IP address.

If you haven't tweaked the prefix or *localstatedir* options in your configure process, then this file is located in */usr/local/var/krb5kdc*. In general, this file (along with all of the KDC databases) lives under the *krb5kdc* directory of *localstatedir*, which defaults to *<prefix>/var*. Let's look at a skeleton *kdc.conf* file:

```
[kdcdefaults]
    kdc_ports = 88,750

[realms]
    WEDGIE.ORG = {
        database_name = /usr/local/var/krb5kdc/principal
        admin_keytab = /usr/local/var/krb5kdc/kadm5.keytab
        acl_file = /usr/local/var/krb5kdc/kadm5.acl
        dict_file = /usr/local/var/krb5kdc/kadm5.dict
        key_stash_file = /usr/local/var/krb5kdc/.k5.WEDGIE.ORG
        kadmind_port = 749
        max_life = 10h 0m 0s
        max_renewable_life = 7d 0h 0m 0s
        master_key_type = des3-hmac-sha1
        supported_enctypes = des3-hmac-sha1:normal des-cbc-crc:normal
    }
```

More information on the parameters accepted by the Kerberos KDC in the *kdc.conf* file can be found in the manpage for *kdc.conf*. With the configuration files out of the way, we're ready to actually initialize the Kerberos database. To perform this step, we'll be using the *kdb5_util* program, included with the Kerberos distribution. This program performs various administrative tasks on the Kerberos database, which we'll investigate later. For now, we're going to use the create parameter to create a skeleton database for our new realm.

The following command line creates a new realm:

```
# /usr/local/sbin/kdb5_util create -s
```

Of course, adjust the path as necessary. The -s option indicates that we'll be using a stash file to store what Kerberos calls the *master key*.

The master key is an encryption key that is used to encrypt the entire Kerberos database on disk. When the Kerberos KDC daemon starts, it first queries the console for the master key password; once the password is given, it can load the database in memory, decrypt it, and continue. Unfortunately, this password prompt prevents the KDC from starting automatically, since it requires human intervention to enter the password. Therefore, the password can be saved to disk in the form of a stash file. The -s option specifies that we want to create a stash file so that the KDC daemon can start without manual intervention.

 It is important to note that the master key as described above is not the same as the Ticket Granting Ticket principal's key (the key belonging to *krbtgt/REALM@REALM*). The master key is only used to encrypt the database on disk.

Let's take a look at the dialog that is presented during a kdb5_util create command:

```
# /usr/local/sbin/kdb5_util create -s
Initializing database '/usr/local/var/krb5kdc/principal' for realm 'WEDGIE.ORG',
master key name 'K/M@WEDGIE.ORG'
You will be prompted for the database Master Password.
It is important that you NOT FORGET this password.
Enter KDC database master key:
Re-enter KDC database master key to verify:
```

If you see an error such as:

```
Configuration file does not specify default realm while retreiving configuration
parameters
```

This means you haven't created a valid */etc/krb5.conf* file with at least a default_realm defined.

Now the realm has been initialized, and some of the essential principals have already been created. Let's take a quick look at what kdb5_util created for us. First, here are the files that we now have in our Kerberos database directory:

```
# ls -a /usr/local/var/krb5kdc
.                       principal           principal.ok
..                      principal.kadm5
.k5.WEDGIE.ORG          principal.kadm5.lock
```

The *principal* and *principal.ok* files are our Kerberos database files. The *principal.kadm5* and *principal.kadm5.lock* files are the Kerberos administrative database and administrative database lock files, respectively. Finally, the *.k5.WEDGIE.ORG* file is our stash file, created by adding the -s option to kdb5_util.

Let's see what principals were created for us. The program we'll use is kadmin.local. Kadmin is the administrative interface to the Kerberos database; inside of kadmin, a Kerberos administrator can add principals, modify principals, delete principals, change passwords, and other administrative tasks. Normally, kadmin is run over a network from another machine, and requires you to authenticate (using Kerberos, of course) to a principal that has administrative privileges. *Kadmin.local* is a fail-safe copy of kadmin; it must be run locally on the KDC as root and modifies the KDC databases directly. Since we haven't yet added any principals, let alone administrative principals, we have to use *kadmin.local* to access our newly formed database.

Let's start *kadmin.local*:

```
# /usr/local/sbin/kadmin.local
Authenticating as principal jgarman/admin@WEDGIE.ORG with password.
kadmin.local:
```

Once in *kadmin.local*, we can list the principals we currently have in our KDC:

```
kadmin.local: listprincs
K/M@WEDGIE.ORG
kadmin/admin@WEDGIE.ORG
kadmin/changepw@WEDGIE.ORG
kadmin/history@WEDGIE.ORG
krbtgt/WEDGIE.ORG@WEDGIE.ORG
```

(Don't worry, we'll cover all of the commands available in kadmin in the Appendix.)

Now we'll create an administrative principal. The traditional naming scheme for principals with administrative privileges is the username of the administrator with an instance of admin. Therefore, if your normal username is jdoe, your admin principal would be *jdoe/admin*. The following kadmin command will add a principal named *jdoe/admin* to your KDC:

```
kadmin.local:  addprinc jdoe/admin
WARNING: no policy specified for jdoe/admin@WEDGIE.ORG; defaulting to no policy
Enter password for principal "jdoe/admin@WEDGIE.ORG":
Re-enter password for principal "jdoe/admin@WEDGIE.ORG":
Principal "jdoe/admin@WEDGIE.ORG" created.
```

There is no need to worry about the policy warning; the policy that it is referring to is a password-aging and strength-checking policy. Since one hasn't been created yet (we'll see how to do that in Chapter 6), it warns us that none will be applied to our new principal.

Now when you perform a listprincs again, you'll see your new administrative principal in the list. At this point, let's go ahead and start our KDC. The KDC daemon process is named krb5kdc, and is located in *<prefix>/sbin*. Let's go ahead and start it:

```
# /usr/local/sbin/krb5kdc
```

Here, no news is good news. If we get a prompt back with no error messages, the daemon should now be running in the background, responding to Kerberos client requests. Let's go ahead and test it by logging in as our administrative user:

```
# /usr/local/bin/kinit jdoe/admin
Password for jdoe/admin@WEDGIE.ORG:
```

Once again, no news is good news.

Now, we're going to add our new administrative user to the administrative access control list. Right now, *jdoe/admin@WEDGIE.ORG* has no administrative rights on the Kerberos server; we'll have to define what rights that user has in the ACL file.

By default, the ACL file is named *kadm5.acl* and located in the same directory that your KDC databases are kept. The location and filename can be overridden by the *acl_file* parameter in *kdc.conf*. The file should contain a list of principals with administrative privilege, one per line, with several fields per line, separated by whitespace. The fields are:

- Principal name
- Permissions
- Target principals for which the permissions apply (optional)

So, each line represents a permission granted or denied to a particular principal. The permission is defined by the principal name (the administrator the permissions apply to), the permissions being granted, and what principals those permissions can operate on (called the *target principal*). Each line can override the line above; that is, permissions granted to a principal can be taken away by a later line.

In the principal name and the target principal parameters, a glob character of * can be used to match all of a given portion of a principal. For example, */admin@WEDGIE.ORG matches all usernames with an admin principal in the WEDGIE.ORG realm. * by itself matches all principals in all realms.

The permissions parameter is composed of single-letter permission options. A lower-case letter means that the user is granted the particular right the letter represents. An upper case letter means that the user is denied that right. Here are the possible permissions options:

a

Addition of users or policies into the KDC database

d

Deletion of users or policies from the KDC database

m

Modification of users or policies in the KDC database

c

Changing principals' passwords in the KDC database

i

Inquiries into the database, to list principal information

l

Listing of the principals contained in the database

* (or x)

Grants the user all of the above permissions

So, for example, a permissions string of "acil" permits the user to add new users, change passwords of existing users, get detailed information about a principal, and list all principals in the database. All of the other permissions are denied.

The negative (uppercase) equivalents to these permissions do not become useful until you begin to combine them with the optional target principal parameter. This way, you can permit administrators to perform some administrative tasks on all users, then add negative permissions to deny them the permissions to administer other users.

Let's take a look at an example. Our fictitious Wedgie organization has several administrators. We have two individuals in particular, Tyler Durden and Robert Paulson. Tyler is the senior system administrator at Wedgie, and Robert is a junior system administrator who is responsible for the maintenance of the normal user accounts. Therefore, we want to set up permissions so that Tyler has full access to modify any user principals, including administrative user principals and service principals. Since Robert is only responsible for normal user principals, we want to restrict his access so that he cannot modify administrative principals. Let's see how we would accomplish this with the MIT ACL file:

```
tdurden/admin@WEDGIE.ORG    *
rpaulson/admin@WEDGIE.ORG   *
rpaulson/admin@WEDGIE.ORG   ADMICL    */admin@WEDGIE.ORG
```

To continue with our exercise, let's give *jdoe/admin* permissions to administer all principals:

```
jdoe/admin@WEDGIE.ORG       *
```

 The kadmind process will have to be restarted before changes in the *kadm5.acl* file will take effect.

Before we can use kadmin over the network, we need to create a keytab file containing the kadmin principals that were created when we initialized our realm. We'll have to return to *kadmin.local* to perform this step, so restart it if you've exited out of it already. From the kadmin> prompt:

```
kadmin.local: ktadd -k /usr/local/var/krb5kdc/kadm5.keytab kadmin/admin kadmin/
changepw
Entry for principal kadmin/admin with kvno 3, encryption type Triple DES cbc mode
with HMAC/sha1 added to keytab WRFILE:/usr/local/var/krb5kdc/kadm5.keytab.
Entry for principal kadmin/admin with kvno 3, encryption type DES cbc mode with CRC-
32 added to keytab WRFILE:/usr/local/var/krb5kdc/kadm5.keytab.
Entry for principal kadmin/changepw with kvno 3, encryption type Triple DES cbc mode
with HMAC/sha1 added to keytab WRFILE:/usr/local/var/krb5kdc/kadm5.keytab.
Entry for principal kadmin/changepw with kvno 3, encryption type DES cbc mode with
CRC-32 added to keytab WRFILE:/usr/local/var/krb5kdc/kadm5.keytab.
```

Of course, if you have changed the *localstatedir* to put the Kerberos database files in a different directory, adjust the */usr/local/var/krb5kdc* path to the path where your database files reside.

Starting the servers

Now we're ready to start the KDC server processes. There are several daemons that are included with the MIT Kerberos 5 package, and we'll detail them in Table 4-2. Unless otherwise specified, these daemons run on the master KDC only. All of these servers can be found in */usr/local/sbin* (for the default installation prefix of */usr/local*).

Table 4-2. MIT Kerberos 5 daemons

Daemon	Purpose
krb5kdc	The Kerberos 5 KDC itself. It runs on both the master and all of the slave KDCs.
krb524d	A daemon to translate Kerberos 5 service tickets into Kerberos 4 tickets. Used for backwards-compatibility with Kerberos 4–based services. For more information on running krb524d, see Chapter 8.
kadmind	The Kerberos 5 administration daemon. This daemon is the server component to the kadmin administrative client. It also handles password change requests.
kadmind4	The Kerberos 4 administration daemon. This daemon is only necessary for compatibility with the Kerberos 4 version of kadmin. Not required for Kerberos 4 compatibility unless you're using the Kerberos 4 administrative tools for some reason. Not recommended for new installs.
v5passwdd	Implements an old version of the Kerberos 5 password-changing protocol. This daemon is not needed on most installations, and there are only a few clients which speak this older password-changing protocol.
kpropd	This is the Kerberos 5 database propagation daemon. Unlike the daemons above, this daemon is run only on the slave KDCs.

Typically, you'll only need to run the krb5kdc and kadmind processes on your master KDC. If you need compatibility with older Kerberos 4 based services, such as the AFS filesystem, then you also may need to run the krb524d daemon, covered in Chapter 8. Let's start the Kerberos daemon now (we started krb5kdc earlier):

```
# /usr/local/sbin/kadmind
```

Your MIT Kerberos 5 KDC is now ready to answer client authentication requests.

A quick test

Now let's login with the administrative user that we created earlier, and use it to add a few other principals using the kadmin program. The commands that we'll be using to perform this quick test can be run on any machine that has MIT Kerberos installed.

First, we'll obtain tickets manually for our *jdoe/admin@WEDGIE.ORG* principal:

```
$ kinit jdoe/admin
Password for jdoe/admin@WEDGIE.ORG:
```

 There are a few errors that can occur here. If you see Cannot contact any KDC for requested realm, ensure that the KDC daemon krb5kdc is running, and the realm that is printed when you run kinit matches the name of the realm that you just set up. Another possible error is Preauthentication failed, which simply means that you typed in your password incorrectly. More information about troubleshooting Kerberos error messages can be found in Chapter 5.

Now let's go ahead and log into the kadmin administration server:

```
$ kadmin
Authenticating as principal jdoe/admin@WEDGIE.ORG with password.
Enter password:
kadmin:
```

 If you see the error Cannot set GSS-API authentication names, you probably have not created the admin keytab correctly, or it is located in the wrong place.

Now let's test your permissions; if you created the *kadm5.acl* file earlier, you should have full permissions for all principals in the database. Let's go ahead and create a normal day-to-day user:

```
kadmin: addprinc jdoe
WARNING: no policy specified for jdoe@WEDGIE.ORG; defaulting to no policy
Enter password for principal "jdoe@WEDGIE.ORG":
Re-enter password for principal "jdoe@WEDGIE.ORG":
Principal "jdoe@WEDGIE.ORG" created.
```

Note that even if you don't have permissions to create users, the kadmin program will continue to ask for a password for the new principal before giving an error message of:

```
add_principal: Operation requires ``add'' privilege while creating "jdoe@WEDGIE.ORG".
```

If you see this error message, make sure that the administrative user you're logged in as has the permissions to create principals, as defined in the *kadm5.acl* file. The kadmind daemon needs to be restarted before changes in the ACL file become active.

Adding slave KDCs

If you're setting up a network with only one KDC, you can stop here. We're going to continue, and create some slave KDCs that will replicate the master Kerberos database and respond to client requests.

With MIT Kerberos, slave KDCs can answer client requests by issuing tickets, but cannot perform any operations that would modify the Kerberos database (such as changing passwords). In other words, slave KDCs have a read-only copy of the Kerberos database. All updates must go through the master KDC. Updates are periodically distributed to the slave KDCs in a push model. A cron job running on the master KDC periodically sends a complete copy of the Kerberos database to the slave KDCs over an encrypted and authenticated connection.

The first step is to build the MIT Kerberos distribution on each of the slave KDCs. The same procedure detailed above in "Building the distribution" should be repeated on each of your slave KDCs.

Once MIT Kerberos is installed, we can continue by extracting host keytabs for each of the slave KDCs. The Kerberos database propagation mechanism uses these keytabs to securely transfer the database between the master and slave KDCs. Log into each KDC, connect to kadmin, create a host principal for the machine, and extract the new key into the hosts' keytab:

```
slave# /usr/local/sbin/kadmin
Authenticating as principal jgarman/admin with password.
Enter password:
kadmin: addprinc -randkey host/slave.wedgie.org
WARNING: no policy specified for host/slave.wedgie.org@WEDGIE.ORG; defaulting to no
policy
Principal "host/slave.wedgie.org@WEDGIE.ORG" created.
kadmin: ktadd host/slave.wedgie.org
Entry for principal host/slave.wedgie.org with kvno 3, encryption type Triple DES cbc
mode with HMAC/sha1 added to keytab WRFILE:/etc/krb5.keytab.
Entry for principal host/slave.wedgie.org with kvno 3, encryption type DES cbc mode
with CRC-32 added to keytab WRFILE:/etc/krb5.keytab.
```

Enter these kadmin commands on each slave, using the slave's hostname as the name of the host principal. Follow the same procedure on the master KDC to create a host principal for the master KDC.

Once all of the principals have been created and appended to the keytabs of the KDC machines, add the names of these principals to the database propagation ACL file on each KDC. Log into each KDC and create a file in the Kerberos database directory (by default, */usr/local/var/krb5kdc*) named *kpropd.acl*. This file must contain the host principals of all KDCs participating in your realm, with one principal listed per line. An ACL file for our test network would look like the following:

```
host/freebsd.wedgie.org@WEDGIE.ORG
host/slave.wedgie.org@WEDGIE.ORG
```

If this file does not exist, or does not contain the host principals for all participating KDCs, you will get an error message in the system log when attempting to distribute the Kerberos database to slave KDCs.

The *kpropd.acl* file lists all of the principals that are authorized to connect to the KDCs Kerberos database propagation service. In a typical setup, only the master KDC distributes the Kerberos database to slave machines; so you only need to list the master KDC's host principal in each slave KDC's *kpropd.acl* file. However, it is a good strategy to put all KDCs in this file, so that it is easier to make another KDC temporarily the master in case the master KDC fails and is unavailable for a long period.

Next, create an entry in each KDC's */etc/inetd.conf* file so that they listen for connections to the Kerberos database propagation server. Insert a line such as the following, changing the program path as necessary on each KDC:

```
krb5_prop  stream  tcp nowait  root  /usr/local/sbin/kpropd kpropd
```

Ensure that you have an entry for krb5_prop in your */etc/services* file. If an entry does not exist, add the following line to your */etc/services* file:

```
krb5_prop  754/tcp
```

After modifying the *inetd.conf* file, restart inetd so the changes take effect.

Now that we have an ACL file, we can go ahead and dump the database, and send a copy to our slave KDC. The following commands, executed on the master KDC, will create a copy of the Kerberos database and then send that copy to the slave KDC:

```
master# /usr/local/sbin/kdb5_util dump /usr/local/var/krb5kdc/slavedump
master# /usr/local/sbin/kprop -f /usr/local/var/krb5kdc/slavedump slave.wedgie.org
Database propagation to slave.wedgie.org: SUCCEEDED
```

If, instead of the above success message, you receive an error message, check to make sure that the machine's hostname and DNS name match, the keytabs have been created on each KDC with the appropriate host principals, and the ACL file on your slave KDCs list the host principals of the other KDCs.

We'll have to create a stash file to hold the Kerberos master key on each of our slave KDCs. Remember that the Kerberos database is encrypted on disk by a master key. When the database is dumped and transferred over the network to the slave KDCs, the database is still protected by the master key and cannot be read without it. So now we'll initialize the slave KDCs' stash files by entering our master key. The master key entered here must match the master key given when initializing the realm on the master KDC.

```
slave# /usr/local/sbin/kdb5_util stash
kdb5_util: Cannot find/read stored master key while reading master key
kdb5_util: Warning: proceeding without master key
Enter KDC database master key:
```

If you get an error after entering your master key, then it does not match the master key that the realm was created with.

Now for one last step. While we've succeeded in transferring our master KDC's database over the network to a slave, we'll need to automate the process if we expect it to happen on a regular basis. To that end, we need to create a cron job that will dump the Kerberos database and distribute it to our slave KDCs. Here is an example shell script that performs this task:

```
#!/bin/sh

# Distribute KDC database to slave servers
# Created by Jason Garman for use with MIT Kerberos 5

# Configurables
slavekdcs="slave.wedgie.org slave-2.wedgie.org"
krb5prefix="/usr/local"
slavedata="${krb5prefix}/var/krb5kdc/slavedata"

success=1

${krb5prefix}/sbin/kdb5_util dump ${slavedata}
error=$?
if [ $error -ne 0 ]
then
        echo "Kerberos database dump failed with exit code $error.  Exiting."
        exit 1
fi

for kdc in $slavekdcs
do
        ${krb5prefix}/sbin/kprop -f ${slavedata} ${kdc}
        error=$?
        if [ $error -ne 0 ]
        then
            echo "Propagation of database to host ${kdc} failed with exit code $error."
            echo "Continuing with other slave servers."
            success=0
        fi
done

if [ $success -eq 1 ]
then
        echo "Kerberos database successfully replicated to all slaves."
fi
```

Finally, place this shell script in the crontab of your master KDCs so that it executes on a regular basis. A typical interval between database replications is an hour.

At this point, your Kerberos realm has at least one KDC, and possibly several additional slave KDCs, ready to serve Kerberos clients. A Kerberos realm is not complete without clients and application servers; we'll cover adding them to your Kerberos realm later in the "Client and Application Server Installation" section, later in this chapter.

Heimdal

Just like MIT, Heimdal is also an open source implementation of Kerberos 5. Many Unix distributions have pre-built Heimdal packages, but like MIT, we will cover building Heimdal from source.

Since Heimdal is under development and is distributed from Sweden, it is unencumbered by United States export restrictions and is freely available for download worldwide. Heimdal is a complete clean-room implementation of the Kerberos 5 protocol specification, and as such contains no MIT Kerberos 5 code.

The current version of the Heimdal Kerberos 5 package as of this writing is 0.6. Don't let the small version number dissuade you from using Heimdal; while it hasn't been in development quite as long as MIT Kerberos 5, it is feature-complete for the basic Kerberos 5 protocol, and includes as standard features some features that MIT Kerberos doesn't have, such as incremental database propagation.

Heimdal depends on another package, kth-krb, to enable Kerberos 4 backwards-compatibility. We won't cover building kth-krb; it has a build process similar to Heimdal, and the only configuration option that you may want to tweak is the prefix directory for the installed binaries and libraries (*/usr/athena* by default). The source distribution of kth-krb is available from *http://www.pdc.kth.se/kth-krb/*.

The Heimdal home page is *http://www.pdc.kth.se/heimdal/*, where you'll be able to download the latest version of the Heimdal source code.

Building the distribution

After unpacking the *tar* file, you'll have a *heimdal-0.6* directory (or whatever the latest version is). Heimdal uses the GNU autoconf configure process. Table 4-3 lists some of the more important options that the Heimdal configure script recognizes.

Table 4-3. Heimdal options

Option	Description
--prefix=<dir>	Sets the directory prefix where the Kerberos binaries, libraries, documentation, and KDC databases are located. By default, everything will be installed under */usr/local*; however, some sites may want to change this to something else that fits their naming scheme.
--with-krb4=<dir>	Gives the configure program the prefix directory where the Kerberos 4 include files and libraries are located. If you installed the kth-krb distribution, this option can be used to tell the Heimdal configure program where you've installed the kth-krb Kerberos 4 libraries.
--with-openssl=<dir>	Heimdal can either link against OpenSSL or an internal DES library for cryptography support. By default, Heimdal will look for OpenSSL in some standard locations, such as */usr* and */usr/local*. If you have OpenSSL installed in another directory, set this configuration option to the root directory of your OpenSSL installation.
--without-ipv6	By default, Heimdal will compile support for IPv6 in the KDC and user libraries (if your operating system supports IPv6 sockets). Use this option to disable the IPv6 support in Heimdal.
--with-openldap=<dir>	By default, Heimdal keeps its Kerberos database in a local file on the KDC's file system. It can keep the database in LDAP, however. We won't cover putting the KDC database in LDAP, but this option allows you to specify the root directory of your OpenLDAP installation. For more information about using an LDAP backend to Heimdal, see *http://www.padl.com/Research/Heimdal.html*.

Typically, the default parameters are sufficient. Remember that if you need your KDC to service Kerberos 4 clients, or have services that require Kerberos 4 tickets, you'll need to specify the --with-krb4 option, indicating the directory where you have kth-krb installed. We'll go ahead and configure with the default options, and make the distribution:

```
% ./configure && make
```

If all went well, install the distribution:

```
# make install
```

The installation process doesn't create the directory where the KDC databases are kept, namely */var/heimdal*. This directory is hardcoded in the Heimdal distribution so the easiest solution to place the database in another directory is to symlink */var/heimdal* to the desired location. We'll create the /var/heimdal directory now, and set the permissions so that unauthorized users cannot access the contents of this sensitive directory:

```
# mkdir /var/heimdal
# chown root /var/heimdal
# chmod 700 /var/heimdal
```

Creating your realm

In this step, we will create the skeleton database files that will define the principals in our new realm. These steps are only performed on the master KDC server.

Just like with MIT Kerberos, we must create a few configuration files before we continue. Also, these configuration files are similar to the ones we use with MIT. They are broken into stanzas, or categories, contained in brackets, with key/value pairs separated by an equal sign. Our first file is */etc/krb5.conf*. Here is a sample */etc/krb5.conf*:

```
[libdefaults]
        default_realm = WEDGIE.ORG

[realms]
        WEDGIE.ORG = {
                kdc = 192.168.0.4
                admin_server = 192.168.0.4
        }

[domain_realm]
        .wedgie.org = WEDGIE.ORG
```

We'll come back to examine the *krb5.conf* file format in more detail in the Appendix. For now, you'll want to ensure that your default_realm parameter is set to the realm name you're about to set up. Define your KDC address in the realms stanza, and that domain_realm contains a mapping from your KDC's domain name (with a leading dot prepended) to your new realm name.

If your KDCs' domain name is equal to the realm name (ignoring case), then you can omit the libdefaults and domain_realm stanzas, since the Kerberos libraries will be smart enough to figure those out on their own.

Heimdal can encrypt the KDC database on disk with a master key. Heimdal will save the password to a stash file also located in */var/heimdal*. This feature is mostly used to protect backups of the KDC database from being easily readable by attackers, assuming that the database is backed up separate from the stash file. If you wish to create a master key and a stash file, use the kstash command:

```
# /usr/heimdal/sbin/kstash
Master key:
Verifying password - Master key:
/usr/heimdal/sbin/kstash: writing key to `/var/heimdal/m-key'
```

Now we will initialize our realm. We will use the kadmin program, which can be used from any Heimdal client to administer principals on the KDC. Since our KDC isn't running yet, we'll have to run it in the local mode, to access the database directly on disk. This is accomplished by giving the -l option to kadmin:

```
# /usr/heimdal/sbin/kadmin -l
```

You should get back a prompt of kadmin>. This is the kadmin interface. We'll use the init command to create our new realm:

```
kadmin> init WEDGIE.ORG
Realm max ticket life [unlimited]:1d
Realm max renewable ticket life [unlimited]:1w
```

At this point, kadmin asks us some questions about the ticket policies in the new realm. Good defaults for the maximum ticket life and renewable ticket life are typically one day and one week, respectively. Shorthand date formats such as the ones above will work, including h for hour and m for minute. We'll cover kadmin in detail in the Appendix.

Now you have a realm with a skeleton set of principals. Let's see what principals are there:

```
kadmin> list *
  default@WEDGIE.ORG
  kadmin/admin@WEDGIE.ORG
  kadmin/hprop@WEDGIE.ORG
  kadmin/changepw@WEDGIE.ORG
  krbtgt/WEDGIE.ORG@WEDGIE.ORG
  changepw/kerberos@WEDGIE.ORG
```

We'll cover the kadmin command set in more detail later in Appendix A; for now, I'll say that the list command lists principals that match a glob pattern—in this case *, meaning every principal. The default principals that are created out of the box include default, which is a pseudoprincipal (tickets cannot be issued for it) whose attributes are used as the defaults for any new principals that are created. Also, we have a few kadmin principals; these principals are internal KDC service principals that handle the administrative interface protocol, database replication, and the Kerberos password change service. Finally, we have the krbtgt principal, which is the Ticket Granting Ticket principal for our realm.

Inside our Kerberos database directory, we now have a few files. First, we have *m-key*, which is the master key password for the Kerberos database. Then, Heimdal creates the KDC log file by default as *kdc.log* inside of this directory. Last but not least, we have the Kerberos database file itself, *heimdal.db*.

Next, we'll add an admin user. By convention, this should be your usual username with an instance of admin. You can name it whatever you like; however, I recommend that it be separate from the principal that you use for everyday use, and of course with a different password. To create our principal, we first must be in kadmin (if you've exited it already, simply run it again with the -l option).

At the kadmin> prompt:

```
kadmin> add jdoe/admin
Max ticket life [1 day]:
Max renewable life [1 week]:
Principal expiration time [never]:
Password expiration time [never]:
Attributes []:
jdoe/admin@WEDGIE.ORG's Password:
Verifying password - jdoe/admin@WEDGIE.ORG's Password:
```

For now, we'll take the defaults.

Next, we have to create an Access Control List so that this new administrative user can actually log in via kadmin. Heimdal stores the ACL file in the Kerberos database directory (the default location is */var/heimdal/kadmind.acl*). Each line of this file contains the following three fields, separated by whitespace:

- Administrative principal
- Permissions
- Target principal (optional)

Each line of the ACL file defines a permission or list of permissions granted to the principal (first field) to perform on the target principal. Both the principal and target principal fields can contain shell glob characters to specify a set of principals. The permissions field can be a comma-separated list of any of the following permissions:

add
> The user can add principals into the Kerberos database.

change-password (or cpw)
> The user can change the password of an existing principal in the Kerberos database.

delete
> The user can delete principals in the Kerberos database.

get (or list)
> The user can retrieve detailed information on a given principal or set of principals from the Kerberos database.

modify

The user can modify principal's attributes in the Kerberos database.

all

A combination of all the above rights.

An example ACL line would be:

```
jdoe/admin@WEDGIE.ORG all
```

This ACL entry will give the user *jdoe/admin@WEDGIE.ORG* administrative rights to perform any operation on all principals in the realm. Note that adding an ACL entry with an empty target principal field applies the permissions to all principals on the KDC. If a * were placed in the target principal field, it would only match principals with no instance component (for example, * would match *jdoe*, but not *jdoe/admin*).

If a permission is not specified in the permissions field, it is not granted by default. Since the permission field itself is optional, by not granting any permissions to an administrative principal, you deny it all permissions. Note that there is currently no way to specify negative permissions, so an approach to give an administrator control over all users who do not have admin instances could not be expressed as giving the administrator all privileges over all principals, then giving the administrator no privileges over admin instance principals. Instead, you can give the administrator all privileges over all principals with no instance (by using a single * in the target principal field). While this differs slightly from what we originally set out to do (what about principals with instances other than admin, such as service and host principals?), it is probably what was intended in the first place, and permissions to act on other instances can be added to the ACL file if needed.

Since all of these rules can be confusing, let's take an example:

```
jgarman/admin@WEDGIE.ORG    all    *
jgarman/admin@WEDGIE.ORG    get    */otherinstance
jdoe/admin@WEDGIE.ORG       all    */admin
```

This set of permissions allows the *jgarman/admin* principal to perform all operations on principals with no instance component, and only perform get (or list) operations on principals with an instance component of "otherinstance." All other operations on other principals are denied. Similarly, *jdoe/admin* is allowed to perform all administrative operations only on principals with an admin instance, but no others. All other principals have no administrative rights.

 Note that Heimdal is very sensitive to whitespace in the *kadmind.acl* file—a stray space or tab at the end of the target principal will be treated as part of the target principal. Since principals cannot contain spaces, the line in the ACL file will not match any principal and will not work as intended.

To continue with the exercise, place the following in your *kadmind.acl* file:

```
jdoe/admin@WEDGIE.ORG all
```

This statement will allow the *jdoe/admin@WEDGIE.ORG* principal to perform all administrative operations on every principal in the realm.

Starting the servers

Now that our Kerberos database has been successfully initialized, we're ready to start the Kerberos daemons on the master KDC. There are several daemons that are included with Heimdal (shown in Table 4-4), each of which serves a different purpose. If you did not change the prefix when building the software, you can find these servers in */usr/heimdal/libexec*. Unless otherwise specified, these daemons should be run only on the master KDC.

Table 4-4. Master KDC daemons

Daemon	Purpose
kdc	This is the KDC server process. The Heimdal kdc server includes support for Kerberos 5, Kerberos 4, and the Kerberos 5-to-4 ticket translator (the latter two are only enabled if Kerberos 4 support was compiled in to the distribution at build time). This process should be run on all KDCs on your network.
kadmind	This is the administrative daemon for the Heimdal KDC. This process must be run on the master KDC (and only the master KDC) if you want to administer the Kerberos database over the network.
kpasswdd	This server handles Kerberos password-change requests. Heimdal separates out password-changing from the kadmind server, and uses this process to handle client password-change requests. This daemon should be run only on your master KDC, since it changes the Kerberos database directly.
hpropd	This server receives the Kerberos database from the master KDC and writes it to a slave KDC's disk. Therefore, this daemon should only be run on slave KDCs. It can work in tandem with the iprop-server and iprop-client to support incremental propagation, which we'll cover in a bit when we add slave KDCs to our network.

Let's start the common services we'll need (kdc, kadmind, and kpasswdd):

```
# /usr/heimdal/libexec/kdc &
# /usr/heimdal/libexec/kpasswdd &
# /usr/heimdal/libexec/kadmind &
```

A quick test

Now that our realm is established, let's test our installation to make sure everything is functioning. Login with the jdoe/admin principal:

```
% kinit jdoe/admin
jdoe/admin@WEDGIE.ORG's Password:
```

As long as no errors are output, everything went well. Let's go ahead and login to the kadmin server:

```
% kadmin
kadmin> list -l jdoe/admin
jdoe/admin@WEDGIE.ORG's Password:
                Principal: jdoe/admin@WEDGIE.ORG
        Principal expires: never
         Password expires: never
     Last password change: never
```

```
             Max ticket life: 1 day
         Max renewable life: 1 week
                        Kvno: 6
                       Mkvno: 0
                      Policy: none
       Last successful login: never
          Last failed login: never
          Failed login count: 0
               Last modified: 2002-11-10 15:53:34 UTC
                    Modifier: jgarman/admin@WEDGIE.ORG
                  Attributes:
Keytypes(salttype[(salt-value)]): des3-cbc-sha1(pw-salt), des-cbc-md5(pw-salt), des-
cbc-md4(pw-salt), des-cbc-crc(pw-salt)
```

Adding slave KDCs

If you're setting up a network with only one KDC, you can stop here. Otherwise, we're going to create some slave KDCs that will replicate the master Kerberos database and respond to client requests.

With Heimdal Kerberos, slave KDCs can answer client requests by issuing tickets, but cannot perform any operations that would modify the Kerberos database (such as changing passwords). In other words, slave KDCs have a read-only copy of the Kerberos database. All updates must go through the master KDC. Updates are periodically distributed to the slave KDCs in a push model. A cron job running on the master KDC periodically sends a complete copy of the Kerberos database to the slave KDCs over an encrypted and authenticated connection.

The first step is to build the Heimdal Kerberos distribution on each of the slave KDCs. The same procedure detailed above in "Building the distribution" should be repeated on each of your slave KDCs.

First, we'll have to add a host principal for each slave server. We will log into each slave server in turn, create a new principal, and extract it into a keytab. The ktutil program included with Heimdal can create a principal with a random key and extract it into a keytab with one operation, so we'll use it to create our host principal.

```
slave# /usr/heimdal/sbin/ktutil get host/slave.wedgie.org
```

Now, we'll add the Heimdal propagation server to the slave's *inetd.conf* file. A line such as the following should be sufficient:

```
krb5_prop  stream tcp  nowait root /usr/local/libexec/hpropd hpropd
```

Note that krb5_prop must be a valid entry in */etc/services* that maps to the Heimdal Kerberos propagation port, namely 754. Once inetd has been restarted so that the hpropd is listening on the slave, we can force the master to distribute a full copy of the Kerberos database to our new slave:

```
master# /usr/heimdal/sbin/hprop slave
```

Obviously, you'll want to automate this process so that it happens on a regular basis. You can enter the hprop command above in your crontab to occur regularly. Most Kerberos sites set this up to replicate hourly; however, your site may have different requirements. Multiple slave Kerberos servers can be updated at the same time by listing their hostnames on the hprop command line.

Heimdal also supports incremental database propagation, where instead of transferring the entire database at preset intervals, updates are sent to slaves as changes are made to the master database. This option is much more efficient with network resources and also makes updates appear to slaves (and consequently to end users) almost immediately. As this feature is still undergoing development, we won't cover the details here, but the Heimdal documentation available at *http://www.pdc.kth.se/heimdal/heimdal.html* describes the procedure required to enable incremental database propagation.

Windows Domain Controller

The Windows 2000 and 2003 Domain Controller is the Windows equivalent of a Unix-based KDC. You'll need Windows 2000 Server or Windows 2003 Server to create a domain controller.

Therefore, to establish a Windows-based KDC, you must establish an Active Directory domain. Microsoft has a wizard that steps you through this process. While this book doesn't cover the intricacies of Active Directory, we will explore the basic steps required to create a domain controller on a Windows 2000 or 2003 Server machine.

Once again, this quick guide to setting up a Kerberos realm using a Windows server machine is not intended to be a full introduction to Active Directory. Instead, this section will guide you through the necessary steps to establish a working Kerberos realm using your Windows server as a KDC, where both Windows machines and Unix boxes can participate as clients.

Creating your realm

First, log into the machine that will become the new domain controller with an account that has local Administrator privileges. Start by executing the dcpromo command from the command line. This command starts the Active Directory Wizard. If the machine isn't already a domain controller, you'll see the window shown in Figure 4-1.

When you click Next, it will continue to the next step of the wizard, shown in Figure 4-2.

You'll want to create a new domain. Continue with the defaults until you get to the domain name dialog, shown in Figure 4-3.

Figure 4-1. Active Directory Wizard welcome screen

Figure 4-2. Active Directory Controller Type dialog

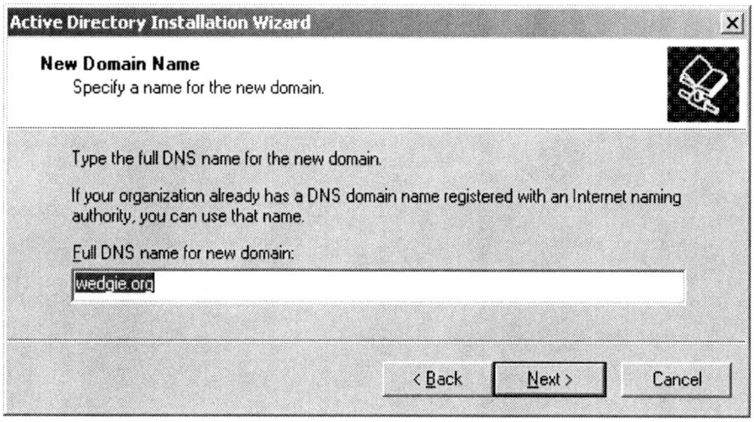

Figure 4-3. Selecting the domain name for the new Active Directory domain

The answer to this dialog box will become the name for the new Active Directory domain, and should be the same as your organization's DNS name. Note that the resulting Kerberos realm created by the wizard will be this name, converted to uppercase. So if your domain name is *example.com*, the Kerberos realm that the Active Directory wizard creates for you will be named EXAMPLE.COM.

The NetBIOS name that you choose in the next dialog does not affect your Kerberos realm in any way; the default should be sufficient. The next step presents you with the option of where to place the Kerberos database files and log files (Figure 4-4).

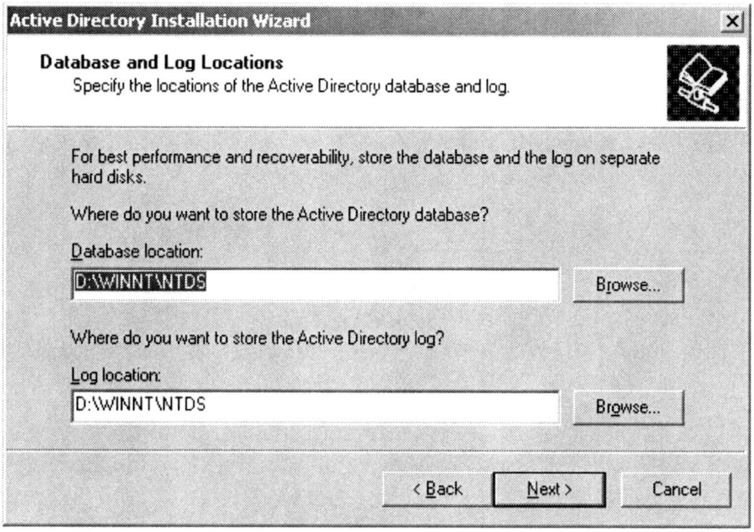

Figure 4-4. Active Directory Database Location dialog

As we discussed earlier, it is good practice to store these files on separate disks, separate from each other and the disk holding the operating system.

The next dialog asks where the SYSVOL files should be kept. Once again, this option has no bearing on the functioning of the Kerberos KDC and the default is sufficient. Once you've clicked Next on that dialog box though, you may encounter the message depicted in Figure 4-5.

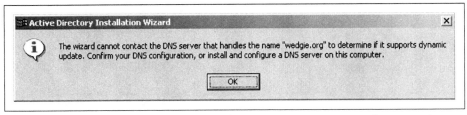

Figure 4-5. Active Directory warning message when no DNS server supporting dynamic updates is authoritative for the new domain

This message appears if there is no Windows or other DNS server supporting or dynamic updates that are authoritative for the DNS domain associated with your realm. In this case, you'll probably want to set up DNS on your new domain controller, and you'll see the configure DNS dialog pictured in Figure 4-6.

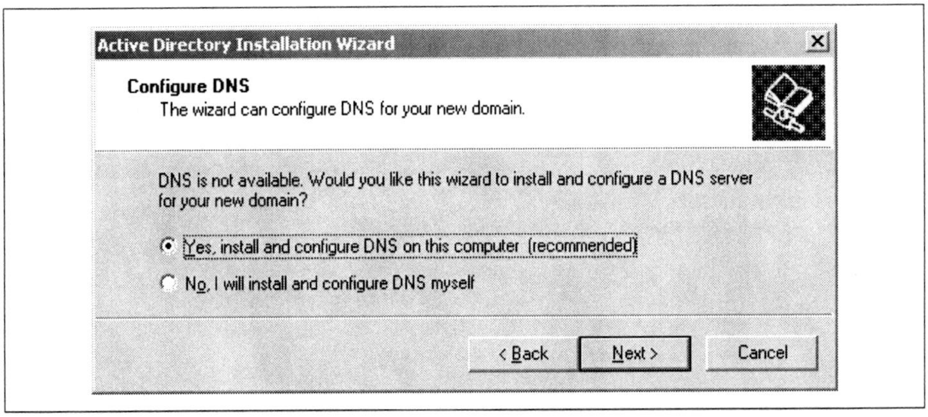

Figure 4-6. Creating a DNS server for your new Active Directory domain

The next two steps in the AD wizard ask for information that is irrelevant to the proper operation of Kerberos. For our purposes, the defaults work fine.

After you click the Finish button on the wizard, the configuration process is automatically started. This process may take several minutes, depending on the speed of your machine. Once the process finishes, the wizard will ask you to reboot the computer. Once the machine reboots, it is now a Domain Controller and a Kerberos KDC. Other Windows 2000/XP/2003 machines that join the new Windows domain will now use Kerberos to authenticate domain user logins. Interoperability between Windows domain controllers and Unix Kerberos clients and application servers will be covered in depth in Chapter 8.

 Note that this process does not affect the primary or secondary DNS server settings of the local system. If the system is set up to use a DNS server that does not delegate the new DNS domain created during this process to the new Active Directory server, then the dynamic DNS updates and other Active Directory processes will fail. See Q244669 on the Microsoft Support site for more details.

DNS and Kerberos

A properly functioning DNS server for your domain and functioning DNS resolvers on machines participating in your Kerberos realm is essential for the proper operation of your realm.

Traditional Unix Kerberos 5 implementations use the flat file */etc/krb5.conf* file for hostname-to-Kerberos realm mapping, much like */etc/hosts* can be used for name-to-IP mapping. The Kerberos configuration file contains two major pieces of information: the DNS domain name to Kerberos realm mappings, and a list of KDCs for each Kerberos realm. Obviously, this method does not scale, so just as DNS now serves the purpose of the old */etc/hosts* file, DNS can also be used to provide Kerberos configuration.

Kerberos can use DNS as a service location protocol, by using the DNS SRV record as defined in RFC 2052. In addition, Kerberos can use a TXT record to locate the appropriate realm for a given host or domain name. These DNS entries are not required to run a Kerberos realm, but they do eliminate the need for manual configuration of clients. With these DNS records, Kerberos clients can find the appropriate KDCs without the use of a configuration file. Windows will establish the necessary SRV records automatically when an Active Directory domain is created. Those using Unix for their KDCs can create these DNS entries manually in their zone files as a convenience to clients.

 Note that while Windows will use DNS to locate KDCs, it will not use DNS to locate any KDCs for any non-Windows Kerberos realms. Configuration information for non-Windows Kerberos realms must be entered manually using the ksetup tool. More information on this tool and enabling interoperability between Windows and other Kerberos implementations can be found in Chapter 8.

Setting Up KDC Discovery Over DNS

In order to use KDC discovery over DNS, the following records should be placed in the zone file corresponding to the Kerberos realm. In most cases, since the Kerberos realm name is simply an uppercase version of the DNS domain owned by the organization, these DNS entries are placed into the organization's existing DNS zone file. However, if the Kerberos realm and DNS domain differ, then a new zone must be created with the name of the Kerberos realm.

A SRV DNS Resource Record describes the KDCs available for a particular realm and contains the following information:

Service
> This item represents the service that this SRV record provides location information for. The service name for the Kerberos KDC is always _kerberos. Other Kerberos related services include _kerberos-adm for the kadmin server, and _kpasswd for the Kerberos 5 password-changing service.

Protocol
> The protocol can either be _tcp or _udp. The latest Kerberos Clarifications document requires that all future KDCs accept both TCP and UDP connections from authentication clients.

Realm
> This is the realm that the KDC is authoritative for. Since DNS is case-insensitive while realm names are case-sensitive, you cannot represent multiple realms with different cases in the same DNS zone. For example, since REALM.ORG and Realm.ORG differ only in case, they will both map to the same case-insensitive DNS zone. Therefore, KDC discovery through DNS is not possible when the names of two or more Kerberos realms differ only by capitalization.

Time to Live (TTL)
> The TTL field has the same meaning here as in any DNS record; it represents the amount of time that this record can be cached by DNS clients. Once the TTL time has expired, the cached information is invalidated and any further requests for this record have to be sent to the DNS server.

Priority
> Just like MX records, several KDCs can be listed with differing priorities. Clients will try the listed KDCs in order, from lowest number to highest. If the KDC with the lowest-numbered priority is not available, it will try the next highest number until the client is able to successfully connect to a KDC.

Weight
> The weight field implements simple load-balancing characteristics. For identical records with the same priority, clients will use a probabilistic algorithm to give more preference to hosts with a higher weight than those with a lower weight.

To disable this load-balancing feature so that clients choose from equal priority records randomly, use a zero for this field.

Port

This is the TCP or UDP port on which the service is listening.

Target

This is the fully qualified DNS name of the machine providing the Kerberos service.

Here is an example of a set of SRV records for several Kerberos KDCs:

```
_kerberos._udp.WEDGIE.ORG.     IN SRV 1  0 88  kerberos-1.wedgie.org.
_kerberos._tcp.WEDGIE.ORG.     IN SRV 1  0 88  kerberos-1.wedgie.org.
_kerberos._udp.WEDGIE.ORG.     IN SRV 10 0 88  kerberos-2.wedgie.org.
_kerberos._tcp.WEDGIE.ORG.     IN SRV 10 0 88  kerberos-2.wedgie.org.
_kerberos-adm._tcp.WEDGIE.ORG. IN SRV 1  0 749 kerberos-1.wedgie.org.
_kpasswd._udp.WEDGIE.ORG.      IN SRV 1  0 464 kerberos-1.wedgie.org.
```

This example includes two Kerberos KDCs, kerberos-1 and kerberos-2. Both listen to the standard Kerberos 5 port, 88, on both UDP and TCP. Kerberos-1 is the master KDC, so it also handles all of the administration requests and password change requests. Since kerberos-1 has a lower priority than kerberos-2 (1 versus 10), clients will prefer using kerberos-1 for queries over kerberos-2.

> Note the trailing period after the domain names above. The trailing period specifies that these entries are absolute domain names. The default behavior of BIND is to treat all domain names as relative to $ORIGIN (the DNS domain contained in the zone file).

DNS Domain Name-to-Realm Mapping

Kerberos can also use DNS for domain name-to-realm mapping. This mapping, provided by the domain_realm stanza in MIT-style krb5.conf files, can also be provided through TXT records in DNS. The TXT record format for specifying domain name-to-realm mappings is similar to the SRV record format for locating Kerberos KDCs within a given Kerberos realm. It contains three major fields:

Service

This field is always _kerberos.

Domain/host name

This field is the DNS domain name or hostname.

Realm name

This field is the Kerberos realm associated with the domain name in the previous field.

An example, mapping all hosts within the domain *wedgie.org* to the Kerberos realm WEDGIE.ORG is shown below:

```
_kerberos.wedgie.org. IN TXT "WEDGIE.ORG"
```

Note that the latest Kerberos Clarifications call for less dependence on the insecure DNS service to perform domain name-to-realm mapping for future implementations of Kerberos. This DNS-to-realm mapping is used by Windows' Active Directory services to locate realm information, and was documented as part of an Internet Draft. However, the most recent Kerberos Clarifications drafts obsoletes the older Internet Draft and strongly recommends against using unsecured DNS services to provide this mapping.

Client and Application Server Installation

Before a client machine or Kerberized application server can use Kerberos authentication, it must have the proper libraries, configuration files, and in some cases, service and host principals added to a local keytab file. We will limit the discussion (for now) to using the same Kerberos implementation both on the KDC and the clients. Most of the setup information below can be used to interface with a different vendor's KDC, but we will take a closer look at interoperability later in Chapter 8.

Unix as a Kerberos Client

There are three major steps to setting up a Unix-based Kerberos client or Kerberized application server: compiling the distribution, installing configuration files, and creating host and service principals if necessary. The first step, compiling the distribution, has already been discussed in the "Building the distribution" sections (under the appropriate heading for your chosen Kerberos implementation); follow the directions to build and install the client libraries.

Next, we'll create configuration files on each of the clients. Both MIT and Heimdal use a configuration file located in */etc/krb5.conf*. This configuration file contains the name and addresses of all KDCs that the client can communicate with. Alternatively, this information can be placed in DNS, as discussed in the section "DNS and Kerberos." Since most Kerberos installations are still using configuration files, we'll discuss them.

We saw a simple *krb5.conf* file earlier, when we set up the MIT KDC above. That template still applies for clients, and in fact, the */etc/krb5.conf* configuration file can be copied straight from the KDC to all of the clients. If you want to tweak the configuration file anyway, there are three stanzas that are important for client configuration: libdefaults, realms, and domain_realm.

Let's start with a sample configuration file. It should look familiar; it is the same one presented in the KDC installation section:

```
[libdefaults]
    default_realm = WEDGIE.ORG

[realms]
```

```
    WEDGIE.ORG = {
        kdc = freebsd.wedgie.org:88
        admin_server = freebsd.wedgie.org:749
        default_domain = wedgie.org
    }

[domain_realm]
    wedgie.org = WEDGIE.ORG
    .wedgie.org = WEDGIE.ORG
```

The libdefaults stanza contains parameters that apply to all applications using the Kerberos libraries. The only option that you may have to tweak in this stanza is the default_realm option. This option specifies the default realm that the Kerberos libraries will use when trying to find a service principal for a given service. Normally, the Kerberos realm and DNS domain name are the same, but they can be different. If your Kerberos realm differs from the DNS domain that this machine resides in, then you should set this parameter to your Kerberos realm.

The realms stanza includes information about every Kerberos realm that this client can communicate with. Every realm that the client has to communicate with must either have an entry in the realms section on the clients' *krb5.conf* file or be included in the DNS as described above in "DNS and Kerberos." The only required parameter inside of a realm declaration is kdc, which gives the address and optional port number of a KDC that is authoritative for that realm. Multiple kdc declarations can be given if there are multiple KDCs serving that realm. An optional admin_server declaration lists the address and optional port number of the master KDC that handles client password changes and other administrative tasks.

The domain_realm stanza maps DNS domain names to Kerberos realm names. Whenever an application contacts a Kerberized service, it has to ask a Kerberos KDC for a ticket to that service. The Kerberos client libraries use the DNS domain name of the server to determine what Kerberos realm, and consequently, what Kerberos KDC to contact in order to request the tickets. The domain_realm stanza defines these mappings. In addition, as discussed above in "DNS and Kerberos," these mappings can be stored in DNS.

Each mapping consists of a key/value pair, where the key is a DNS domain name or hostname, and the value is the corresponding realm. In the example above, the hostname *wedgie.org*, as well as any hosts inside of the *wedgie.org* domain (note the initial dot on the second item in domain_realm) are mapped to the WEDGIE.ORG realm.

Once the configuration files are in place on all clients and application servers, we are ready to configure a sample Kerberized application: the Kerberized telnet included with both MIT and Heimdal.

Your */etc/inetd.conf* file probably already contains an entry for your system's telnet daemon. If you're using an inetd replacement such as xinetd, your configuration may be in a different location with a different file format, but the concepts will remain the same. You'll want to enable the telnet server if it isn't already, and change the path to the telnet daemon so that it matches the new Kerberized telnet daemon that you installed as part of the Kerberos distribution. An example for inetd.conf to call the MIT Kerberos telnet daemon is below:

```
telnet  stream  tcp    nowait  root    /usr/local/sbin/telnetd telnetd
```

Restart your inetd and your new Kerberized telnet daemon is ready to use.

To test, you'll need to first authenticate yourself to Kerberos. Right now, we'll use kinit to manually perform this step. You can kinit from any machine that has the Kerberos distribution and configuration files installed.

```
% kinit jgarman
Password for jgarman@WEDGIE.ORG:
```

Now you should have a Ticket Granting Ticket for your realm. You can verify this by using the klist command:

```
% klist
Ticket cache: FILE:/tmp/krb5cc_1000
Default principal: jgarman@WEDGIE.ORG

Valid starting     Expires           Service principal
12/02/02 01:02:30  12/02/02 11:02:30 krbtgt/WEDGIE.ORG@WEDGIE.ORG


Kerberos 4 ticket cache: /tmp/tkt1000
klist: You have no tickets cached
```

This output is from MIT; Heimdal's klist shows similar information, but in a different format.

Now we're ready to attempt logging into our new telnet server through Kerberos authentication:

```
% /usr/local/bin/telnet -a freebsd.wedgie.org
Trying 192.168.0.5...
Connected to freebsd.wedgie.org (192.168.0.5).
Escape character is '^]'.
[ Kerberos V5 accepts you as ``jgarman@WEDGIE.ORG'' ]
Last login: Mon Dec  2 01:07:25 from 192.168.0.4
FreeBSD 4.7-STABLE (PII) #0: Thu Oct 17 02:30:53 GMT 2002
....
```

If everything works, you should see the above message that Kerberos V5 accepts you.

Note that we're using the telnet client included with your Kerberos distribution; for Heimdal Kerberos, the default location for this binary is */usr/heimdal/bin/telnet*. You need to use the Kerberized telnet client in order for Kerberos authentication to work correctly. In addition, the -a option is used to tell the telnet client to automatically log us in with our previously obtained credentials. Without the -a option, the Kerberos telnet client will behave exactly the same as a traditional non-Kerberized telnet client—by asking the user for a login and password to send to the server in clear text.

If you're having trouble, the first item to check is whether you are using the correct DNS name for the telnet server in your telnet command line. If, for example, you are on the same system as the telnet server and you attempt to "telnet -a localhost," the Kerberos negotiation will fail. This is because the telnet client is attempting to acquire a service ticket for *host/localhost@YOUR.REALM*; you probably don't have a principal named that. (And you shouldn't!) Instead, you must use a DNS name or IP that reverse resolves to the DNS name that was used to create the host principal.

Mac OS X as a Kerberos Client

Mac OS X 10.2 and higher contain built-in support for Kerberos. The Kerberos included with Mac OS X is actually a modified version of the MIT Kerberos 5 distribution. As a result, the best way to approach Kerberos client functionality in Mac OS X is to simply treat it as a special case of a generic MIT Kerberos client running Unix. However, there are a few quirks and some added functionality included with the Mac OS X implementation as compared to a stock MIT Kerberos 5 distribution.

First, while Kerberos is included with the base Mac OS X distribution, it is recommended that administrators install the MIT Kerberos Extras for Mac OS to add some of the functionality that was omitted from the Apple distribution (*http://web.mit.edu/macdev/Development/MITKerberos/Common/Documentation/osx-kerberos-extras.html*). These Extras add support for Carbon-based applications that use the CFM Kerberos libraries, as well as placing an alias to the Kerberos graphical ticket utility included with Mac OS X into a more suitable location (namely, */Applications/Utilities*).

The location of the configuration file is different than the traditional MIT file location. Instead of */etc/krb5.conf*, the Kerberos configuration file is located in */Library/Preferences/edu.mit.kerberos*, which follows more closely the naming conventions in Mac OS X. Unfortunately, there is currently no graphical utility included with Mac OS X to create or edit this file. Nonetheless, the contents of the file are the same as the *krb5.conf* file, so you can simply copy a working *krb5.conf* file from a Unix machine into the *edu.mit.kerberos* Preferences file.

GUI users need not despair, however, since Mac OS X contains a graphical credential cache and ticket manager application. This application is located in */System/Library/CoreServices/Kerberos*, and if you've installed the Kerberos Extras, there is a link to it located in */Applications/Utilities*. When that application is launched, the GUI credential cache window appears, shown in Figure 4-7.

In addition, if there are valid tickets in the credential cache, the Kerberos application's dock icon shows the remaining lifetime of the active principal's TGT, in hours and minutes, shown in Figure 4-8.

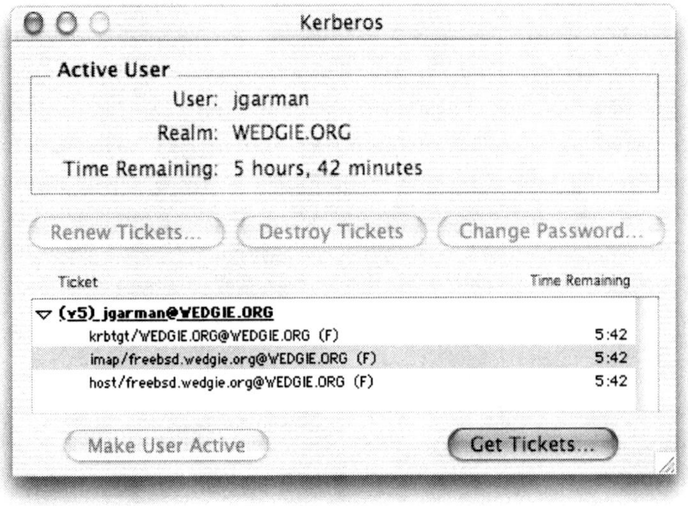

Kerberos

Active User

User: jgarman

Realm: WEDGIE.ORG

Time Remaining: 5 hours, 42 minutes

(Renew Tickets...) (Destroy Tickets) (Change Password...)

Ticket	Time Remaining
▽ **(v5) jgarman@WEDGIE.ORG**	
krbtgt/WEDGIE.ORG@WEDGIE.ORG (F)	5:42
imap/freebsd.wedgie.org@WEDGIE.ORG (F)	5:42
host/freebsd.wedgie.org@WEDGIE.ORG (F)	5:42

(Make User Active) **(Get Tickets...)**

Figure 4-7. Mac OS X graphical Kerberos ticket manager

Figure 4-8. Mac OS X Kerberos dock icon, showing remaining TGT lifetime in hours and minutes

This GUI application segues into the major difference between Mac OS X's implementation of Kerberos and the stock MIT Kerberos 5 distribution. To ensure consistent behavior of Kerberos applications running on Mac OS X, whether those applications are native Carbon or Cocoa apps or older OS 9 applications running under the Classic environment, Mac OS X uses a memory-based credential cache as opposed to a file-based credential cache.

In addition, the Mac OS X Kerberos libraries and applications support multiple client principals, and switching between these principals. Traditionally, with MIT Kerberos, if you wish to be authenticated in two or more realms at the same time, you have to manually swap credential cache files by setting the KRB5CCACHE environment variable to a different file for each principal, and then running kinit with the appropriate credential cache for each principal. Then, you have to remember to change the KRB5CCACHE environment variable to the appropriate credential cache for the principal you wish to use before starting a Kerberized client program.

Obviously, this is a rather convoluted procedure, and since the Mac OS X Kerberos libraries already use a memory-based credential cache instead of a file-based credential cache, the solution is simple. The memory-based credential cache includes support for multiple credential caches that are managed automatically by the Kerberos libraries.

The initial credential cache in Mac OS X is named "API:Initial default ccache" and additional credential caches start their naming at "API:0", where the zero indicates the sequence in which the caches were created for this user. The active principal is underlined in the GUI Kerberos application, and the Kerberos dock menu has a checkmark next to the active principal. Switching active principals in the Kerberos application is as easy as using the dock menu to select the appropriate principal, or clicking on the principal in the Kerberos application and selecting "Make user active". In addition, Mac OS X includes a command-line utility, kswitch, that can switch between active principals, either by specifying the name of the credential cache or the client principal associated with the credential cache. Also note that destroying the current credential cache will not only delete the current credential cache but also automatically switch the active principal to the next most recently used principal, if one exists.

Of course, if you prefer the traditional Unix CLI Kerberos tools, those are available in Mac OS X as well. The kinit, klist, and other command-line Kerberos tools are available in Mac OS X and work very similarly to their MIT counterparts, with slightly different semantics to support the credential switching and memory-based credential cache capabilities. The kinit program will create a new credential cache if a user already has tickets for one principal and acquires tickets for another principal, unlike MIT kinit which would destroy the tickets for the previous principal and store the tickets for the new principal. In addition, the klist command is extended with an -A option, which lists the tickets for all credential caches associated with the currently logged in user. For example, here's a user who has tickets for both the *jgarman@WEDGIE.ORG* and *tdurden@SAMPLE.COM* principals:

```
> klist -A
Kerberos 5 ticket cache: 'API:Initial default ccache'
Default Principal: jgarman@WEDGIE.ORG
Valid Starting     Expires              Service Principal
05/29/03 09:23:41  05/29/03 19:23:41   krbtgt/WEDGIE.ORG@WEDGIE.ORG
05/29/03 09:23:42  05/29/03 19:23:41   imap/freebsd.wedgie.org@WEDGIE.ORG


--------------------------------------------------------------------------------
Kerberos 5 ticket cache: 'API:0'
Default Principal: tdurden@SAMPLE.COM
Valid Starting     Expires              Service Principal
05/29/03 15:12:38  05/30/03 01:12:39   krbtgt/SAMPLE.COM@SAMPLE.COM
> kswitch -p tdurden@SAMPLE.COM
> klist
Kerberos 5 ticket cache: 'API:0'
Default Principal: tdurden@SAMPLE.COM
Valid Starting     Expires              Service Principal
05/29/03 15:12:38  05/30/03 01:12:39   krbtgt/SAMPLE.COM@SAMPLE.COM
```

The command-line telnet client that is shipped with OS X has Kerberos support compiled by default. Therefore, once you have a Kerberos configuration file installed and you've logged into Kerberos, either through kinit or through the graphical

Kerberos login program, you can use the standard Unix telnet command (with the -a option, as shown above) to use Kerberos authentication to log into a Kerberized telnet server.

Graphical Mac OS X applications such as Mail, Fetch, and Eudora also include Kerberos support. Once the Kerberos preferences file is in place, graphical Classic Mac OS and native Mac OS X applications will automatically launch the GUI Kerberos login application when necessary. Note that Carbon-based applications require the CFM Kerberos libraries to be installed from the Kerberos Extras package mentioned earlier before Kerberos support will function in these applications. We'll discuss how to require valid Kerberos credentials to log into a Mac OS X box in Chapter 7.

Windows as a Kerberos Client

If a Windows 2000/XP/2003 host is part of a Windows domain, then there is no extra work required to implement Kerberos-based login and Windows services that use Kerberos for authentication. However, for mixed environments where Windows clients will also be connecting to Kerberized services running on Unix hosts, you'll want to install the MIT Kerberos for Windows distribution on your Windows clients.

We'll explore the possibilities and implementation details of a mixed Windows/Unix Kerberos environment later. For now, let's take a look at how to install the Kerberos for Windows distribution from MIT, and some of the applications that come bundled with it.

First, retrieve the latest Kerberos for Windows distribution from the MIT Kerberos home page located at *http://web.mit.edu/kerberos/www/*, if you're a U.S. or Canadian citizen. Unfortunately the Cryptography Publishing Project does not currently distribute the MIT Kerberos for Windows binary distribution for overseas users. The current non-beta version as of this writing is Kerberos for Windows 2.1.2. The Kerberos for Windows distribution is packaged as several Zip files, so ensure that WinZip or some other unarchiver is installed.

The only required distribution is the main binary distribution. Another distribution that may need to be installed is the extra redistributable components—if you receive errors about missing DLLs, the Microsoft redistributable components distribution needs to be installed. Each distribution contains a rather deep directory structure, starting with a directory named with the distribution name. If you're installing multiple distributions, you'll have to manually copy the binaries and DLLs installed by the other distributions to the main distribution's *rel* directory.

To make the Kerberos libraries available to all Windows applications, copy the Kerberos DLLs to your Windows SYSTEM32 directory:

```
C:\krb5>copy comerr32.dll gssapi32.dll kclnt32.dll krb5_32.dll krb5cc32.dll
%SystemRoot%\SYSTEM32
```

You'll also need to create a *krb5.ini* configuration file. This file has the same syntax as the */etc/krb5.conf* file on Unix systems, so copying the *krb5.conf* file over from a Unix system in your Kerberos realm will suffice. Ensure that the *krb5.ini* file is in the SYSTEM32 directory as well so that all applications can access it. Note that if there is a *krb5.ini* file in the application's directory as well, it will take precedence over the system-wide file and may cause problems.

The MIT Kerberos for Windows distribution enables its memory-based credential cache by default, but also retains support for the older style, file-based credential caches. The in-memory cache support has the advantage of not exposing users' Kerberos credentials to the filesystem. Note that Kerberos credential cache, while now memory-based, is separate from the internal Windows credential cache, maintained by the LSA (Local Security Authority). The LSA cache contains, among other things, the Kerberos TGT for the currently logged in user, as well as any service tickets that were obtained through the Windows SSPI interface. To bridge this gap between the MIT and LSA credential caches, MIT Kerberos now includes a program, ms2mit, to copy TGTs out of the LSA cache into the MIT credential cache. This program, when run, will produce no output but should copy the Ticket Granting Ticket from your Windows LSA cache into the MIT credential cache.

However, there are still circumstances where a manual Kerberos login is appropriate, and MIT provides a graphical Kerberos credential cache management utility called leash32 that allows users to acquire and delete Kerberos tickets from the MIT credential cache. Leash32 also allows users to view their current Kerberos tickets graphically. The leash32 application is shown in Figure 4-9.

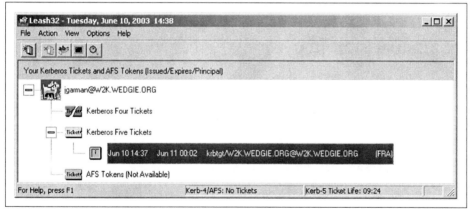

Figure 4-9. MIT Kerberos for Windows leash32 application

The MIT distribution also contains the traditional command-line utilities kinit, klist, and kdestroy, which act just like their Unix counterparts. In addition, all applications using MIT Kerberos for Windows honor the KRB5CCNAME environment variable to specify alternative credential cache locations.

## CHAPTER 5

Troubleshooting

Working with Kerberos can seem like an exercise in futility. The combination of complex software, interoperation between Kerberos implementations and diverse operating systems, and terse (at best) error messages tend to bring premature balding to the administrators responsible for the smooth operation of their systems. However, working with Kerberos does not have to be this frustrating.

To provide a systematic approach to solving problems in Kerberos, this chapter begins with a discussion of the various debugging tools and techniques, including a sample decision tree to follow when facing a new problem. Becoming familiar with these tools and techniques before disaster strikes will be helpful when the inevitable problem occurs. The second section will use those tools and techniques to diagnose some typical problems that occur in a Kerberos system. It will describe the symptoms of these common problems and then show possible solutions to solve them.

A Quick Decision Tree

So you're having a problem with your Kerberos installation. The first step to solving this problem, like debugging any other issue, is to narrow down the root cause. We'll determine if the problem falls into three distinct categories, and continue our analysis from there.

An easy way to categorize an error involving Kerberos authentication is through what tickets the client can acquire for a service. Let's look at the three top-level categories:

Client can't get an initial Ticket Granting Ticket. This is most likely a client-specific problem, especially if logging in with the user principal and password works on other clients. Of course, it could also mean that the password entered for the user principal is incorrect.

The most likely culprits include time-synchronization problems and issues reaching the Kerberos server due to misconfiguration of the client. It is also possible that the client does not share a compatible encryption type for the users' secret key with the KDC. This can happen, for example, when attempting to interoperate between a Unix client and a Windows domain controller. By default, Windows domain controllers create user entries with an RC4-HMAC encryption type, which most Unix Kerberos implementations do not understand. Newer versions of Heimdal and MIT Kerberos 5 will support this encryption type.

Client has valid TGT but gets error before a service ticket is acquired. Once again, this is most likely a problem with the client. The usual suspects in this scenario include Kerberos misconfiguration on the client, which we'll cover in a subsequent section.

Another possibility is that the service principal that the client requested simply does not exist. Examining the KDC log files is a good way to determine if the client is reaching the KDC, and if so, if it is attempting to acquire tickets for a principal that does not exist, or is in a different realm.

Client has valid TGT and service ticket, but reports error on connection to Kerberized service. There is most likely a problem with the server. At this point, the client has received a ticket for the service and presented it to the service for authentication. The most common cause for a failure at this point is a mismatch in the encryption types or key version numbers for the Kerberos service between the service's keytab and the KDC. The KDC may have issued a ticket with an encryption type that the service did not understand, or perhaps the service's keytab contains an incorrect encryption key. The service may not be able to read its keytab at all; ensure that the service's keytab is readable by the user the service runs as, and that the appropriate configuration is in place to point the service to the location of the keytab.

Another possibility is that the server's DNS or Kerberos configuration file is not configured correctly. Make sure that the target server's hostname can be correctly resolved by using diagnostic tools such as ping and nslookup.

General root causes that should be investigated include time synchronization and correct hostname and DNS settings on all machines.

Finally—this may seem obvious—it is easy to overlook the final step: recording the error and the solution that was used to solve the problem. All too often, especially with some of the more esoteric errors that Kerberos can produce, administrators experience an error one day, solve the problem, then experience the same error a week later, and have to track down the root cause again, only to find that the solution is vaguely familiar.

Debugging Tools

The MIT Kerberos distribution includes a small sample Kerberized client/server application. These example applications are located in the *src/appl/sample* subdirectory of the MIT Kerberos 5 distribution.

Just like any other Kerberized server, the sample server requires a service principal and access to the secret key associated with that principal through a keytab file. By default, the sample server uses a principal name of "sample," with an instance of the hostname that it is running on. If you're having trouble with a particular service principal, the sample server and client can use any principal name to communicate with each other, given the sample server has read access to the service's keytab file.

The command-line arguments accepted by the sample server are:

```
> ./sserver -h
usage: ./sserver [-p port] [-s service] [-S keytab]
```

The -p argument specifies what TCP port that the server will listen on for client requests. If this argument isn't specified, then sserver will immediately exit. The -s option can be used to specify a particular service principal (instead of the default, "sample"). For example, the host principal can be specified by -s host. Finally, the -S option specifies a keytab file in which the server can find the secret key for the service principal. By default, sserver will use /etc/krb5.keytab.

Ensure that a valid keytab entry for the principal you're using to test exists in a keytab file and is readable by the user you're starting sserver as. Note that the server won't test for the readability of the keytab until a client connects to it, and your client will report "Permission denied".

The command-line arguments that the client accepts are similar:

```
> ./sclient
usage: ./sclient <hostname> [port] [service]
```

A successful exchange looks like the following, assuming that you have shells open on both of the hosts freebsd and slave, and their prompts are freebsd> and slave> respectively:

```
freebsd> ./sserver -p 8888 -s sample -S /tmp/sample.keytab
slave> ./sclient freebsd 8888 sample
sendauth succeeded, reply is:
reply len 27, contents:
You are jgarman@WEDGIE.ORG
```

If you choose a service name other than "sample," specify the service name on the command lines to both the server and the client. Just like with any other Kerberos client/server application, you'll see that you now have Kerberos tickets for the sample service principal:

```
client> klist
Ticket cache: FILE:/tmp/krb5cc_p27758
Default principal: jgarman@WEDGIE.ORG

Valid starting     Expires            Service principal
02/26/03 02:34:47  02/26/03 10:58:19  krbtgt/WEDGIE.ORG@WEDGIE.ORG
02/26/03 02:35:51  02/26/03 10:58:19  sample/freebsd.wedgie.org@WEDGIE.ORG
```

A similar set of programs exists for Heimdal Kerberos. Heimdal actually includes several sample client/server applications, and the two client/server sets that are the most useful for our debugging purposes are the tcp_client/tcp_server applications and the gssapi_client/gssapi_server applications, both found in the *appl/test* directory inside of the Heimdal source distribution. The tcp_client and tcp_server applications use the Kerberos 5 API directly, and the gssapi_client and gssapi_server applications are simple applications that utilize the GSSAPI for authentication.

The command-line arguments for these programs are similar to the MIT Kerberos sample applications:

```
> ./gssapi_server -h
Usage: gssapi_server [-fh] [--port=port] [-p port] [--service=service]
    [-s service] [--keytab=keytab] [-k keytab] [--fork] [--help] [--version]
-p port, --port=port        port to listen to
-s service, --service=service service to use
-k keytab, --keytab=keytab   keytab to use
-f, --fork                   do fork
> ./gssapi_client -h
Usage: gssapi_client [-fh] [--port=port] [-p port] [--service=service]
    [-s service] [--keytab=keytab] [-k keytab] [--fork] [--help] [--version] host
-p port, --port=port        port to listen to
-s service, --service=service service to use
-k keytab, --keytab=keytab   keytab to use
-f, --fork                   do fork
```

The arguments accepted by tcp_client and tcp_server are the same as the gssapi_client and gssapi_server applications, respectively. Unlike the MIT Kerberos sample applications, the default principal name used by the Heimdal testing applications is "test".

When testing these programs, it was noted that the keytab command-line option did not function correctly; instead, the application continued to try and access */etc/krb5.keytab* regardless of the filename passed through the -k parameter.

An example of successful output:

```
freebsd> ./gssapi_server -s sample -p 8888
slave> ./gssapi_client -s sample -p 8888 freebsd
User is 'jgarman@WEDGIE.ORG'
gss_verify_mic: hej
gss_unwrap: hemligt
```

Another tool that can be helpful is the Kerberized telnet daemon. It has rather verbose output so that errors can be readily gleaned from the messages it prints when connecting. When creating the realm in Chapter 4, we set up a telnet daemon to test the new realm. Make sure that, when using telnet to test Kerberos functionality, you use the -a option on the client to tell it to automatically attempt Kerberos authentication. Also, ensure that the telnet client program is actually a Kerberized version, and not the system telnet that may not be Kerberized.

Errors and Solutions

With the debugging tools presented above, we'll run through a few problem scenarios, from the initial symptoms of a problem through to its solution.

Errors Obtaining an Initial Ticket

Several errors can occur when attempting to obtain an initial Ticket Granting Ticket from a Kerberos KDC. Since there are many ways to obtain a TGT, such as through integrated login with a PAM Kerberos module, the best way to narrow down problems is by using the Unix kinit program manually. This will work even if your KDC is a Windows domain controller, given that the principal you're testing has been set up for DES encryption (see Chapter 8).

Let's go through a few examples:

```
> kinit
Password for jgarman@WEDGIE.ORG:
kinit(v5): Preauthentication failed while getting initial credentials
```

If your realm requires pre-authentication (see Chapter 6), then this message is typically just Kerberos-speak for "incorrect password." Note that Windows domain controllers require pre-authentication by default. Also note that this message can result from a client that does not support the pre-authentication type required by the KDC. However, all of the Kerberos implementations we cover here support the Encrypted Timestamp (PA-ENC-TIMESTAMP) pre-authentication method. Of course, if you are interoperating with a Kerberos implementation that does not support pre-authentication, and your realm requires it, you will have to disable pre-authentication in the KDC policy.

Next, there is a possibility that the KDC could not find an appropriate encryption key with which to encrypt the response. When a Kerberos 5 client contacts a KDC through the AS exchange for an initial Ticket Granting Ticket, the client sends a list of encryption types that it understands. If the KDC cannot find a secret key associated with one of the encryption types included in the request, it will return an error.

Encryption type mismatches can also occur later on in the Kerberos exchange, and we'll cover that in a later section. Errors obtaining an initial ticket can also be caused by hostname/DNS misconfiguration, or a missing or incorrect Kerberos configuration file. These possibilities will also be covered soon in a later section.

Finally, another common error that can cause the pre-authentication failed message is a clock synchronization problem (which can cause all sorts of other strange problems, as well), covered next.

Unsynchronized Clocks

Another common root cause of Kerberos problems is the lack of clock synchronization between all participating hosts. Usually the error message produced when there is a clock mismatch is self-explanatory. For example:

```
krb5_rd_req failed: Clock skew too great
```

It is recommended that all participating hosts in a Kerberos realm be synchronized to a central time source. The Network Time Protocol (NTP) fits this bill perfectly. NTP is discussed briefly in the "Before You Begin" section in Chapter 4, and more information can be found at the NTP home page at *http://www.ntp.org*.

Since NTP and Kerberos both use Universal Coordinated Time (UTC) to compare clocks, time zone differences do not affect the operation of Kerberos.

Incorrect or Missing Kerberos Configuration

Every client needs to know two things: the realm that every host it wishes to communicate with belongs to, and the KDCs that are responsible for those realms. Therefore, a client requires a mapping between domain names and realms, as well as realms and their KDCs. Traditionally, these mappings are hardcoded inside a configuration file, */etc/krb5.conf*, on Unix hosts. However, with the advent of Windows 2000, DNS realm and KDC mapping is becoming more popular, as Windows 2000 and above use DNS to find realm and KDC information by default.

Either way that your realm (and other realms your hosts may communicate with) handles its Kerberos configuration, incorrect or missing Kerberos configuration information will cause requests for tickets to fail, sometimes silently—giving no error messages to point toward the cause of failure, or worse yet, misleading error messages that give no indication of the root cause of failure.

Let's begin with some simple examples from a Unix client running MIT. Our client has no */etc/krb5.conf* file. If there is a pre-existing credential cache (pointed to by the environment variable KRB5CCACHE, by default */tmp/krb5cc_UID* where UID is the Unix UID of the current user), then kinit will request a ticket as that principal from the KDC. When there is no pre-existing credential cache, MIT kinit forms the user principal by using the Unix username as the username portion of the principal, and the realm is determined by the default_realm variable in the libdefaults stanza of */etc/krb5.conf*. Since, in this case, there is no */etc/krb5.conf* file, kinit will complain:

```
> whoami
jgarman
> kinit
kinit(v5): Configuration file does not specify default realm when parsing name
jgarman
```

Now let's create a minimalist */etc/krb5.conf* file:

```
[libdefaults]
    default_realm = WEDGIE.ORG
```

With this in place, MIT Kerberos can now determine the default realm. Note that even if a correct DNS domain name-to-realm mapping is available in DNS, MIT still requires a default_realm entry in */etc/krb5.conf* to work correctly. Also, without a default realm defined, some GSSAPI applications may also behave incorrectly, giving "generic error" messages.

Note that this minimalist */etc/krb5.conf* file will only work if you have correct DNS entries for your Kerberos realm, as discussed in "DNS and Kerberos" in Chapter 4. There has to be a way for the client to find its KDC, either through static configuration files or through DNS. If the client cannot find the KDC for a given realm, it will report back accurately:

```
kinit(v5): Cannot resolve network address for KDC in requested realm while getting
initial credentials
```

 MIT Kerberos has a bug in which a KDC returns an error message claiming that it has no support for the requested encryption type to all ticket requests if the KDC has no */etc/krb5.conf* file. Creating a */etc/krb5.conf* file on the KDC, even if it is blank, will fix this problem.

Heimdal kinit also uses an existing credential cache file, if there is one, to determine the principal that kinit will acquire tickets for. If there is no */etc/krb5.conf* file, or if it does not specify a default realm, it will use the domain name component of the local hosts' hostname as the realm. Heimdal will also consult DNS for DNS hostname-to-Kerberos realm mapping as well as KDC location, or use static configuration in */etc/krb5.conf*.

In all cases, static configuration in */etc/krb5.conf* will short-circuit the location of KDCs and domain-realm mappings. If static information is located in the configuration file, the static entries will override any DNS information available.

If issues remain, there could be a problem with your DNS domain name-to-Kerberos realm mapping. This is especially apparent when the DNS domain name and Kerberos realm names do not match. Every time a client acquires a ticket to communicate with a Kerberized application server, it needs to determine the realm that the application server belongs to. This mapping is controlled by the domain_realm stanza in the */etc/krb5.conf* file, or TXT entries in the DNS (as described in the "DNS and Kerberos" section in Chapter 4). Failing to find an appropriate entry either in the configuration file or the DNS, the Kerberos libraries will try the host's DNS domain name, converted to uppercase, as the realm name. Problems related to the domain name-to-Kerberos realm mapping can be diagnosed by narrowing down the problem to a particular problematic domain or host.

Unfortunately, this problem can cause mysterious failures with no error messages. The most direct way to find whether there are mismatched realm-DNS mappings is to check the KDC logs for the client's default realm. If the client attempts to contact a Kerberized service that it thinks is in a different realm, it will attempt a cross-realm authentication to that other realm.

For example, we are on *slave.wedgie.org*, authenticated as *jgarman@WEDGIE.ORG* and attempting a Kerberized telnet to host *freebsd.wedgie.org*, which the slave thinks is in the BOGUS.COM realm, due to a configuration error. Therefore, it is trying to acquire service tickets for *host/slave.wedgie.org@BOGUS.COM*, but first needs to acquire cross-realm tickets for BOGUS.COM. In this example, the following log entries are located in the log file of the KDC responsible for WEDGIE.ORG:

```
Feb 26 21:32:20 freebsd krb5kdc[520]: TGS_REQ (3 etypes {16 3 1}) 192.168.0.5(88
): UNKNOWN_SERVER: authtime 1046294981, jgarman@WEDGIE.ORG for krbtgt/BOGUS.COM
@WEDGIE.ORG, Server not found in Kerberos database
```

The solution to a DNS-to-realm mismatch is to ensure that all clients have the correct mappings in place. In this rather contrived example, the default behavior of Kerberos is sufficient, since all machines in the DNS domain *wedgie.org* belong to the WEDGIE.ORG Kerberos realm. However, other organizations may have a realm name different from their DNS domain name, and it is this situation that requires special care.

Server Hostname Misconfiguration

Undoubtedly, you'll find yourself in the following situation. You've just installed Kerberos 5; your KDC works, as you can acquire tickets for your user principal. You've dutifully established a host principal for your test application server, and you're ready to test the first application.

Your shell output looks something like this:

```
> hostname
freebsd.wedgie.org
> klist
Ticket cache: FILE:/tmp/krb5cc_p82191
Default principal: jgarman@WEDGIE.ORG

Valid starting     Expires          Service principal
01/29/03 04:52:21  01/29/03 10:30:11  krbtgt/WEDGIE.ORG@WEDGIE.ORG

Kerberos 4 ticket cache: /tmp/tkt1000
klist: You have no tickets cached
> ftp freebsd
Connected to localhost.
220 freebsd.wedgie.org FTP server (Version 5.60) ready.
334 Using authentication type GSSAPI; ADAT must follow
GSSAPI accepted as authentication type
GSSAPI error major: Miscellaneous failure
GSSAPI error minor: Server not found in Kerberos database
GSSAPI error: initializing context
GSSAPI authentication failed
334 Using authentication type KERBEROS_V4; ADAT must follow
KERBEROS_V4 accepted as authentication type
Kerberos V4 krb_mk_req failed: You have no tickets cached
Name (localhost:jgarman):
331 Password required for jgarman.
Password:
```

What just happened? It *should* work, after all. Let's double-check the principals in our Kerberos database:

```
% kadmin
Authenticating as principal jgarman/admin@WEDGIE.ORG with password.
Enter password:
kadmin: listprincs
K/M@WEDGIE.ORG
host/freebsd.wedgie.org@WEDGIE.ORG
ftp/freebsd.wedgie.org@WEDGIE.ORG
host/desktop.wedgie.org@WEDGIE.ORG
host/slave.wedgie.org@WEDGIE.ORG
imap/freebsd.wedgie.org@WEDGIE.ORG
ldap/freebsd.wedgie.org@WEDGIE.ORG
krbtgt/WEDGIE.ORG@WEDGIE.ORG
kadmin/admin@WEDGIE.ORG
kadmin/changepw@WEDGIE.ORG
kadmin/history@WEDGIE.ORG
jgarman@WEDGIE.ORG
jgarman/admin@WEDGIE.ORG
```

According to our Kerberos KDC, we have the correct service principal installed (specifically, *ftp/freebsd.wedgie.org@WEDGIE.ORG*). But still, ftp reports "Server not found in Kerberos database."

A hint to the problem can be seen in the ftp output. Note that the first line of the ftp client's output reads:

```
Connected to localhost.
```

This means that the hostname "freebsd" resolves to the loopback address. Sure enough, our */etc/hosts* file contains the following line:

```
127.0.0.1  localhost localhost.wedgie.org freebsd freebsd.wedgie.org
```

Therefore, the ftp server receives the connection on the loopback interface. When the ftp daemon generates the service principal that it will use to validate the user's ticket, it performs an IP-to-name lookup on the interface on which it received the request. Therefore, if we examine the KDC request logs, we'll see a failed request for the nonexistent principal *ftp/localhost@WEDGIE.ORG*:

```
Jan 29 04:52:21 freebsd krb5kdc[35553]: TGS_REQ (3 etypes {16 3 1}) 192.168.0.5(88):
UNKNOWN_SERVER: authtime 1043800211,  jgarman@WEDGIE.ORG for ftp/localhost@WEDGIE.
ORG, Server not found in Kerberos database
```

Once the */etc/hosts* file has been corrected with the correct IP-to-hostname mapping for our host, we get the intended result:

```
> ftp freebsd
Connected to freebsd.wedgie.org.
220 freebsd.wedgie.org FTP server (Version 5.60) ready.
334 Using authentication type GSSAPI; ADAT must follow
GSSAPI accepted as authentication type
GSSAPI authentication succeeded
Name (freebsd:jgarman):
232 GSSAPI user jgarman@WEDGIE.ORG is authorized as jgarman
```

This example illustrates the importance of consistent resolver and DNS information to the proper functioning of Kerberos. This problem can manifest itself in many ways, but all with the same root cause of incorrect data in DNS or local host databases. The particular scenario depicted above can occur with most Linux distributions, which, out of the box, alias the hostname of the machine to the machine's loopback address. Similar scenarios occur with Solaris machines, which, by default, create */etc/hosts* files that list the "short" hostname first, before the FQDN that Kerberos needs to form the correct service principal.

To ensure that Kerberized services can construct proper service principals, your local hosts database needs an entry like the following:

```
192.168.0.5  freebsd.wedgie.org  freebsd
```

Note that the hostname is mapped to the IP address of the appropriate interface (as opposed to the loopback IP address), and that the FQDN is given precedence over the short hostname.

Here's a similar error message that results from DNS and hostname misconfiguration:

```
Hostname cannot be canonicalized while verifying initial ticket
```

Essentially, this is caused when the application attempts to find its service principal name by performing a reverse lookup on the interface IP address that this request was received on. If that IP address does not resolve to a hostname, this message or the earlier "cannot find service principal" message will be generated.

Multi-homed hosts that have a different hostname for every interface also pose a problem for Kerberos. Depending on what interface a client's request arrives on, a different server hostname may be associated with that request. Therefore, each interface that has a different hostname has a different set of service principals based on that hostname, which can cause a problem if there is only one set of service principals defined for the host. It is recommended that multi-homed hosts have a single FQDN associated with all interfaces on the machine.

Encryption Type Mismatches

The extensible encryption type support in Kerberos 5 can result in some strange interactions when mixing different Kerberos 5 implementations. Most of the time the KDC can automatically determine the optimal set of encryption types for a given protocol exchange; however, sometimes it needs a little manual help.

This is necessary when you have keys stored for "stronger" encryption types in the KDC for a given service, but the service can only handle weaker encryption types. Since there's no direct communication between the service and the KDC, there is no way for the service to communicate its encryption-type support to the KDC. Instead, when the KDC returns a ticket to the client for use with the service, the KDC will use the strongest encryption type it has in its database for the service. Let's take an example.

We have a KDC *freebsd.wedgie.org*, running the MIT KDC, and an application server, *slave.wedgie.org*, running a Kererized telnet daemon with the MIT client libraries. We've created a host keytab for *slave.wedgie.org*, and copied it into that host's */etc/krb5.keytab*. The KDC database and the keytab include keys for both triple DES and single DES encryption types, as illustrated below:

```
freebsd# /usr/local/sbin/kadmin
Authenticating as principal jgarman/admin@WEDGIE.ORG with password.
Enter password:
kadmin: getprinc host/slave.wedgie.org
Principal: host/slave.wedgie.org@WEDGIE.ORG
Expiration date: [never]
Last password change: Sun Nov 24 00:42:14 GMT 2002
Password expiration date: [none]
Maximum ticket life: 0 days 10:00:00
Maximum renewable life: 0 days 00:00:00
Last modified: Sun Nov 24 00:42:14 GMT 2002 (jgarman/admin@WEDGIE.ORG)
Last successful authentication: [never]
Last failed authentication: [never]
Failed password attempts: 0
Number of keys: 2
Key: vno 3, Triple DES cbc mode with HMAC/sha1, no salt
Key: vno 3, DES cbc mode with CRC-32, no salt
Attributes:
Policy: [none]
```

The keytab on *slave.wedgie.org* contains both encryption types, and consequently Kerberized telnet works fine between the two hosts:

```
> telnet -a -f slave
Trying 192.168.0.6...
Connected to slave.wedgie.org (192.168.0.6).
Escape character is '^]'.
[ Kerberos V5 accepts you as ``jgarman@WEDGIE.ORG'' ]
[ Kerberos V5 accepted forwarded credentials ]
Last login: Sun Feb 16 15:22:30 from 192.168.0.7
...
```

Now, let's see what happens when we erase the triple DES encryption key from slave's keytab. We'll use this to simulate a service that does not support triple DES encryption types. After we edit the keytab to remove the triple DES encryption key, we attempt another telnet into slave:

```
> telnet -a -f slave
Trying 192.168.0.6...
Connected to slave.wedgie.org (192.168.0.6).
Escape character is '^]'.
[ Kerberos V5 refuses authentication because telnetd: krb5_rd_req failed: Key table
entry not found ]
[ Kerberos V5 refuses authentication because telnetd: krb5_rd_req failed: Key table
entry not found ]
[ Trying KERBEROS4 ... ]
mk_req failed: You have no tickets cached
```

```
[ Trying KERBEROS4 ... ]
mk_req failed: You have no tickets cached
Password for jgarman:
```

This error message can be somewhat misleading; after all, we do have a key table entry for *host/slave.wedgie.org*; however, the keytab entry contains a single DES key, when the KDC has issued the client a service ticket encrypted with triple DES. Since the service can't find an appropriate encryption key to decrypt the ticket, it gives up and returns this error message.

The solution here is to identify which encryption types your service supports and ensure that the Kerberos database only contains those key encryption types for that service. For example, in this case, if our telnet server only supports single DES encryption, we need to remove the triple DES encryption key from the Kerberos KDC, so that the KDC will only issue tickets for that service encrypted with single DES. In general, all Kerberos 5 implementations must support single DES encryption, so if there is suspicion of encryption type incompatibilities, it is recommended that you recreate the relevant principals with a single DES encryption type. Unfortunately, this reduces the security of those principals.

To solve this problem, we delete the host key for slave.wedgie.org, re-create it with only a single DES encryption type, and extract that keytab onto the host. Since the KDC now only has a single DES encryption key available, it will encrypt the service ticket with the single DES key.

The process of creating principals with a subset of encryption types varies from implementation to implementation.

CHAPTER 6

Security

Cerberus, the fierce three-headed creature that guarded the entrance to Hades, prevented the living from entering the underworld and devoured the brave souls who attempted to leave. While Cerberus was successful in keeping the living from visiting the netherworld, like all great characters in mythology, he had a fatal flaw. In the *Aeneid*, when the Trojan hero Aeneas descends to visit his father, he encounters the menacing Cerberus. He tosses Cerberus a spiced cake laced with honey and poppy seeds, and Cerberus promptly devours it and falls unconscious. With hell's keeper fast asleep, Aeneas swiftly crosses into the underworld.

We'd hope that the modern equivalent to the ancient Cerberus would not have such a simple, fatal flaw. While Kerberos is the most popular cross-platform, network-wide authentication system available, it by no means has a perfect security record. It is certainly true that a lot of thought was put into making Kerberos as secure as possible; however, there are still security issues that require careful attention. Thankfully, unlike proprietary security software, Kerberos has been scrutinized for holes both in the basic protocol itself as well as the most common reference implementation from MIT.

It is important to recognize that implementing Kerberos on your network does not guarantee perfect security. While Kerberos is extremely secure in a theoretical sense, there are many practical security issues to be considered. In addition, it is important to remember that Kerberos provides only an authentication service; it does not prevent compromises caused by buggy server software, administrators granting permissions to unauthorized users, or poorly chosen passwords.

While most documentation on the subject of Kerberos security simply says to "secure the KDC," there is much more to the story of Kerberos security than turning off unnecessary services on your KDC machines (although that is certainly good advice!). In this chapter, we will begin with a discussion of potential attacks against your Kerberos authentication system, follow up with steps that should be taken to prevent these attacks, and finally examine Kerberos KDC logs. After reading this chapter, you should understand the security implications that Kerberos presents and how to protect your network from the attack scenarios presented.

Kerberos Attacks

While it may not be possible for a hacker to feed your Kerberos KDC a spiced cake to put it to sleep, there are some electronic attacks that can compromise the security of your Kerberos system. Listed below are potential compromise scenarios, and their effect on the security of the Kerberos system.

Root compromise of a Kerberos KDC machine. A root-level compromise of a KDC machine (master or any of the slaves) gives the attacker full control over the entire Kerberos authentication system. Even though the Kerberos database is encrypted on disk with the Kerberos master key, the master key is also kept on the KDC's disk so no manual intervention is required (to enter in the master password) when the KDC service is started. In addition, since all Kerberos implementations provide fail-safe access to the Kerberos database for the root or Administrator user on the KDC, your entire Kerberos database should be considered compromised in the event of attackers gaining root access to any KDC on your network. See "Protecting Your KDC" later in this chapter for tips on preventing a successful attack against your KDC.

Compromise of a Kerberos administrator's credentials. If an attacker obtains the password of a Kerberos administrative principal, that attacker has complete access to the entire Kerberos database. Most KDC implementations allow administrators to remotely dump the contents of the database for backup purposes, and an attacker can use this functionality to make a complete copy of your authentication database. With full access to the database, the attacker can also create and modify any Kerberos principal. Ensure that only a very small set of users have administrative access, and set policies on those users that enforce strict password checking and at least monthly password changes.

Root compromise of a server machine. For Kerberos's mutual authentication to work, a service must have access to a service principal. These service principals, as explained in Chapter 4, reside on the server's filesystem, either as part of a keytab typically used by Unix implementations, or the LSA Secrets in Microsoft implementations (see Q184017 on Microsoft's support site). If an attacker obtains root access to a server machine, all Kerberized services running on that machine are compromised. In addition, some services, such as the AFS distributed filesystem, share a single service principal across all servers. In this case, root access to an AFS file server machine would compromise all file and database servers in the AFS cell. Once an attacker has access to a service principal's credentials, the attacker can impersonate that service and also decrypt encrypted traffic sent between clients and the compromised service. The security of Kerberized services running on a server depends on the security of that individual server; therefore, all servers should be secured in proportion to the value of the resources stored on that server.

It is important to note that while the compromise of a server machine does compromise the services running on that machine, it does not compromise individual users' credentials. At no time in the Kerberos protocol exchange does a Kerberos service receive any information that would allow it to reconstruct the authenticating user's password directly. However, it's still possible to mount a brute-force or dictionary attack against credentials presented to services, as the authenticator is encrypted with the user's long-term key.

Root compromise of a client machine. A root compromise of a client machine will provide an attacker with all cached tickets on that machine. Since tickets are time-limited, it is not as critical a compromise as an attacker obtaining the users' password. However, with root access to a client machine, the attacker can surreptitiously install a keyboard sniffer to capture a users' password when logging into their machine. Therefore, when a client machine is compromised, passwords of all users who have logged into that machine should be considered compromised as well. In the event of a client compromise, the users who have logged into that client should immediately change their passwords.

Compromise of user credentials. There are two possibilities in this scenario: either the user's credential (ticket) cache is exposed, or a user's password is compromised. If an attacker obtains a user's unencrypted credential cache, the tickets contained in that cache are only valid for the time period specified in the tickets. On the other hand, if an attacker acquires the user's password, the attacker can impersonate that user until the user changes his password.

From the above list, the one fact that underlies all of those scenarios is the importance of keeping all machines on your network secure. Installing Kerberos on your network does not diminish the importance of keeping all machines, even end user desktops, secure from outside attack. The compromise of any machine in your network will have some detrimental effect on the security of your Kerberos authentication system.

Other Attacks

Since Kerberos only provides an authentication service, there are several security threats that a Kerberos installation will not protect against. The following attacks are not attacks directly against the Kerberos system itself, but are problems related to providing a secure, available authentication service in general. These techniques can be used to attack any authentication system, and Kerberos is no exception:

Denial of service
    A denial of service attack can be mounted against your organization's KDCs by flooding them with authentication requests. The large numbers of requests arriving can slow down response times to legitimate requests, or even, in extreme

cases, crash the machines on which your KDCs reside. Kerberos cannot protect against denial of service attacks and it is generally recommended that your network, including your Kerberos KDCs, be firewalled from the Internet to prevent this type of attack. Adding additional KDCs to your network for redundancy can also mitigate the effects of a DoS attack.

The "insider"

Kerberos cannot protect against an internal authorized user who decides to misuse their privileges. For example, a rogue Kerberos administrator could modify or remove information from the Kerberos database.

Social engineering and password exposure

Similarly, Kerberos cannot protect against individual users who divulge their passwords to attackers, either inadvertently or as a result of a social engineering attack. The use of Kerberos does not diminish the importance of user training on keeping passwords secure and not revealing their passwords to anyone, including those who claim to be part of your computer staff. Similarly, Kerberos cannot prevent users from reusing their passwords at other, less secure sites that may handle passwords in the clear. Hackers who successfully attack a less secure site where a user has recycled their Kerberos password will obtain a valid username and password for your Kerberos realm.

Security holes in the Kerberos software itself

This risk cannot be overstated. Unfortunately, with the current state-of-the-art in software engineering, it is very difficult to write secure code. Just like all other software packages available, every Kerberos implementation has had security issues at some point or another, and these issues can sometimes lead to a compromise of your KDCs. Therefore, it is extremely important to keep informed of your Kerberos vendor's patches, and apply them as soon as they become available.

Now that we've covered the attacks that can be performed against a Kerberos network, we'll take a look at some security issues in the Kerberos protocol itself.

Protocol Security Issues

First, let's revisit the underlying reason why the Kerberos protocol was developed. Kerberos was designed to protect authentication data from passing over a network in the clear. Before Kerberos, when a user wished to log into a remote service, the client software would pass the user's credentials (a password) to the server in clear text. Since networks are broadcast mediums, where every station connected to a network segment can "hear" all traffic on that segment, sending passwords in the clear over a network is extremely insecure. Therefore, Kerberos encrypts all authentication exchanges that occur over the network. Encryption is only part of the solution, however, and the designers of Kerberos have put much thought into ensuring as secure a system as possible. In this section, we'll explore several attacks against the distributed authentication systems, such as Kerberos. We'll also discuss the particular techniques that Kerberos employs to mitigate the threats posed by these attacks.

Dictionary and Brute-Force Attacks

In the original Kerberos 4 protocol, the KDC issues an encrypted TGT to any client that requests it. Recall from Chapter 3 that this TGT is encrypted with the user's secret key (derived from her password). The security of the entire system is dependent on not being able to decrypt this message, since if an attacker is able to retrieve the key used to encrypt the message, he now has the user's password and can impersonate that user at will. Therefore, if an attacker wishes to obtain a user's password, he can ask the KDC for a valid TGT for the victim's username. While there are no ways to break the encryption methods used in Kerberos tickets directly, the attacker can then continue to brute-force the decryption of the TGT by launching an *offline dictionary attack*.

During a dictionary attack, an attacker feeds a list of commonly used passwords, or a *dictionary*, to a cracking program. For each entry in the dictionary, a program attempts to decrypt the message using the password. If a hit is made, the program reports back to the attacker the user's password.

Since the transformation from the user's password to the encryption key is known (the string-to-key transformation covered in Chapter 3), it is trivial for an attacker to build a program that can translate common passwords into Kerberos encryption keys. Then, the attacker collects a large number of valid TGTs from the KDC and continues the work of cracking the TGTs off-line; that is, for each decryption attempt, he does not have to contact the KDC. Instead, once these TGTs are acquired from the KDC, no further communication is necessary to attack the passwords.

This method is made possible since there is a known plaintext included in the TGT, namely the string "tgt" itself. The Kerberos Ticket Granting Service principal name is always "krbtgt," and that principal name is the signal that indicates a successful decryption. By the time the attacker has successfully determined the password, the now unencrypted ticket has expired; however, the attacker now has a valid username/password combination to the Kerberos server and can obtain new tickets using that valid username and password.

Code is available to perform this attack against Kerberos 4 KDCs via a patch to the password cracker program John the Ripper. The code is available from Dug Song's web site at *http://www.monkey.org/~dugsong/john-1.6.krb4.patch-3*.

A dictionary attack forms a lower bound on the security of any password-based authentication system. No matter what kind of fancy encryption scheme is utilized, if the user's password is a simple, easily guessed word, then it will quickly succumb to a dictionary attack. Another attack, the *brute-force attack*, forms an upper bound on the security of Kerberos. Instead of attempting to decrypt messages by iterating over words in a pre-defined dictionary, a brute-force attack tries every encryption key, one by one, until the right key is found. Cryptosystems are designed with a large key space to make brute force attacks impractical. However, with the very fast pace of technology, key spaces that were once considered impractical to search are now within the grasp of even a moderately motivated attacker.

The encryption used in Kerberos v4, as well as the most common encryption type in Kerberos v5, is single DES. Single DES, designed in the late 1970s, has a 56-bit key length. When Kerberos was designed (in the late 1980s), brute-forcing a 56-bit key was not practical given the speed of the processors available. By today's standards, the 56-bit key space of single DES is considered relatively insecure. In 1998, the Electronic Frontier Foundation demonstrated that with a $200,000 investment, a determined attacker can build a specialized "DES cracker" which can brute-force the encryption key from a DES message within a matter of days.* With the processing power available today (in 2002), the time to decrypt a message encrypted using single DES has fallen into the range of a couple of hours. The most dramatic demonstration of the fallibility of DES came on January 19, 1999, when *distributed.net* cracked a 56-bit DES key in 22 hours,† using the spare cycles of thousands of computers worldwide and the EFF DES cracker in tandem.

Bits and the Strength of Cryptosystems

When reading about symmetric key cryptosystems such as DES, numbers of "bits" of encryption are invariably mentioned. However, what exactly does a "56-bit key" mean? How long would it take to try every key? What about a 128-bit key?

The number of bits in a cryptosystem's key represents its key length, or the number of possible encryption keys that the cryptosystem can handle. DES, for example, has a 56-bit key length. That means that there are 2^{56}, or 72,057,594,037,927,936 possible keys. While that seems like a large number, a network of off-the-shelf personal computers can search that key space in the matter of only a few weeks. For the more determined attacker, specialized machines such as the DES cracker can be built to speed the process along.

Since the number of keys grows exponentially with the number of bits in the key, a key length of 57 bits has twice the number of keys than a 56-bit key length. So, a 128-bit key contains more possible keys than there are protons in the visible universe. Brute-forcing that key with current computer technology would be impractical, to say the least.

Finally, when comparing the strength of cryptosystems, the key length of symmetric key cryptosystems such as DES and triple DES cannot be compared directly with the key length of asymmetric key (or public key) cryptosystems such as RSA. Roughly speaking, a public key algorithm with a 512-bit key length is equivalent to a 56-bit key length in a symmetric key encryption algorithm.

---

* *http://www.eff.org/descracker.html*
† *http://www.distributed.net/des/*

Thankfully, in Kerberos v5, some new protocol features were introduced to mitigate this threat. First is the extensible encryption type support, which allows for the addition of stronger encryption techniques as computer power continues to grow. In addition, pre-authentication was added, which forces a client to prove their identity before the KDC issues encrypted tickets to the client. Pre-authentication limits the problem of an offline brute-force or dictionary attack. Instead, a remote attacker must contact the KDC every time she attempts a new password.

However, Kerberos v5's new encryption type support and pre-authentication features do not completely solve the dictionary and brute-force attacks. New encryption types will undoubtedly make a brute force attack less viable by increasing the difficulty of brute-forcing an encrypted message by many, many orders of magnitude. However, all servers, clients, and KDCs on the network must support new encryption types. If, for example, you have many different Kerberos client and server implementations installed across your network (for instance, a set of MIT Kerberos servers along with some Windows clients), you can only use a common encryption type supported by all machines in your network. MIT supports triple DES keys, but Windows does not, so communications between Windows- and MIT-based Kerberos implementations will be limited to single DES. The upcoming 1.3 release of the MIT Kerberos 5 distribution will support the RC4 cipher used by Windows, and therefore strengthen the encryption used for communications between the two implementations.

With pre-authentication in place, an attacker can no longer obtain valid, encrypted tickets on request from the KDC. However, the attacker can instead use a network "sniffer" to obtain KDC responses as they are sent through the wire to clients. These responses will include tickets encrypted with client's keys. While the attack has increased in difficulty by an order of magnitude, it is still a potential problem. In addition, most implementations of Kerberos (notably MIT) do not force clients to use pre-authentication by default, negating the security benefit that pre-authentication would provide.

Replay Attacks

Another attack that can be mounted against Kerberos is known as a *replay attack*. Since all protocol exchanges are simply electronic messages that are sent over a computer network, an attacker can listen to the network messages involved in a successful authentication exchange, make a copy of the messages, and replay them at a later time. The attacker doesn't need to guess the users' password or decrypt any messages in this scenario. Since the replay attack requires access to listen to all network messages as well as the ability to send fake messages, a replay attack is an *active attack*. A theoretical replay attack is pictured in Figure 6-1.

In this figure, we see that Alice (the innocent end user) successfully obtains tickets to authenticate to her mail server. Bob, the evil hacker, is surreptitiously listening to all

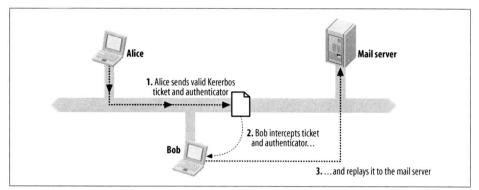

Figure 6-1. Kerberos replay attack

network traffic between Alice, the mail server, and the Kerberos KDC. Bob cannot directly use the TGT that Alice requests in the first step, since the TGT must be decrypted with Alice's password, which Bob does not know (although he can certainly try to brute-force the password, as discussed in the previous section). However, when Alice sends her encrypted ticket and authenticator, Bob can intercept that message and *replay* it to impersonate Alice to the mail server.

The ticket is encrypted with the mail server's key, and the authenticator is encrypted with the session key shared between Alice and the mail server. When the mail server receives the ticket and authenticator, it decrypts the ticket with its key, retrieves the session key from the ticket, and uses the session key to decrypt the authenticator. If all decryptions are successful, then authentication succeeds.

Kerberos has several built-in protections to prevent successful replay attacks. As an administrator, you do not have to worry about enabling any of these protections; they are built in to the particular Kerberos implementation that you're using. These protections are:

Address field in tickets

When a client requests a ticket from the KDC, it lists the network addresses from which the ticket is valid. For example, if the IP address of the workstation is 192.168.1.1, the workstation would fill that address in the address field in the ticket request, and the KDC would copy that into the ticket it returns to the workstation. This protection solves the problem of an attacker who attempts to replay a valid ticket on a workstation not listed in the ticket's address field. However, this protection is not enough to completely thwart replay attacks; the address field may be left blank, and the ticket would be valid for all addresses. Or, if the attacker had access to a machine listed in the addresses field, he could login and replay the ticket from there.

Time-based authenticators

Since address-based security is imperfect, Kerberos employs another scheme to thwart replay attacks. Every time a client wishes to use a Kerberized service, she generates an authenticator, which is submitted with the ticket to the service for authentication. The authenticator contains nothing but a timestamp, encrypted with the session key generated by the KDC for this particular ticket exchange. When the service receives this authenticator, it checks the decrypted timestamp against its system clock. If the two times differ by more than five minutes in either direction, the service will reject the ticket and refuse to authenticate the user. The 5-minute time period is designed to allow for some variation between different clocks on the network. However, even five minutes may be more than enough time for an attacker to replay valid tickets, especially if he employs an automated program to capture and replay tickets.

Replay caches

The last line of defense that Kerberos has against replay attacks is the replay cache. Both the Kerberos v4 and v5 protocols include the time-based authenticator. Kerberos v5 introduces the replay cache to avoid attackers reusing tickets in the short time period that authenticators are valid. Every Kerberized service maintains a cache of the authenticators it has recently received. When the service receives an authenticator, it checks the replay cache. If the service finds a copy of the authenticator already in the replay cache, it rejects the request. Otherwise, the service accepts the request and adds the authenticator to the replay cache to validate further requests.

Man-in-the-Middle Attacks

Finally, a *man-in-the-middle attack* affects most any protocol that attempts to verify the identity of connection endpoints (in this case, a user and the machine they wish to reach). A man-in-the-middle attack is an *active attack*, meaning that the attacker must be able to read all messages on the network as well as send out arbitrary messages of his own design.

The goal of the man-in-the-middle attack is to impersonate the server, resulting in the user thinking that he connected to the legitimate server, when in fact he is talking to the attacker. Once the attacker has control of the session, she can act as a simple pass-through (passing messages between the user and the legitimate server, without modification), or she can actively inject, modify, or delete messages between the user and the server. The attacker now is part of the conversation between the user and the legitimate server, and can modify any messages that pass through her, hence the name "man-in-the-middle."

The good news is that the Kerberos protocol has built-in protection against man-in-the-middle attacks. Since Kerberos performs mutual authentication, by confirming not only the end user's identity but also the server's identity, man-in-the-middle attacks are thwarted.

To prevent against man-in-the-middle attacks, some mechanism to validate the server's encryption key must exist. Other protocols use manual verification (such as

Secure Shell, where the "fingerprint" of the server's public key is printed on the screen when the user first connects), or signing authorities (in the case of SSL-enabled web sites). Kerberos uses the fact that a copy of all of the keys for both services and users are stored on the KDC to ensure protection against man-in-the-middle attacks. Since the session key generated by the KDC and then sent to the service is encrypted with the service's key, an attacker cannot recover the session key without the service's secret key.

A client can then detect whether the server he is talking to is genuine by requesting *mutual authentication,* where the server must demonstrate her identity by recovering the session key, encrypting a response, and sending it back to the client. If the server is not genuine, and does not have a copy of the service key, then the server cannot send back a valid encrypted message, and the client disconnects.

While Kerberos provides the ability to perform mutual authentication, applications must have code to enable that protection. In addition, several applications, such as the PAM modules available for authentication against Kerberos passwords, do not use the ticket-based authentication process. Instead, they take in a password over the network (hopefully encrypted) and verify it on the server side by asking the KDC for a TGT and then decrypting the TGT. This is where a practical man-in-the-middle attack can be mounted against Kerberos.

In this case, the attacker wants to place herself in between the server and the KDC, so that she can spoof the application server into thinking she is the real KDC. Since KDC requests and responses are simple UDP messages, it is easy for an attacker to send out fake messages that purport to be from the KDC's real IP address. Thus, the attack is carried out through the following procedure:

1. The attacker picks a password to use for the account she wishes to gain access to.

2. The attacker then sets up a program to listen to network requests, to see when clients request a TGT for the target user. When a TGT arrives, the program sends a TGT response back to the requestor encrypted with the chosen password.

3. Then, the attacker logs in to the server, gives the target username and the chosen password. At that point, the program sends the server the TGT encrypted with the password that the attacker has chosen instead of the real password.

4. If the server receives the fake response first, it will successfully decrypt the TGT since the passwords match.

To prevent this attack, the server must retrieve its host service key from its keytab, and then request a service key from the KDC using the TGT it just obtained on behalf of the user. Since only the server and the KDC know the host service key, an external attacker cannot produce a fake message and the account is denied access.

The KDCspoof program is a practical exploit of this vulnerability, and is available from *http://www.monkey.org/~dugsong/kdcspoof.tgz.*

Security Solutions

Now that you have a solid understanding of the security issues and limitations of Kerberos, let's examine how to work around these limitations and ensure that your Kerberos implementation is as secure as possible.

Requiring Pre-Authentication

First, we will start with pre-authentication. The Microsoft Windows KDC is the only implementation of those covered in this book that requires clients to pre-authenticate by default. In some implementations, a command-line option or flag can be used to require all clients to use pre-authentication. Other implementations require the administrator to explicitly specify which principals need to pre-authenticate before being granted a TGT.

MIT

The MIT KDC allows administrators to require the use of pre-authentication on a per-principal basis. Pre-authentication can be enabled for a principal in the MIT KDC through the following kadmin command:

```
kadmin: modify_principal +requires_preauth principal
```

Heimdal

The Heimdal KDC also allows administrators to require the use of pre-authentication on a per-principal basis. To require pre-authentication for a principal in the Heimdal KDC database, use the following kadmin command:

```
kadmin> modify principal
Max ticket life [1 day]:
Max renewable life [1 week]:
Principal expiration time [never]:
Password expiration time [never]:
Attributes []:+requires-pre-auth
```

The Heimdal KDC also allows you to turn off pre-authentication on all principals when starting the KDC, for emergency or testing purposes. The -p or --no-require-preauth switches disable pre-authentication checks for all principals until the KDC restarts.

Windows domain controllers

The Windows domain controller KDC service enables pre-authentication for all principals by default. To view the current pre-authentication settings for a principal in the Windows Active Directory, use the following procedure:

1. Log into a Windows machine that has the Active Directory administrative snap-ins installed. You must have Domain Administrator privileges to modify these settings.

2. Open the MMC console, and add the "Active Directory Users and Computers" snap-in.

3. Navigate to the user you wish to view, and double-click to open the properties page.

4. Switch to the "Account" tab on the properties page.

You will see a screen similar to the one shown in Figure 6-2.

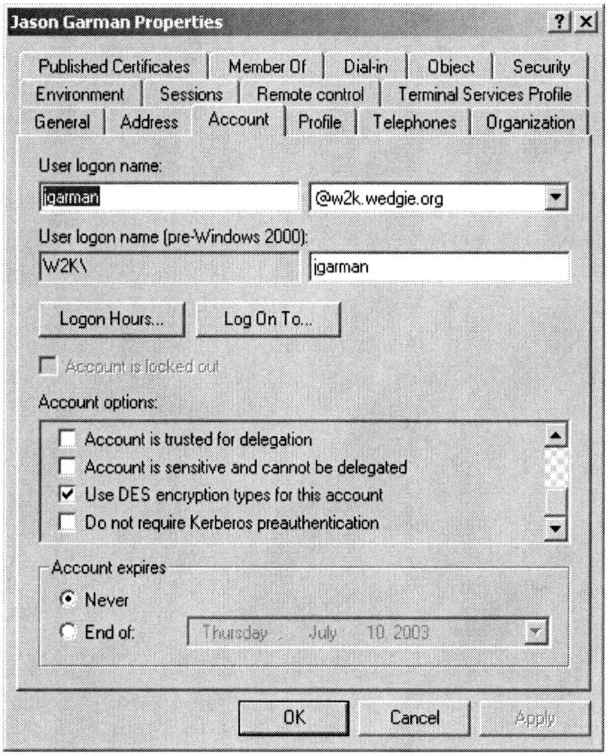

Figure 6-2. Pre-authentication setting in user properties dialog box

Pre-authentication can be enabled or disabled using the "Do not require Kerberos pre-authentication" checkbox.

Enforcing Secure Passwords

The security of your entire network depends on your users choosing secure passwords. However, experience shows that most users choose quite poor passwords. In one realm that already had password strength-checking in place,[*] over 2,000

---

[*] *A Real-World Analysis of Kerberos Password Security.* Thomas Wu, Stanford University Computer Science Department. May 1998. Available at *http://citeseer.nj.nec.com/418833.html*.

passwords in a Kerberos realm consisting of 25,000 principals were successfully brute-forced during a 2-week period. This experiment was performed with spare CPU cycles available on systems readily available in 1998. A determined attacker with more resources available would have an even easier time. A related experiment was made in 2002 to determine the feasibility of password attacks against the Windows 2000 Kerberos implementation, with similar results.[*]

Clearly, these discoveries proved to the researchers it was a cop-out to say that brute-force attacks were outside the scope of the authentication system in the original Kerberos specification. Pre-authentication, as discussed earlier, is a solution that prevents the most egregious of brute force attacks, but another important step to take is to enforce the quality of users' passwords.

Whenever users can choose their own passwords, there is a chance that they will find a way to choose an insecure password, but enforcing some simple heuristics on passwords users choose gives the administrator some guarantee that passwords won't be too simple. Many organizations have policies that outline standards for password strength; these policies usually specify password length as well as the amount of non-alphabetic characters that must be contained in the password. However, the enforcement of these policies is essential to their success. By centralizing authentication, Kerberos also centralizes the enforcement of password policies, making the administrator's life significantly easier.

All of the KDC implementations that we cover support some form of password policy enforcement. We'll take a look at how to configure each one.

Heimdal

The Heimdal KDC does not include any password strength-checking code by default. Instead, it only enforces a password minimum of six characters. To perform more stringent password strength checks, Heimdal provides a powerful method to link in an external library in order to verify the strength of user-provided passwords. While this method is powerful, since any external function can be provided to check password strength, it is much harder to set up than the built-in capabilities available in the other KDCs.

In the latest version of the Heimdal KDC, a sample password-check function is available in the source distribution. It uses the freely available cracklib to verify passwords against commonly used passwords and other identifiers. To use this password-checking function, obtain cracklib from *http://www.users.dircon.co.uk/~crypto/*. Once you've built cracklib, the function is located in *lib/kadm5/sample_passwd_check.c*. This file

---

[*] *Feasibility of attacking Windows 2000 Kerberos Passwords.* Frank O'Dwyer. March 2002. Available at *http://www.brd.ie/papers/w2kkrb/feasibility_of_w2k_kerberos_attack.htm*.

must be built into a shared library; the exact command varies depending on your system and compiler, but a sample would be:

```
gcc -shared -o sample_passwd_check.so sample_passwd_check.c -lcracklib
```

Once the shared library is built, add the following lines in your */etc/krb5.conf file* to enable the password checking:

```
[password_quality]
        check_library = path to sample_passwd_check.so
        check_function = check_cracklib
```

When you restart *kpasswdd*, the password checking is enabled.

MIT

The MIT KDC can evaluate user-supplied passwords based on two metrics: the number of *character classes* it contains, and its length. The length of a password is obvious, but what is a character class? The MIT KDC defines five different character classes:

- Lowercase letters
- Uppercase letters
- Numbers
- Punctuation
- Other characters

For example, given a password policy with a minimum length of six and minimum of two character classes, the password "MITkdc" would be accepted, while the password "mitkdc" would be rejected. However, a simple password based on a dictionary word such as "Tokens" will pass through fine given a minimum of two character classes. A minimum of three character classes will prevent any dictionary word from being used directly, as a nonalphabetical character is required somewhere in the password.

When specifying the number of character classes required in a password, there is no way to enforce that a number of characters of each class must be included in a password before it is accepted. If the minimum number of character classes is three, then the password is valid as long as there is at least one character from each class in the password.

To enforce certain standards on the strength of passwords used in the MIT KDC, a user policy can be established which can then be applied to a set of principals. To establish or modify an existing policy, the following kadmin commands can be used. More information on these commands can be found in the Appendix.

```
kadmin: add_policy [-maxlife time] [-minlife time] policy_name
kadmin: modify_policy [-maxlife time] [-minlife time] policy_name
```

Windows domain controllers

The Windows domain controller evaluates user-supplied passwords on two metrics: the length and the complexity of the password. But default, Windows tests a password's complexity by confirming that it:

- Does not contain all or part of the user's account name
- Is at least six characters in length
- Has at least one character from three of the four character classes: lowercase letters, uppercase letters, numbers, and nonalphanumerical symbols

To enable password strength-checking on all accounts in a Windows domain, open the Domain Security Policy Administrative Tool. You will see a screen similar to the one in Figure 6-3. Open Security Settings → Account Policies → Password Policy. Inside you will find two settings: "Minimum password length" and "Passwords must meet complexity requirements". Enabling the complexity requirements will enable the checks outlined above.

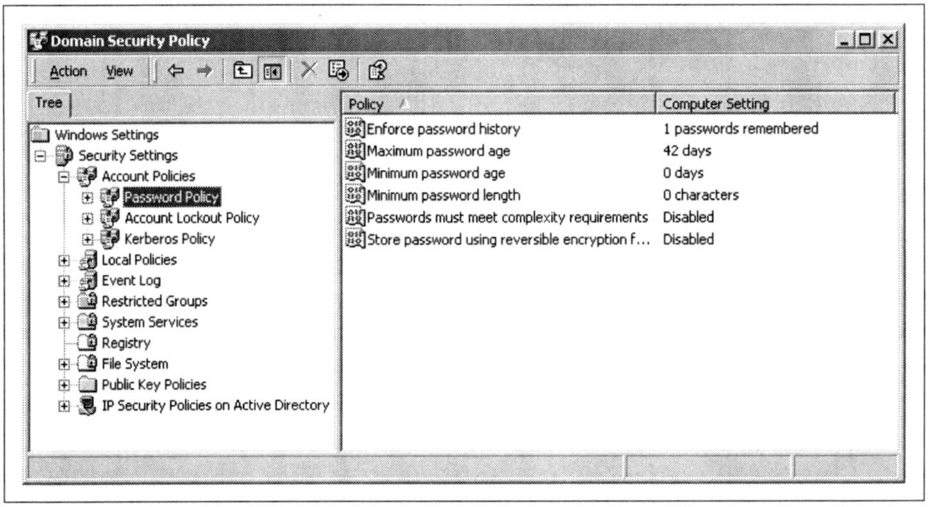

Figure 6-3. Windows Domain Security Policy

Enforcing Password Lifetimes and History

In addition to policies on password strength, many organizations also specify a maximum lifetime for user passwords after which the user must change to a new password. Most Kerberos KDC implementations can enforce a maximum and minimum lifetime for user passwords, as well as a password history to ensure that users do not simply reuse previous passwords to evade the mandatory password change.

While it may be tempting to specify a very short maximum lifetime for user passwords to prevent brute-force attacks and reduce the effectiveness of a stolen password, it is important to realize that mandatory password change policies represent a quality versus quantity trade-off. As the frequency of password changes goes up, the quality of each password chosen goes down, or else the user will resort to writing her password down.

In addition, most of the KDCs covered in this book have a facility to remember previous passwords that the user has chosen, to prevent the user from flip-flopping back and forth between a few passwords.

MIT

To enforce mandatory password lifetimes in the MIT KDC, a user policy can be established which then can be applied to a set of principals, or lifetimes can be set on a per-principal basis. Let's first take a look at how to set password lifetimes on a policy:

```
kadmin: modify_policy [-maxlife time] [-minlife time] [-history num] policy_name
kadmin: add_policy [-maxlife time] [-minlife time] [-history num] policy_name
```

In each command, the optional maxlife parameter specifies the maximum lifetime of the user passwords subject to the policy *policy_name*. Similarly, the optional minlife parameter specifies the minimum lifetime for user passwords subject to the policy.

In addition, the number of historical passwords kept for user principals subject to this policy can be specified with the *history* parameter. The only argument that the history parameter takes is the number of historical passwords to check against when changing passwords.

If you already have a policy established (for example if you've already set up a policy from the last section), then you can use the first command to modify your existing policy to add a mandatory minimum and maximum lifetime and password history.

Heimdal

The Heimdal KDC only includes the ability to expire a principal's password at a given time. Once the password expires, the user is prompted to change it, and the new password is now active. However, the password expiration is not recurring; that is, if you set a principal's password to expire in 30 days' time, once the password expires, it will not automatically set the user's password to expire 30 days from that day. Instead, the administrator must set the password to expire again.

To set a password expiration date on a principal, use the following kadmin command:

```
kadmin> mod jgarman
Max ticket life [1 day]:
Max renewable life [1 week]:
Principal expiration time [never]:
Password expiration time [never]:2002-08-05
Attributes [requires-pre-auth]:
```

This sets the *jgarman* principal's password to expire on Aug 5, 2002.

Windows domain controllers

The Windows domain controller has the ability to set both maximum and minimum password lifetimes, as well as establish a password history to prevent reuse of previous passwords. The administrative interface to adjust these parameters is located in the Domain Security Policy. Open Security Settings → Account Policies → Password Policy. The window shown in Figure 6-3 will appear. Inside you will find three settings: "Minimum password age", "Maximum password age", and "Enforce password history".

Protecting Your KDC

Since the KDC contains the secret encryption keys for all of the users as well as all of the services in your administrative realm, it is obviously very important that the KDC be well protected. It is both an advantage and a disadvantage of Kerberos that all key information is centralized; on one hand, it is easier to heavily secure one machine than to try to heavily secure a lot of distributed machines, but on the other hand, a compromise of the KDC machine compromises all authentication information in the realm.

Therefore, the machines that run KDC software should be specially prepared and dedicated solely to this purpose. During the operating system install, the machine should be physically separated or firewalled from the network to prevent exposure to the outside world. The machine is most vulnerable to outside attack during the installation of the operating system and KDC software, since the safeguards protecting the machine have not been set up yet. For example, automated worms such as Code Red have exploited unpatched Windows boxes running IIS within less than 10 minutes of exposure to the outside world.

No other server software should be installed on the KDC, especially servers that have high public visibility such as mail, web, and database servers. Remote login, if required, should be limited to a very small subset of administrative users who have local login passwords separate from their Kerberos passwords. Passwords for the administrator or root account on the KDC machines must be tightly controlled and changed periodically to prevent compromise.

Finally, physical security of the KDC machines is paramount. Physical access to any machine implicitly gives an attacker administrator-level access to that machine. Since the KDC contains all of your Kerberos realm's secret keys, physical access to the KDC would compromise all of those keys. Therefore, KDCs should be located in a locked room with limited access, preferably with some type of entry/exit logging. And remember to always log out of the console of the KDC after performing any necessary administrative tasks.

Protecting a Unix KDC

First, choose a Unix operating system that you are intimately familiar with. Good selections for a dedicated KDC machine include the free Unix systems, such as FreeBSD, OpenBSD, and Linux. These operating systems can be downloaded for free, include full source code, and are well supported by the online community, which addresses security issues quickly. Other Unix operating systems such as Solaris are also good choices, but more care must be taken in preparing commercial operating systems, as they usually ship with more network services enabled by default.

When installing the operating system, choose the smallest distribution of software possible. Since there will not be any users directly logging into this machine's console, do not install X Window System servers or clients, or desktop environments such as CDE, Gnome, and KDE. The only optional component that should be installed is a C compiler to compile the KDC software, if you are going to use one of the open source Kerberos implementations.

After operating system installation, download and install all recommended security patches applicable to your operating system.

Where to Get Unix Security Patches

Security patches are a first, important step to setting up a secure system, and are especially important when building a system that will act as a Kerberos Key Distribution Center. Listed below are sites where you can download important security updates for your particular Unix operating system:

Sun Solaris
    Sunsolve: *http://sunsolve.sun.com/*

Hewlett-Packard HP-UX
    HP IT Resource Center: *http://us-support.external.hp.com*

FreeBSD
    FreeBSD Security page: *http://www.freebsd.org/security/index.html*

OpenBSD
    OpenBSD security page: *http://www.openbsd.org/security.html*

Linux
    RedHat security page: *http://www.redhat.com/solutions/security*
    Caldera security page: *http://www.caldera.com/support/security*
    Slackware security list archive: *http://www.slackware.org/lists/archive*
    SuSE security page: *http://www.suse.com/us/support/security/index.html*

An important factor in the security of your KDC is its network visibility. It is important to disable all network-based services on your KDC other than the KDC software itself, as well as a Secure Shell server if remote login is required. To determine what network services are installed, use the netstat command from a shell prompt. Let's take a look at an example output from a Linux machine:

```
% netstat -an
Active Internet connections (servers and established)
Proto Recv-Q Send-Q Local Address          Foreign Address        State
tcp        0      0 192.168.1.83:749        0.0.0.0:*              LISTEN
tcp        0      0 127.0.0.1:749           0.0.0.0:*              LISTEN
tcp        0      0 0.0.0.0:22              0.0.0.0:*              LISTEN
tcp        0      0 192.168.1.83:88         0.0.0.0:*              LISTEN
tcp        0      0 127.0.0.1:88            0.0.0.0:*              LISTEN
tcp        0      0 192.168.1.83:4444       0.0.0.0:*              LISTEN
tcp        0      0 127.0.0.1:4444          0.0.0.0:*              LISTEN
tcp        0    180 192.168.1.83:22         192.168.1.20:61096     ESTABLISHED
udp        0      0 192.168.1.83:464        0.0.0.0:*
udp        0      0 127.0.0.1:464           0.0.0.0:*
udp        0      0 192.168.1.83:88         0.0.0.0:*
udp        0      0 127.0.0.1:88            0.0.0.0:*
udp        0      0 192.168.1.83:4444       0.0.0.0:*
udp        0      0 127.0.0.1:4444          0.0.0.0:*
Active UNIX domain sockets (servers and established)
Proto RefCnt Flags       Type       State         I-Node Path
unix  2      [ ACC ]     STREAM     LISTENING     1353   /dev/gpmctl
unix  5      [ ]         DGRAM                    948    /dev/log
unix  3      [ ]         STREAM     CONNECTED     1459649
unix  3      [ ]         STREAM     CONNECTED     1459648
unix  2      [ ]         DGRAM                    1376
unix  2      [ ]         DGRAM                    1085
unix  2      [ ]         DGRAM                    957
%
```

The netstat command outputs the state of the system's networking stack. It has a variety of options depending on your particular flavor of Unix, and each vendor's may produce different output. In order to see the full list of options available for your operating system, pull up the manual page for netstat. Another tool that is useful for enumerating network ports and the programs that are listening on those ports is lsof; it is available from *ftp://vic.cc.purdue.edu/pub/tools/unix/lsof*.

The above machine only has OpenSSH and Kerberos servers listening to the network. This is a recommended configuration; it minimizes the network visibility of your KDC as much as possible. See the following section, "Firewalls, NAT, and Kerberos," for a full list of the port numbers that the Kerberos protocol uses for communication between KDCs and clients. Once a clean port configuration has been established, it is recommended that you produce a file that contains a netstat, ps, and preferably an lsof listing, so that any differences between your clean configuration and possible backdoors (installed as part of an intrusion) can be easily spotted later. These files, as well as a copy of the tools that were used to generate these files, should be placed on a CD-ROM or other write-protected, removable media to prevent modification by an attacker.

Hardening Your Unix KDC Against Attack

By installing the appropriate security patches for your Unix operating system and shutting off unnecessary network services, you've taken the first step to ensuring the security of your KDC. Effective security, however, is a multilayered process, and there are several guides online that will give you tips on further securing, or *hardening*, your system from attack.

Bastille Linux (also for HP-UX)
   http://www.bastille-linux.org/

Solaris Security Toolkit
   http://wwws.sun.com/software/security/jass/index.html

I recommend using OpenSSH to enable administrators to login remotely to your KDC. OpenSSH is an open source implementation of the Secure Shell protocol suite and can be compiled on all major Unix operating systems. Be sure to download and install the latest version of OpenSSH from its home page, *http://www.openssh.com*, since earlier versions have contained security problems. If all administrators have local accounts on the KDC, you do not have to enable any special Kerberos-related options in OpenSSH so that it will do authentication against the local user password file instead of Kerberos. For more information on Secure Shell and OpenSSH, see *SSH, The Secure Shell: The Definitive Guide* by Daniel J. Barrett and Richard Silverman (O'Reilly).

Protecting a Windows Domain Controller

Every Windows domain controller in your network also acts as a KDC, and needs to be secured appropriately. The general advice that pertains to Unix KDCs also applies to a Windows domain controller. Just like a Unix KDC, the Windows domain controller contains all of the authentication information (and much more). To properly secure a Windows domain controller, first disable all unnecessary services, disallow logins to the server except for a small number of administrative users with secure passwords, and apply the latest set of service packs from Microsoft.

Unfortunately, a default installation of Windows 2000 Server will install and enable Internet Information Services (IIS), which, unpatched, contains several security vulnerabilities that allow an attacker to gain administrative control of your server. Therefore, it is recommended to keep the machine disconnected from the network until IIS is disabled or removed. To remove IIS, open the Add/Remove Programs item in the Control Panel, choose Add/Remove Windows Components, and uncheck Internet Information Services.

 Note that thanks to Microsoft's new "Secure by Default" philosophy, Windows 2003 Server no longer installs and activates IIS by default. Readers who are using Windows Server 2003 to build a Kerberos KDC will not have to manually disable and remove IIS.

With IIS out of the way, a good next step is to apply the latest batch of service packs from Microsoft. Doing this as early as possible in the process reduces the chances of a strange conflict arising that renders some critical service unusable. The easiest way to accomplish this is to use the Windows Update tool; updates are also available at Microsoft's site at *http://www.microsoft.com/windows2000/downloads/servicepacks/ default.asp.*

Finally, we'll set some restrictive policies on the domain controller itself. Fortunately, Windows provides for a special set of policies that apply to the domain controllers separate from the rest of the machines in the domain. Those policies can be found in the Domain Controller Security Policy snap-in, located in the Microsoft Management Console application.

First, let's restrict login privileges to a small set of users. Inside of the Domain Controller Policy window, open the Windows Settings → Security Settings → Local Policies → User Rights Assignment folder. The following are a few items that should be altered from their defaults:

Access this computer from the network
> The recommended value is "Authenticated Users, Administrators." If this machine had IIS previously installed and enabled, you will find IUSR and IWAM account names listed here. They will reappear under this policy setting after every reboot if IIS is installed.

Force shutdown from a remote system and shut down the system
> The recommended value is "Administrators."

Log on as a batch job
> Since, under Windows 2000 and 2003, the Task Scheduler automatically grants this right as necessary, there should be no users or groups listed under this setting.

Log on locally
> This policy determines the groups or users that are allowed to log into the domain controller locally, or through a Terminal Services connection. The recommended value is "Administrators." No regular users, and definitely no guests, need to log into the domain controller directly.

Next, we'll tweak some settings in the Security Options folder (which is also located inside of the Windows Settings → Security Settings → Local Policies folder). Here are some items that should be changed from their default settings:

Additional restrictions for anonymous connections
> By setting this to "Do not allow enumeration of SAM accounts and shares," you can prevent an anonymous user from listing the local users on your domain controller.

Message text for users attempting to log on and Message title for users attempting to log on
> These settings allow you to define a message box that is displayed before a user is presented with the system's login dialog box. Set these to your organization's

standard login banner, which should include text declaring that activity is subject to monitoring, and that unauthorized activity is subject to prosecution.

Finally, we'll tweak the following setting, located in the Windows Settings → Security Settings → Event Log → Settings for Event Log folder.

Restrict guest access to <application, security,system> log
All three of these settings should be set to "Enabled" to prevent an attacker from reading potentially sensitive information that may be located in your system's event logs.

Just like with a Unix KDC, it is recommended that you generate a "clean" network port listing and process listing and keep a copy in a safe place, such as on floppy. A good tool that can be used to generate a network port listing similar to lsof on Unix is Active Port, available from *http://www.webattack.com/get/activeports.shtml*.

These are good first steps for securing a Windows domain controller. Further information is available from Microsoft, including the Microsoft Solutions for Securing Windows 2000 Server located at *http://www.microsoft.com/technet/security/prodtech/ windows/secwin2k/default.asp* and the Windows 2000 Hardening Guide, located at *http://www.microsoft.com/ technet/security/prodtech/Windows/Win2kHG/default.asp*.

Continual Maintenance

The focus on securing the KDC should not end with the successful implementation of a Kerberos network authentication system; the administrator must continue to monitor security mailing lists, such as Bugtraq, and vendor-specific mailing lists that announce the latest security patches for both the operating system and the Kerberos KDC software. While keeping the KDC up-to-date with security patches may cause occasional downtime and service outage, it saves days of lost productivity caused by reinstalling the KDC, re-keying all services, and resetting all user passwords in the aftermath of an intrusion.

The Bugtraq mailing list information and an online security vulnerability database is located at *http://www.securityfocus.com/popups/forums/ bugtraq/intro.shtml*. A similar mailing list for Windows NT and 2000, called NTBugtraq, is available at *http://www.ntbugtraq.com/*.

In particular, a continual maintenance policy should include periodic reviews of the KDC event or system logs, as we'll discuss later in the "Auditing" section. Also, a periodic review of the open network ports and active processes against the clean configuration you generated in the previous section should be performed to detect any changes. Changes that have occurred due to documented maintenance and software updates must be integrated into your clean configuration port and process dumps. Other changes should be investigated, as they may be signs of attack.

While the above discussion outlines the basics involved in securing your KDC machines, more detailed information about securing Unix and Windows hosts can be found in *Securing Windows NT/2000 Servers for the Internet* by Stefan Norberg (O'Reilly), as well as *Practical Unix and Internet Security* by Simson Garfinkel, Gene Spafford, and Alan Schwartz, also available from O'Reilly.

Firewalls, NAT, and Kerberos

Since Kerberos relies heavily on the proper functioning of DNS and some protocol messages include IP addresses in them, firewalls and NAT in particular pose obstacles to the proper functioning of Kerberos. First, let's examine what ports must be opened on a firewall if Kerberos protocol messages need to pass through it, and then look at the thorny issue of using NAT and Kerberos together.

There are several situations to consider from the perspective of a firewall administrator. The most common is a setup where client machines are located outside of a corporate firewall, and the KDCs and application servers are located inside of the firewall. All machines involved have public IP addresses and NAT is not in use. This setup is pictured in Figure 6-4.

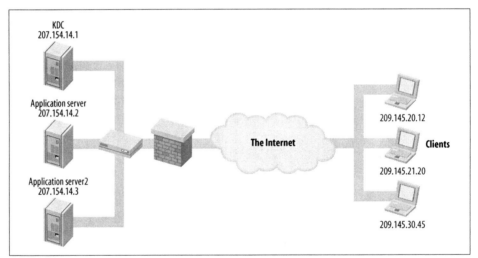

Figure 6-4. Clients outside firewall, KDC and application servers inside firewall

In order for outside clients to obtain tickets for your Kerberos realm, several ports need to be opened through the firewall to your KDCs. These ports are required in addition to whatever ports are already open to communicate with the application servers. In a scenario like this one, it is very important that no plain text passwords pass through the firewall through your application servers; therefore, it is still recommended that individual applications use a layer of encryption on top of their usual protocol to prevent an accidental password exposure.

Kerberos Network Ports

To enable the clients outside of the corporate firewall to communicate with the KDC and Kerberized services inside the firewall, some ports must be opened on the corporate firewall (Table 6-1).

Table 6-1. Kerberos 5 ports for client-to-KDC communication

Machine	Local port (server)	Remote port (client)	Description
All KDCs	88/udp 88/tcp	Above 1024	Kerberos 5 ticket service
All KDCs	749/tcp	Above 1024	Kerberos 5 kpasswd service for client password changes
All KDCs	4444/udp	Above 1024	Kerberos 5 to 4 ticket conversion service
All KDCs	749/tcp	Above 1024	Kerberos 5 administration service (MIT and Heimdal)
Master/Administrative KDC	464/udp	Above 1024	Kerberos 5 password changing service (older password-changing protocol)

Strictly speaking, the only port that needs to be open for Kerberos to function properly is 88. The other ports can be opened as needed to provide their respective services to clients outside of the firewall.

Because of the inherent flaws in the Kerberos 4 protocol, it is not recommended that you open Kerberos 4 to the Internet. However, if you must open Kerberos 4 through your firewall, Table 6-2 lists the ports that it uses for client/KDC communication.

Table 6-2. Kerberos 4 ports for client-to-KDC communication

Machine	Local port (server)	Remote port (client)	Description
All KDCs	750/udp 750/tcp	Above 1024	Kerberos 4 ticket service
All KDCs	751/udp 751/tcp	Above 1024	Kerberos 4 admin service
All KDCs	761/tcp	Above 1024	Kerberos 4 password changing service

Kerberos and NAT

The next firewall scenario to consider is pictured in Figure 6-5. In this scenario, all of the KDCs and application servers are behind a corporate firewall, with publicly accessible, routable IP addresses. Clients are located outside of the corporate firewall but live in private IP address space behind a small NAT firewall.

Network Address Translation, or NAT, enables multiple machines to share a single IP address. In a NAT setup, clients inside of the NAT device have private, non-routable IP addresses, as defined in RFC 1918. These IP addresses, while valid, are

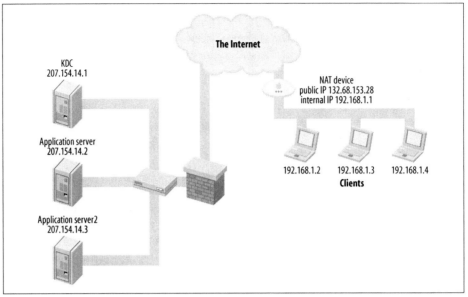

Figure 6-5. KDCs and application servers behind firewall, with clients using NAT

not directly accessible to the Internet at large. The NAT device takes care of relaying requests between the internal machines and the larger Internet. NAT presents a problem to Kerberos since ticket requests contain the requestor's IP address. Because the clients requesting tickets in this case are using NAT, the IP address they provide to the KDC will be nonroutable. Since the private address on the ticket does not match the public address of the NAT device, Kerberized services will not honor any tickets issued for NAT clients.

For example, you have a user on a cable modem with a small NAT device. The public IP address of the NAT device is 132.68.153.28, and the internal network is the RFC 1918 range 192.168.1.0 to 192.168.1.255. A client at 192.168.1.2 requests a TGT from the Kerberos KDC inside of the corporate firewall. A TGT, valid only for the IP address of 192.168.1.2, is returned to the client.

The TGT exchange works fine, but the only valid address listed on the returned TGT is the internal NAT address of the client. As soon as the client attempts to obtain a service ticket using this TGT, the application will fail. Since the address listed on the ticket does not match the public address of the NAT device, an "incorrect net address" error will be returned to the client, and the authentication attempt will fail.

There are two approaches to solving this issue. Either every client in the NAT network can be configured to request tickets with the IP address of the external interface on the NAT device, or clients can be configured to request "addressless" tickets, that is, tickets that can be used from any IP address.

For MIT and Heimdal clients, use the -A option to kinit to request addressless tickets. Another, more general, solution if you're using MIT clients is to add the following line to the [libdefaults] section of your */etc/krb5.conf* file:

```
noaddresses = true
```

This line is recognized by all applications that use the MIT Kerberos 5 libraries, and will cause applications to request tickets without addresses.

Using addressless tickets to support clients behind NAT devices presents little degradation in security. The only vulnerability that it presents is that if an attacker were able to obtain a copy of your credential cache, he could use your tickets regardless of his source IP address. It also makes replay attacks a bit easier, but as discussed in the previous "Replay Attacks" section, Kerberos includes other safeguards against replay attacks.

Auditing

Although it is certainly important to ensure that your machines are secure from outside attack, you also need to periodically audit the activity of your KDC to look for any malicious activity. Depending on your KDC vendor, the amount of logging that occurs by default can vary from none (Windows 2000's default configuration) to a lot (Heimdal & MIT). In this section, we will examine the information that KDCs log, how to enable logging on your KDC, and how to read and understand the resulting log files.

The logging facilities built in to these KDC implementations not only serve auditing purposes, but they play a big role in debugging issues that may arise during the operation of your Kerberos system. First, let's take a look back at the Kerberos protocol exchange. At each point where the KDC is contacted, the KDC usually provides an option to log that information to a file.

Enabling Logging

Each KDC has different auditing options, and different procedures for enabling auditing.

MIT

To enable logging in the MIT KDC, the *krb5.conf* file can contain a [logging] stanza with several variables that control where the logging output goes. Here are the variables:

kdc

> The kdc variable controls where the log for the KDC's authentication service and Ticket Granting Service is sent. The logs produced in the file specified in the KDC variable contain all of the transactions between users, servers, and the KDC.

admin_server

> The admin_server variable controls where the logs for the kadmin server are sent. The logs produced in the file specified in the admin_server variable contain all of the transactions between Kerberos administrators and the KDC that are performed through the kadmin interface.

Each option can take several different arguments, depending on the type of file, device, or syslog facility you wish the logs to be sent to. If you want logs sent to several destinations, you can list them, one at a time, on separate lines.

FILE=*filename*
FILE:*filename*

> These options send the specified logs to a file called *filename*. In the first form with a "=", the file is overwritten each time the KDC starts. The second form, specified with a ":", indicates that the file will be appended to each time the KDC starts.

STDERR

> This option specifies that the logs should be sent to the standard error output of the KDC.

CONSOLE

> This option specifies that the logs be sent to the console of the KDC machine.

DEVICE=*devicename*

> This option specifies that the logs be sent to the *devicename*. This can be used to send logs to a particular terminal, or printer.

SYSLOG:*severity*:*facility*

> This option specifies that the logs be sent to the syslog service on the KDC. The severity and facility arguments are optional, and can be used in combination with *syslog.conf* to send KDC output to its own file, or relay to another syslog server. The available severities and facilities vary by operating system vendor, but the syslog manpage will list the options available for your OS. By default, the severity is ERR and the facility is AUTH.

Let's take a look at an example:

```
[logging]
  kdc = FILE:/var/log/kdc.log
  kdc = SYSLOG:NOTICE
  admin_server = FILE:/var/log/kadmin.log
  admin_server = CONSOLE
```

In this example, all of the KDC activity (authentication service and ticket granting service) are logged to a file named */var/log/kdc.log*, to which something is appended to every time the KDC restarts. In addition, KDC activity is logged to syslog, under the AUTH facility and the NOTICE severity. All kadmin requests and responses are logged to */var/log/kadmin.log* as well as the system console.

Heimdal

The controls for the Heimdal KDC logging facility are located in the *krb5.conf* file. The options are similar to the MIT KDC logging options, but have a few important additions. Just like the MIT KDC, all of these options are contained in a [logging] stanza in the configuration file.

Each variable in the logging section of the Heimdal *krb5.conf* configuration file is named after the program that is generating the logs. That is, the logs from the kdc program are sent to the destination specified by the kdc variable. Similarly, logs from the kadmind program are sent to the destination specified by the kadmind variable, and so on. In addition, a "default" variable is provided as a catchall for messages that do not have a more specific destination specified. The destination specifications are as follows:

FILE=*filename*
FILE:*filename*

> These options send the specified logs to a file called *filename*. In the first form with a "=", the file is overwritten each time the KDC starts. The second form, specified with a ":", indicates that the file will be appended to each time the KDC starts.

STDERR

> This option specifies that the logs should be sent to the standard error output of the KDC.

CONSOLE

> This option specifies that the logs be sent to the console of the KDC machine.

DEVICE=*devicename*

> This option specifies that the logs be sent to the *devicename*. This can be used to send logs to a particular terminal, or printer.

SYSLOG:*severity*:*facility*

> This option specifies that the logs be sent to the syslog service on the KDC. The severity and facility arguments are optional, and can be used in combination with *syslog.conf* to send KDC output to its own file, or relay to another syslog server. The available severity and facility arguments are system-dependent By default, the severity is ERR and the facility is AUTH.

In addition, each destination may be preceded by an optional logging level. Logging levels are integers, numbered from zero upwards; zero is the minimum of detail. To specify a logging level, prefix a destination with the range of logging levels (for example, 1–5) followed by a slash. If only one logging level is given, then only messages sent to that level will be logged to the destination.

Here is an example:

```
[logging]
    kdc = 0/FILE:/var/log/kdc.log
```

```
kdc = 1-/SYSLOG:DEBUG
kadmind = FILE:/var/log/kadmin.log
kpasswdd = FILE:/var/log/kpasswdd.log
default = FILE:/var/log/kerberos.log
```

In this example, KDC logs with a logging level of zero are sent to */var/log/kdc.log*, while messages with a higher logging level are sent to syslog, facility AUTH, severity DEBUG. Messages sent from kadmind are stored in the */var/log/kadmin.log* file and kpasswdd logs are sent to */var/log/kpasswdd.log*. All other messages from applications using Heimdal Kerberos are sent to */var/log/kerberos.log*. In all cases, the log file is appended to when the respective programs restart.

Windows domain controllers

Windows 2000 domain controllers do not log any authentication requests by default. Windows Server 2003 is somewhat better in this regard since it logs successful authentication requests by default, but it does not log any denied requests. Thankfully, Microsoft provides very detailed logging facilities that can be enabled. A Windows domain controller can log the Kerberos KDC activity as well as domain logon and logoff events. We'll take a look at both, from a Kerberos perspective.

First, let's enable the logging of authentication requests for your domain. The first thing to configure is the Security Log's maximum log file size. On Windows 2000, machines in your domain will only keep a 512 KB rotating log file by default (overwriting events that are more than 7 days old). With today's large hard drives, there is no reason to constrain log files to less than a megabyte, so we'll increase the file size limit to 10 megabytes in this example.

To change the maximum log file size for the security log, follow these steps:

1. Log into a Windows machine that has the Active Directory administrative snap-ins installed. You must have Domain Administrator privileges in order to modify these settings.
2. Open MMC and load the Active Directory Users and Computers snap-in.
3. Right-click on your domain, and choose Properties.
4. Select the Group Policy tab.
5. Select the Default Domain Policy GPO, and click Edit.
6. Navigate to Computer Configuration → Windows Settings → Security Settings → Event Log → Settings for Event Log.

You will now see the window shown in Figure 6-6.

By double-clicking on Maximum security log size, you'll be presented with a dialog box. Click "Define this policy setting" and set a maximum size (in this case, 10240 Kbytes). If you would like to change the log retention options, you can change the "Retain security log" and "Retention method for security log" settings in this window.

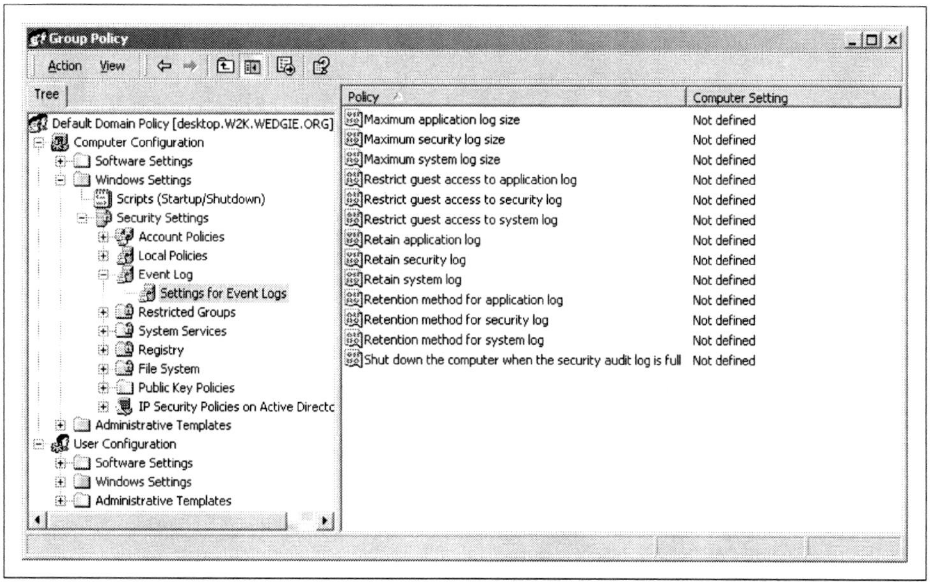

Figure 6-6. Active Directory Group Policy event log settings

Next we'll enable auditing for our domain. There are two different auditing options included in Windows, rather obscurely named "logon auditing" and "account logon auditing." They both audit authentication requests, however, they audit different parts of the login process, and store the information on different hosts. Confused yet? Let's take a look at the two choices:

Logon Auditing

This setting toggles the auditing of local Windows login events. These login events are not constrained to Kerberos-based logins; logon auditing will record login events for every type of authentication that Windows supports, such as NTLM. This type of logging is similar to a Secure Shell (or other application-level) log on a Unix box; it records the start and finish of a user's login session. Therefore, logon auditing occurs on the individual servers that users log in to, and the corresponding audit logs only appear in that server's Event Log.

Account Logon Auditing

This setting enables auditing similar to the other KDC's we have mentioned here. Every time a Kerberos ticket is granted, either through the Authentication Service or the Ticket Granting Service, the domain controller writes the details about that ticket to its Security Log when this setting is enabled. Since there is no concept of a "login session" in Kerberos, there is no way to determine when a user "logs out," and consequently the duration of users' login sessions, with this option alone. However, this option does provide for a nice centralized log of all Kerberos-based authentication requests, since the account logon audit records are written to the domain controllers' event logs, instead of the individual servers' event logs.

Okay, now that we've cleared that up, let's continue on to enable these audit policies on your domain. We're going to start at the same Group Policy window that we opened in the previous exercise.

From the Group Policy window, navigate to Computer Configuration, Windows Settings, Security Settings, Local Policies, Audit Policy. You'll see a window similar to the one shown in Figure 6-7.

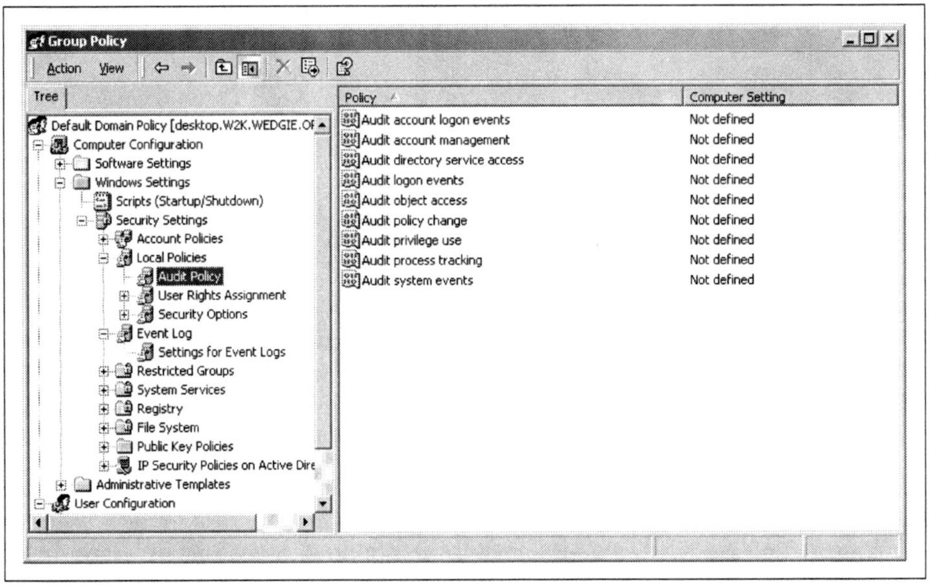

Figure 6-7. Active Directory Group Policy audit policy settings

From this window, you can configure both the "Audit logon events" and "Audit account logon events." It is recommended that both successful and failed attempts should be logged for these events.

Understanding the Logs

Now that you've set up the auditing mechanism on your Kerberos KDC and your KDC is busy logging all of its activity, you need to periodically review these logs for suspicious activity. Enabling the logging activity on your KDC is useless unless the logs are actually analyzed at some point, either automatically by a script that has preset thresholds for suspicious activity, or by hand. In this section, we'll examine the log messages emitted by each Kerberos implementation covered in this book, and describe what each message means.

Each implementation has a dramatically different log format, but since there are only a few protocol exchanges in Kerberos, the number of different log messages is relatively low. Each log message can be directly connected to an exchange between the KDC and a Kerberos client.

MIT

Each time the MIT KDC starts up, it logs the interfaces and ports on which it is listening to the defined KDC log file:

```
Jul 31 03:04:40 www.wedgie.org krb5kdc[10543](info): setting up network...
Jul 31 03:04:40 www.wedgie.org krb5kdc[10543](info): listening on fd 7: 192.168.1.83
port 88
Jul 31 03:04:40 www.wedgie.org krb5kdc[10543](info): listening on fd 8: 192.168.1.83
port 750
Jul 31 03:04:40 www.wedgie.org krb5kdc[10543](info): set up 2 sockets
Jul 31 03:04:40 www.wedgie.org krb5kdc[10544](info): commencing operation
```

In this case, the KDC is listening on both the Kerberos 5 and Kerberos 4 well-defined ports. Similarly, every time the KDC is shut down cleanly, it logs this fact to the log file as well:

```
Jul 31 15:11:57 www1.wedgie.org krb5kdc[779](info): shutting down
```

Now, let's take a look at what is logged during Kerberos protocol exchanges. First, let's take an example user using Kerberos 5, who is obtaining a TGT when he starts his day. The following message is recorded in the log:

```
Jul 30 23:18:26 www1.wedgie.org krb5kdc[10544](info): AS_REQ (3 etypes {16 3 1}) 192.
168.1.83(88): ISSUE: authtime 1028085506, etypes {rep=16 tkt=16 ses=16},
jgarman@WEDGIE.ORG for krbtgt/WEDGIE.ORG@WEDGIE.ORG
```

Let's examine this output piecemeal. First, we have the date, time, and hostname of the KDC. This information appears whether the log is being sent to a file or via syslog. Next, we have the name and process ID of the KDC, as well as the severity of the message (in this case "info").

The next part of this message describes the request that was made to the KDC. It begins with the type of request (AS_REQ, for an Authentication Service request). Then, it follows by listing the encryption types that the client claims to support. In this case, the client listed three encryption types that it understands. Each encryption type is specified by its numeric identifier. A complete listing of currently defined encryption types and their numeric identifiers can be found in the Kerberos Encryption Specifications document, which is on the Kerberos Clarifications site at *http:// www.kerberos.isi.edu*. In this particular example, the encryption types supported by the client are DES-CBC-CRC (1), DES-CBC-MD5 (3), and DES3-HMAC-SHA1 (16). Next, we see the requesting IP address, followed by the port on the KDC that the request arrived on.

The next section of this message indicates the KDC's response to the request. In this example, the KDC issued (ISSUE) a ticket valid beginning at authtime (indicated by the standard Unix time_t value, seconds past January 1, 1970). This ticket's encryption types for the reply, the ticket itself, and the session key, are all DES3-HMAC-SHA1. Finally, we see the principal that requested the ticket (*jgarman@WEDGIE.ORG*) and the service for which the ticket was issued (*krbtgt/WEDGIE.ORG@WEDGIE.ORG*, since the user requested a TGT).

If the realm requires pre-authentication for this user, the KDC first logs a NEEDED_PREAUTH instead of an ISSUE response, then, upon successful pre-authentication, logs the ISSUE response, as in the following example:

```
Aug 01 09:29:09 www1.wedgie.org krb5kdc[17734](info): AS_REQ (3 etypes {16 3 1}) 192.
168.1.6(88): NEEDED_PREAUTH: afsadmin@WEDGIE.ORG for krbtgt/WEDGIE.ORG@WEDGIE.ORG,
Additional pre-authentication required
Aug 01 09:29:11 www1.wedgie.org krb5kdc[17734](info): AS_REQ (3 etypes {16 3 1}) 192.
168.1.6(88): ISSUE: authtime 1028208551, etypes {rep=16 tkt=16 ses=16},
afsadmin@WEDGIE.ORG for krbtgt/WEDGIE.ORG@WEDGIE.ORG
```

Now, once the user has their TGT, he wishes to connect to a remote server, and so requests a service ticket:

```
Aug 02 10:35:37 www1.wedgie.org krb5kdc[17734](info): TGS_REQ (3 etypes {16 3 1})
192.168.1.83(88): ISSUE: authtime 1028298937, etypes {rep=16 tkt=16 ses=16},
jgarman@WEDGIE.ORG for host/www1.wedgie.org@WEDGIE.ORG
```

This message is very similar to the message emitted when requesting a TGT. The only difference between the two messages is that this message is of type TGS_REQ (Ticket Granting Server request) rather than AS_REQ. All of the rest of the fields represent the same data as they did for the AS_REQ.

Now, let's take a look at the messages that turn up in the log when things start going wrong. First, we'll take a user who doesn't exist in the Kerberos principal database. When he tries to kinit, the following message is logged:

```
Aug 02 12:07:19 www1.wedgie.org krb5kdc[17734](info): AS_REQ (3 etypes {16 3 1}) 192.
168.1.83(88): CLIENT_NOT_FOUND: root@WEDGIE.ORG for krbtgt/WEDGIE.ORG@WEDGIE.ORG,
Client not found in Kerberos database
```

Here, we see an AS_REQ message with a response of CLIENT_NOT_FOUND. A similar message is emitted when a valid user attempts to obtain a ticket for a service that does not exist in the KDC database:

```
Aug 02 13:43:28 www1.wedgie.org krb5kdc[17734](info): TGS_REQ (1 etypes {1}) 192.168.
1.83(88): UNKNOWN_SERVER: authtime 1028298840,  jgarman@WEDGIE.ORG for afs/net.
wedgie.org@WEDGIE.ORG, Server not found in Kerberos database
```

Heimdal

Each time the Heimdal KDC starts up, it outputs the network ports it listens on to the KDC log file:

```
2002-08-04T14:44:51 listening on IPv4:127.0.0.1 port 88/udp
2002-08-04T14:44:51 listening on IPv4:192.168.1.83 port 88/udp
2002-08-04T14:44:51 listening on IPv4:127.0.0.1 port 88/tcp
2002-08-04T14:44:51 listening on IPv4:192.168.1.83 port 88/tcp
2002-08-04T14:44:51 listening on IPv4:127.0.0.1 port 750/udp
2002-08-04T14:44:51 listening on IPv4:192.168.1.83 port 750/udp
2002-08-04T14:44:51 listening on IPv4:127.0.0.1 port 750/tcp
2002-08-04T14:44:51 listening on IPv4:192.168.1.83 port 750/tcp
2002-08-04T14:44:51 listening on IPv4:127.0.0.1 port 4444/udp
2002-08-04T14:44:51 listening on IPv4:192.168.1.83 port 4444/udp
2002-08-04T14:44:51 listening on IPv4:127.0.0.1 port 4444/tcp
2002-08-04T14:44:51 listening on IPv4:192.168.1.83 port 4444/tcp
```

By default, the Heimdal KDC acts as a Kerberos 5 KDC, Kerberos 4 KDC, and a Kerberos 5-4 ticket translator. Now let's continue with an example protocol exchange in which a client requests a TGT:

```
2002-08-04T15:40:09 AS-REQ jgarman@WEDGIE.ORG from IPv4:192.168.1.83 for krbtgt/
WEDGIE.ORG@WEDGIE.ORG
2002-08-04T15:40:09 Using des3-cbc-sha1/des3-cbc-sha1
2002-08-04T15:40:09 sending 606 bytes to IPv4:192.168.1.83
```

All of the Heimdal messages begin with a date, followed by the T delimiter and the time. The first message indicates that the KDC received an Authentication Service request (AS-REQ) for the principal *jgarman@WEDGIE.ORG*. Next, it lists the originating IP and the service ticket the client requests.

The next message indicates the encryption types that the KDC will use in responding to the request: in this case, triple DES. Finally, if the KDC accepts the request, it emits the last message indicating the size of the response and the IP address of the client.

If the KDC requires pre-authentication, the following messages will be sent to the log upon successful client authentication:

```
2002-08-04T17:02:09 AS-REQ jgarman@WEDGIE.ORG from IPv4:192.168.1.83 for krbtgt/
WEDGIE.ORG@WEDGIE.ORG
2002-08-04T17:02:09 No PA-ENC-TIMESTAMP -- jgarman@WEDGIE.ORG
2002-08-04T17:02:09 sending 282 bytes to IPv4:192.168.1.83
2002-08-04T17:02:09 AS-REQ jgarman@WEDGIE.ORG from IPv4:192.168.1.83 for krbtgt/
WEDGIE.ORG@WEDGIE.ORG
2002-08-04T17:02:09 Looking for pa-data -- jgarman@WEDGIE.ORG
2002-08-04T17:02:09 Pre-authentication succeded -- jgarman@WEDGIE.ORG
2002-08-04T17:02:09 Using des3-cbc-sha1/des3-cbc-sha1
2002-08-04T17:02:09 sending 624 bytes to IPv4:192.168.1.83
```

The first three messages indicate the original request, and the error response sent back by the KDC to the client requesting pre-authentication. The final five lines are similar to the non-pre–authentication case, with the addition of the pa-data and pre-authentication succeded messages. Requesting a service ticket generates similar output:

```
2002-08-04T17:17:42 TGS-REQ jgarman@WEDGIE.ORG from IPv4:192.168.1.83 for
afs@WEDGIE.ORG [forwardable]
2002-08-04T17:17:42 sending 527 bytes to IPv4:192.168.1.83
```

Note that the ticket options that the client requested are listed on the TGS-REQ line.

Windows domain controllers

As we discussed earlier, the log files for the two different audit options (logon auditing and account logon auditing) are stored on different machines' Event Logs. The account logon auditing produces audit logs that are similar to the other KDC implementations we've covered. Since the account logon auditing is generated by the Kerberos KDC service running on the domain controllers, we're going to examine what those logs look like.

There are several Kerberos-related log events that account logon auditing emits. They are listed below:

- 672 Authentication Ticket Granted
- 673 Service Ticket Granted
- 674 Ticket Granted Renewed
- 675 Pre-authentication Failed
- 676 Authentication Ticket Request Failed
- 677 Service Ticket Request Failed

Any Kerberos client looks the same from the perspective of account logon auditing. It doesn't matter whether the requesting machine is running Windows or Unix; as long as it contacts the KDC running on one of your domain controllers, the KDC service will log both the successful and failed attempts at requesting tickets. So, let's dive in and examine some sample event logs.

Here's an example of a Windows machine successfully authenticating a user "jgarman" in the WEDGIE.ORG realm:

```
Event Type: Success Audit
Event Source: Security
Event Category: Account Logon
Event ID: 672
Date:  10/1/2002
Time:  11:55:10 PM
User:  NT AUTHORITY\SYSTEM
Computer: DESKTOP
Description:
Authentication Ticket Granted:
  User Name:  jgarman
  Supplied Realm Name: WEDGIE.ORG
  User ID: WEDGIE\jgarman
```

```
Service Name:  krbtgt
Service ID:  WEDGIE\krbtgt
Ticket Options:  0x40810010
Ticket Encryption Type: 0x3
Pre-Authentication Type: 2
Client Address:  192.168.1.17
```

The sequence of event log entries begins with a 672 event, signifying that the Authentication Server has issued a TGT. Note that the User field contains SYSTEM, not the end user for whom the ticket was issued. The username component of the requesting principal is contained in the User Name field, which is mapped to an NT-style user name in the User ID field. Unfortunately, this implies that if you want to filter the Event Log to show activity relating to a particular user name, you're out of luck. Also note that the Computer field always lists the domain controller's NetBIOS name (in this case DESKTOP), not the requesting machine's name, once again negating any ability to intelligently filter through the standard Event Viewer interface.

The Service Name field contains the first component of the principal we've been issued a ticket for: in this case simply, "krbtgt." This service name is mapped to a username in the Active Directory, and the resulting name is used for the Service ID field, much like the User Name is mapped to a User ID.

Finally, we see the ticket options (in easy-to-read hexadecimal format).

After the client receives this TGT, it requests service tickets. There are quite a few that Windows requests, and their names are strange to those used to working with Kerberos on Unix machines. Let's take a look at one:

```
Event Type: Success Audit
Event Source: Security
Event Category: Account Logon
Event ID: 673
Date:  10/1/2002
Time:  11:55:10 PM
User:  NT AUTHORITY\SYSTEM
Computer: DESKTOP
Description:
Service Ticket Granted:
  User Name:  jgarman
  User Domain:  WEDGIE.ORG
  Service Name:  WEB$
  Service ID:  WEDGIE\WEB$
  Ticket Options: 0x40810010
  Ticket Encryption Type: 0x17
  Client Address:  192.168.1.17
```

As you can see, this Event ID is 673, indicating that the client contacted the Ticket Granting Service for a service ticket. In this case, a service ticket is granted to the WEB$ service (this is simply the NetBIOS name of the target machine, with a dollar sign appended).

Finally, let's examine an example failed authentication attempt. Since Windows requires pre-authentication by default, you can detect password or brute-force attacks against your KDC by watching for event 675, Pre-authentication Failed messages. Here is an example:

```
Event Type: Failure Audit
Event Source: Security
Event Category: Account Logon
Event ID: 675
Date:  10/4/2002
Time:  11:56:07 PM
User:  NT AUTHORITY\SYSTEM
Computer: DESKTOP
Description:
Pre-authentication failed:
  User Name:  Administrator
  User ID:  WEDGIE\Administrator
  Service Name:  krbtgt/WEDGIE
  Pre-Authentication Type: 0x2
  Failure Code:  24
  Client Address:  192.168.1.1
```

## CHAPTER 7

Applications

Establishing a Kerberos realm and creating KDCs for your realm is only the beginning of creating a Kerberos-based authentication infrastructure. To enjoy the benefits of Kerberos, you, as the network administrator, also have to install Kerberos-enabled services and client software. This chapter illustrates how to enable Kerberos support in several popular server packages and the corresponding client programs.

What Does Kerberos Support Mean?

There are essentially two "types" of Kerberos support that a client/server application can implement. The first, and unfortunately, most common is for the client to send the server the user's Kerberos password in plain text. The server then acquires a TGT on the user's behalf (and hopefully verifies that the TGT is valid by also acquiring a service ticket for itself—see the description of the man-in-the-middle attack in Chapter 6 for details on why this is important). This method has a distinct advantage: most protocols that require authentication only support simple, plain text username and password authentication. Even if the protocol is extensible enough to support stronger authentication methods, these stronger authentication methods are usually not widely supported by the variety of clients in use. This method, of course, has the disadvantage of sending the user's credentials in plain text over the network. Since Kerberos is designed as a single-sign-on solution, exposure of a user's credentials in this way is even more dangerous since the same username and password is accepted for authentication by other Kerberos-enabled services. Finally, this method does not allow for a true single-sign-on solution; instead, it provides users with a single login and password that they have to enter multiple times.

The other method of supporting Kerberos authentication is what I'll call "native" Kerberos authentication support. Native Kerberos authentication support provides a true single-sign-on capability, in which users can login once to their local workstation, and acquire service tickets for Kerberos-enabled servers throughout the day. This requires special support on both the client and server so that the Kerberos tickets are communicated in a secure manner. This method provides for a superior user experience: the user only has to enter her credentials once per login session. Further authentication to Kerberos-enabled services is handled transparently, without user intervention. However, native Kerberos support in client applications is still not widespread, and may require users to change to a client application that does support Kerberos.

Our primary focus in this chapter is to enable native Kerberos support for popular applications. However, there are still some protocols where support for native Kerberos authentication is not currently possible or is not widely available. We will discuss how to use the Kerberos 5 PAM modules to add Kerberos 5 password verification support to those protocols.

Services and Keytabs

Remember that Kerberos provides a service that verifies the identity of two connection endpoints, identified by unique names, or principals. It is rather obvious so far that each user is associated with a principal name that is stored in the Kerberos database, since all authentication schemes by their very nature require that all users be uniquely identified with an associated secret. However, the concept that all services that users contact through Kerberos also require a principal and secret key is a new one to most administrators.

On Windows hosts, service keys are automatically created as needed when Kerberized services are installed. Unix-based Kerberos realms require a bit more manual configuration, and this section discusses the issues that Kerberos administrators have to work with when installing Kerberized services.

As we saw in Chapter 2, a service principal has three major components: the service name, the hostname of the machine that provides the service, and the Kerberos realm to which the machine belongs. Here's a sample service principal:

```
imap/freebsd.wedgie.org@WEDGIE.ORG
```

In this example, the service name is "imap", the host that this service is running on is "freebsd.wedgie.org", and the realm that this machine belongs to is "WEDGIE.ORG".

Of course, a secret key is associated with every principal, and so there is an encryption key or keys (possibly more than one, with different key version numbers, encryption types, and salts) associated with a given service principal. On Unix hosts, service keys are stored on the server providing the service, in a special file called the *keytab*. There can be, and for security reasons, should be, one keytab file per service offered.

Since keytab files contain highly sensitive information, notably encryption keys, it is imperative to ensure proper access controls to these files. Each Kerberized service should run as a different, unique username, and the keytab file for that service should be readable only by that username. As discussed in Chapter 6, the compromise of a service's key allows an attacker to masquerade as any authorized principal when communicating to that service, and also allows an attacker to read any conversation between clients and the compromised service.

The default keytab file—for most Unix-based Kerberos implementations—is */etc/ krb5.keytab*. By convention, this keytab contains the encryption keys associated with the host principal. While generating a host keytab for every machine in your realm is optional, it is highly recommended for those machines that run a Kerberized telnet or SSH daemon, or use Kerberos passwords to determine access to the local machine.

The process of exporting encryption keys from a Kerberos KDC to a keytab varies from one implementation to the next. The process for some common implementations is covered in Chapter 4. When extracting keytabs, ensure that they are protected during transport over the network from eavesdroppers. This can be accomplished by either running `kadmin` on the host you're extracting a keytab to, or using an encrypted file transfer protocol such as SSH's `scp` command to transfer the keytab to the target host.

Transparent Kerberos Login with PAM

When a user logs into his workstation at the beginning of the day, we want that user to acquire a Kerberos Ticket Granting Ticket when he enters his credentials. We'll call this *transparent Kerberos login*. Windows 2000, XP, and 2003 automatically acquire tickets upon login when the user is part of a Windows domain. However, for other systems, we have to configure this step manually. In Unix, the simplest and most portable way to get initial credentials for a user upon login is through the Pluggable Authentication Modules (PAM), which is available on most operating systems. Using PAM, you can acquire Kerberos tickets for logins that occur on the system's console (and any other network-based protocol, but we want to avoid sending passwords over the network).

Historically, applications such as the console login program and the X Windows System login program (xdm) all had to be modified to support new authentication methods. This introduces a maintenance and security nightmare, as locally-maintained patches must be made to system software to enable authentication methods other than the standard Unix password file. Worse yet, if the operating system comes without source, you may not even be able to replace the program with one that performs the necessary authentication method.

PAM solves this problem by providing a standard plug-in interface that both application developers and authentication method developers can write to. A mapping file is created that maps applications' authentication requests to the appropriate authentication methods, so that authentication modules can be added and removed on the fly, without recompiling the application. Linux, FreeBSD, Solaris, and HP-UX all include PAM support, and more operating systems are adding support.

However, PAM is not a panacea. It only supports traditional username and password authentication, so PAM works best when authenticating local (ie., on the console) login requests. Network-based services should use native Kerberos authentication to take advantage of the single-sign-on capabilities of Kerberos and to avoid sending plain text passwords across the network. PAM cannot provide native Kerberos authentication through the Kerberos ticket exchange. In addition, PAM implementations differ slightly from vendor to vendor, so PAM modules that may work on one vendor's OS may not work on another vendor's OS. The differences are usually small enough that they can be easily worked around, but it is something to be aware of when using PAM.

More Information About PAM

The following Unix operating system vendors have web sites that describe their support of the PAM framework:

- HP-UX: *http://www.hp.com/products1/unix/operating/security*
- Solaris: *http://wwws.sun.com/software/solaris/pam*
- Linux: *http://www.kernel.org/pub/linux/libs/pam*
- FreeBSD: *http://www.freebsd.org/doc/en_US.ISO8859-1/articles/pam*

The Linux-PAM page at *http://www.kernel.org/pub/linux/libs/pam/* is also a good resource. A list of available PAM modules is maintained at *http://www.kernel.org/pub/linux/libs/pam/modules.html*.

With the introductions out of the way, let's examine how to set up PAM to support Kerberos 5 logins. There are several PAM modules providing Kerberos authentication support, and unfortunately, they're all named pam_krb5. We'll pick one to work with; we'll use the pam_krb5 module available from *http://www.nectar.cc/krb*, as it is well supported and integrated into the Linux-PAM distribution. If your operating system already includes a precompiled pam_krb5, by all means, use it. However, if you have to compile your own pam_krb5, use this one.

Depending on your site's use of Kerberos, you can configure pam_krb5 to either require valid Kerberos credentials to login, or only to acquire Kerberos tickets if the user's Kerberos password matches some other password that is required to login to the local system (for example, a local password database).

Remember that Kerberos only provides an authentication service; hosts that use PAM to authenticate local users will still need an authorization database, which could be a local */etc/passwd* file, or a network-wide directory service such as NIS, LDAP, or NetInfo. If you are requiring users to login with valid Kerberos passwords, the directory that you choose should not include any password information for the users.

Configuring PAM

PAM is typically configured through a single configuration file, */etc/pam.conf*, or a directory of configuration files representing services that use PAM for their authentication needs. The exact location of the configuration files and their search order varies from implementation to implementation; "man pam" should point you in the right direction.

PAM delegates the task of logging a user into a system to a series of individual modules. Each PAM module provides a distinct set of services to any PAM-enabled application; for example, a Unix password file module may provide the ability for an application to authenticate and authorize access against a Unix password file. A Kerberos 5 PAM module provides authentication support and session establishment support. Applications can call the PAM modules through a standardized API, so that regardless of the underlying authentication mechanism, the API visible to the application remains the same.

PAM further subdivides the task of authenticating and authorizing a user to log into a system into four distinct tasks: account authorization, authentication, password services (such as password changing), and session establishment and teardown. Each PAM module can implement one or more of these tasks.

The PAM configuration (which can be either a monolithic file or a set of files in a directory) serves the purpose of attaching modules to PAM-enabled applications. Therefore, an administrator can specify a PAM module that an application uses to validate potential clients. Figure 7-1 shows the relation between applications, PAM modules, and the PAM configuration file.

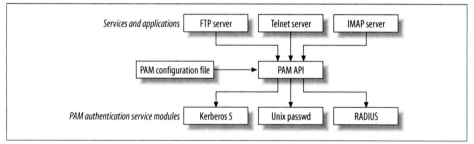

Figure 7-1. PAM architecture

However, confining administrators to a single authentication mechanism per application is limiting. For example, while it may be useful for machines to authenticate against a Kerberos 5 KDC, there are certain users, such as root, that you'd like to keep in a local password file instead of in a centralized database. Another example is a failsafe login ability; in the case of network failure or if the authentication servers are unreachable, it is definitely useful to have a small local password database with administrative users so that you can still access the machine. Therefore, PAM supports multiple authentication sources for a given application. PAM refers to this as *stacking*.

Stacking PAM modules provides for quite a lot of flexibility in configuration, at the cost of some complexity. Specialized PAM modules (such as a PAM module to check if the potential user's shell is listed in */etc/shells*) can be created to further limit access to services.

Let's take a look at an example PAM configuration, for the telnet service:

```
auth       required      /lib/security/pam_env.so
auth       sufficient    /lib/security/pam_unix.so likeauth nullok
auth       sufficient    /lib/security/pam_krb5afs.so use_first_pass tokens
auth       required      /lib/security/pam_deny.so

account    required      /lib/security/pam_unix.so

password   required      /lib/security/pam_cracklib.so retry=3
password   sufficient    /lib/security/pam_unix.so nullok use_authtok md5 shadow
password   sufficient    /lib/security/pam_krb5afs.so use_authtok
password   required      /lib/security/pam_deny.so

session    required      /lib/security/pam_limits.so
session    required      /lib/security/pam_unix.so
session    optional      /lib/security/pam_krb5afs.so
```

 Note that this example assumes a PAM configuration directory, with each service represented by a separate file contained inside. If your system uses a monolithic PAM configuration file, then there is an additional field: the service name that is prepended to every line in the configuration file.

The first field is the PAM task. We briefly discussed the four tasks that PAM defines above; let's take a closer look at them.

auth
> The auth task handles the actual authentication of the user. PAM modules that implement the auth task take in a username and password from the user and return a code determining whether the password is valid for the given user.

account
> The account task performs what the PAM documentation refers to as *account management*. Most of the functions that the PAM documentation associates with this task can also be referred to as authorization related tasks. These include determining whether the user's password has expired and whether the user is permitted access to this service.

password
> The password task handles password changes for the user.

session
> Modules implementing the session task provide services that should be performed before a service is given and before the user disconnects from the session. An example would be writing audit trail entries to a log file.

As you can see in the above example, the stacking of PAM modules is based on the task; every task for every service can have several PAM modules associated with it. The second field, known as the control field, indicates how the failure of a given module affects the outcome of the task as a whole. Traditionally, the control field has four valid values:

required

Success of this module is required for the authentication process to succeed. If this module returns failure, other modules are still executed, but the authentication process will fail regardless. In addition, PAM does not specify the order in which modules marked required are executed, except in the case of intervening modules marked requisite and sufficient. This is done for security reasons, to avoid giving attackers detailed information on failed authentication attempts.

requisite

Failure of this PAM module immediately terminates the authentication process. If this module fails, no module listed after this one is executed.

sufficient

The success of this PAM module immediately causes the authentication process to succeed. If this module succeeds, no module listed after this one is executed.

optional

This module is ignored unless it is the only module for this particular authentication task.

Newer versions of the PAM framework support a more complex syntax for the control field. For more information and to determine what your particular vendors' PAM system supports, check your system's manual page for "pam".

The next field is the name of the PAM module, which can either be expressed as an absolute path or relative to the default directory for modules. The last field is a list of arguments for the module. The arguments vary from module to module but there are some generic options recognized by most modules:

debug

Log debugging information to syslog for this module; this option is useful for troubleshooting PAM configurations.

use_first_pass

If a preceding authentication module has already obtained a password, try authentication using that password. If authentication using that password fails, then the module returns failure.

try_first_pass

First try authentication using the password passed from the preceding authentication module. If that fails, then prompt the user for a new password and attempt authentication with it.

The pam_krb5 PAM module also recognizes the following options:

forwardable
   When obtaining a TGT for the user, request forwardable tickets from the KDC.

ccache=*name*
   When creating the credential cache upon successful authentication, create it with the name specified by *name*. The name argument must be in the form of *type:residual*, where *type* is the type of credential cache, typically FILE. *residual* is the location of the cache, which in the case of the FILE type is a filename. There are two special tokens accepted for this argument, namely %u, which is replaced with the user ID of the authorized user, and %p, which is replaced by the current process ID.

Mac OS X and the Login Window

The initial console login window presented to Mac OS X users is called, appropriately enough, the loginwindow. Unfortunately, loginwindow's PAM support is incomplete. But luckily for Kerberos 5 users, Apple has provided special support in the loginwindow contained in Mac OS X 10.2 and above to provide users with Kerberos tickets when logging into their OS X system.

The procedure for enabling Kerberos support in the Mac OS X loginwindow application is documented in the AppleCare document #107154, "Mac OS X 10.2: How to Enable Kerberos Authentication for Login Window." Note that the method to enable this facility is subject to change in future OS X revisions.

Just like PAM, there are two basic options available when enabling Kerberos login support in OS X. You can either require valid Kerberos credentials for successful local login, or simply acquire Kerberos tickets if the local password is the same as the Kerberos password.

The Mac OS X Security and Authorization Services use the */etc/authorization* file, and this is the file that we'll use to enable Kerberos authentication in loginwindow. First, to require valid Kerberos credentials for login to the local system, Mac OS X can either require a valid host keytab or operate without a host keytab. Note that as we discussed in Chapter 6, a host keytab is required to defend against man-in-the-middle attacks against the Kerberos system.

Since Mac OS X does not include the kadmin utility, the best way to get a host key onto the Macintosh host is to create and extract the host key for the OS X host on the KDC and use Secure Shell (installed by default on OS X) to copy the key securely to the Mac.

In order to require Kerberos credentials when a host keytab is present, search for the system.login.console key in the */etc/authorization* file and replace it with the following:

```
<key>system.login.console</key>
  <dict>
    <key>eval</key>
<string>loginwindow_builtin:login,krb5auth:authenticate,loginwindow_builtin:success
</string>
  </dict>
```

If, on the other hand, you still wish to require Kerberos credentials even though a valid keytab is not present, you can replace the system.login.console key with the following text:

```
<key>system.login.console</key>
  <dict>
    <key>eval</key>
<string>loginwindow_builtin:login,krb5auth:authnoverify,loginwindow_builtin:success
</string>
  </dict>
```

Finally, the OS X loginwindow can acquire a Kerberos TGT as a result of successful local authentication. This method will attempt to acquire a TGT if the local password is the same as the Kerberos principal's password (where the principal name is the local user name, and the realm is the default realm as specified in the Kerberos configuration file). If the passwords differ, no error messages or additional password prompts appear; there will simply be no tickets available in the credential cache.

To enable this method of obtaining Kerberos tickets, search for the system.login.done key in the */etc/authorization* file and replace it with the following:

```
<key>system.login.done</key>
      <dict>
            <key>eval</key>
            <string>switch_to_user,krb5auth:login</string>
      </dict>
```

Kerberos and Web-Based Applications

Web-based authentication is an important issue for many organizations that want to extend their single-sign-on infrastructure to the web, for both internal intranet applications as well as external internet applications. Authentication can either be handled by the web application itself, by providing the user an HTML page with form entries for a username and password, or by the web server, through the HTTP protocol. This section discusses an Apache module that provides administrators the ability to verify Kerberos passwords through an Apache module.

The web server and browser perform HTTP authentication, with the resulting verified username returned by the web server to the web application. When an end user requests a resource on a web server for which the server is configured to require authentication, the web server returns an error 401 (Not Authorized) to the client.

This error message includes an HTTP header, WWW-Authenticate, that provides the client a challenge. Based on the response that the client provides the server, the server may choose to provide the client access to the requested resource, or continue to return 401 errors to the client if the response returned by the client is unsatisfactory. With this generic method, any challenge-response security protocol can be used for HTTP authentication.

The HTTP specification defines two authentication methods based on the above challenge-response architecture: Basic and Digest authentication (defined in RFC 2617). The most widely implemented of the two is the Basic method, in which the challenge consists simply of a realm name (not to be confused with a Kerberos realm) returned by the server to the client defining the resource for which the client is requesting access. Upon receipt of a 401 error with a request for Basic authentication, the browser displays a dialog box with prompts for username and password, and a label containing the name of the realm to which the user is requested to authenticate herself. The username and password is sent back to the server encoded in Base-64 (essentially in the clear, as no encryption is performed, Base-64 is just a transformation to eliminate ambiguity when decoding the response). Digest authentication uses a true challenge-response architecture but is not widely implemented since it requires the server to have the plain text of all users' passwords in order to verify authentication responses.

In addition to Basic and Digest, Microsoft IIS and Internet Explorer also support NTLM authentication, which uses the challenge-response Microsoft NTLM protocol to perform authentication between Microsoft-based browsers and servers. With the introduction of Windows 2000, Microsoft added Kerberos authentication to both IIS and Internet Explorer. Microsoft chose to implement Kerberos authentication through the use of a new HTTP authentication mechanism, Negotiate, layered with the Simple and Protected GSSAPI Negotiation Mechanism (SPNEGO, defined in RFC 2478). Through this mechanism, Internet Explorer can use native Kerberos authentication to access protected resources on an IIS server and provide single-sign-on for these resources. More information on the Microsoft implementation of Negotiate and SPNEGO as a web authentication method can be found at *http://msdn.microsoft.com/library/en-us/dnsecure/html/http-sso-1.asp*.

An implementation of SPNEGO and the Negotiate HTTP mechanism that interoperates with Microsoft Internet Explorer is under development, and the code is availabe at *http://modgssapache.sourceforge.net*. As this code is still under development, installation and configuration is still rough and subject to change. Installation instructions for the current version are available at the above web site, and I'll document my own adventures with it on the O'Reilly Network.

However, no web browsers other than Internet Explorer currently support native Kerberos authentication through the Negotiate mechanism. Therefore, the only true cross-platform solution to Kerberos on the Web at the moment is by passing Kerberos usernames and passwords over the network through Basic authentication, preferably through SSL in order to avoid passing the plain text passwords in the clear. The mod_auth_kerb Apache module, available at *http://modauthkerb.source-forge.net*, provides this capability to Apache. This is the method we will discuss to provide Kerberos authentication to web resources.

There are several problems to this approach from a security standpoint. First is the lack of mutual authentication: while the web server may be able to accurately determine the identity of the requesting user, the user has no way of knowing that he is talking to the legitimate web server. While using SSL mitigates this somewhat, there is still the possibility an attacker could establish a site with a valid SSL certificate and similar content. And since Basic authentication only specifies a simple text "realm name" (not to be confused with Kerberos realm) to be displayed during authentication, this name can easily be spoofed by an attacker intending to acquire passwords from users.

The second issue is passing the plaintext Kerberos password over the network. Again, using SSL mostly solves this problem, and it is highly recommended that web servers using mod_auth_kerb also use SSL to protect users' passwords in transit. Both of these issues would be solved with native GSSAPI support on browsers and servers, and it would also provide the benefit of single-sign-on, but at the moment there is no standard for GSSAPI support other than the Microsoft implementation.

Building the mod_auth_kerb Apache Module

After downloading the mod_auth_kerb C source file, it can be built as a dynamic shared object (dso) that can be loaded into Apache during runtime. The distribution consists solely of a single C source file, *mod_auth_kerb.c*. There is no configure script, so the Apache apxs program must be run manually to compile the source file with the appropriate options to create a valid Apache module. In addition, the Kerberos libraries and include directories have to be specified.

Before beginning, ensure that your Apache has support for loadable modules compiled in. Find the `httpd` binary, and use the `-l` option to list the modules compiled into the Apache binary. As long as `mod_so` is listed, then your Apache has support for dynamically loadable modules:

```
% ./httpd -l
Compiled-in modules:
  http_core.c
  mod_so.c
```

Table 7-1 shows the compile-time options available when building mod_auth_kerb.

Table 7-1. mod_auth_kerb compile-time options

Option	Description
KRB5	Needs to be defined for Kerberos 5 support.
KRB_DEF_REALM	Defines the default realm that is used when authenticating users. This realm is appended to user-names sent by browsers to form a complete principal name. Note that the realm must be contained in quotes, and double-escaped as it is passed through several scripts.

Table 7-1. mod_auth_kerb compile-time options (continued)

Option	Description
APXS2	Define this if you intend to run mod_auth_kerb with an Apache 2.x web server. Otherwise, a module for Apache 1.3.x is built.
KRB5_SAVE_CREDENTIALS	Forces mod_auth_kerb to keep the user's TGT after authentication—useful for CGI scripts that may contact further Kerberos servers with the end user's credentials. When using this option, the credential cache is stored in */tmp/krb5cc_username*, where *username* is the username portion of the authenticated principal.
KRB5_VERIFY_TICKET	Requires the module to retrieve a service ticket for the www/hostname@REALM principal before the user is successfully authenticated. This option is highly recommended to prevent man-in-the-middle spoofing attacks as explained in Chapter 6.
KRB_V5_KEYTAB	This option defines the path to the Kerberos 5 keytab for the *www/hostname* principal, which is used if KRB5_VERIFY_TICKET is defined to ensure that the KDC reply is genuine and not an attacker spoofing the KDC. Similar to the KRB_DEF_REALM option, this option also needs to be enclosed in quotes and appropriately shell-escaped. Since Apache usually does not (and should not) run as root, this keytab should be readable only by the username that Apache runs as.

In addition to these options, the paths to the include and library paths of your Kerberos implementation must also be included on the compile line. Modern Kerberos distributions include a script, krb5-config, that provides this information. Assuming that the module is being built for an Apache 1.3.x web server, a compile line looks like this:

```
% apxs -c -DKRB5 -DKRB5_VERIFY_TICKET -DKRB_V5_KEYTAB=\\\"/etc/apache.keytab\\\"
-DKRB_DEF_REALM=\\\"WEDGIE.ORG\\\" `/usr/local/bin/krb5-config --cflags`
`/usr/local/bin/krb5-config --libs` mod_auth_kerb.c
```

Compiling mod_auth_kerb for Apache 2 is similar; replace apxs with apxs2 and add the -DAPXS2 define to the command line. Hopefully, the build completes successfully and a *mod_auth_kerb.so* file is created in the current directory. Copy this module into your Apache installation's module directory.

Configuring mod_auth_kerb

Once the module has been built and placed in the Apache module directory, then it can be added to the server's *httpd.conf* file. Add the following LoadModule line:

```
LoadModule kerb_auth_module    libexec/apache/mod_auth_kerb.so
```

Also add the following AddModule line to your *httpd.conf* file:

```
AddModule mod_auth_kerb.c
```

Once these lines are in place in the *httpd.conf* configuration file, then the Kerberos authentication module can be configured for use through *htaccess* files or directly inside of the Apache configuration file, like any other Apache authentication module. An *htaccess* file looks like the following:

```
AuthType KerberosV5
AuthName "Kerberos password"
```

```
KrbAuthRealm WEDGIE.ORG
require valid-user
```

This example prompts users to enter in credentials, asking for their "Kerberos password" as defined in the AuthName clause. Note that this will accept any valid credentials for any principal in the WEDGIE.ORG Kerberos realm. If further access control is desired, the standard Apache user list and group functionality can be used to limit authorization to a subset of principal names. An up-to-date list of the configuration directives that can be placed in the *htaccess* file can be found at the mod_auth_kerb site.

The Simple Authentication and Security Layer (SASL)

The Cyrus SASL project forms the basis for several other products' authentication and session encryption support, most notably the Cyrus IMAP mail server and the OpenLDAP directory server. The Cyrus Simple Authentication and Security Layer (SASL) project provides an extensible framework for network protocol authentication. It is more generic than PAM in that SASL supports more complex authentication exchanges, such as Kerberos mutual authentication, and also supports the negotiation of a security layer (encryption) for later protocol exchanges once authentication is complete. SASL is documented as Internet RFC 2222.

SASL supports native Kerberos 5 authentication through the GSSAPI interface. Other authentication methods that SASL provides to applications include Kerberos 4 and standard */etc/password* or */etc/shadow* authentication (optionally through a privileged daemon process for services that don't have the necessary privileges to read the system password database). In addition, SASL supports several database-backed authentication methods, including the sasldb, which uses a lightweight database such as Berkeley DB or GDBM to store username/password pairs, and a mysql driver that uses the MySQL database to store authentication secrets.

SASL also includes a daemon process, saslauthd, which can provide password-based Kerberos 5 support to SASL-based applications similar to that of PAM. We'll cover how to build and enable this password verification method as well.

The Cyrus SASL home page is located at *http://asg.web.cmu.edu/sasl*, and the latest version of the Cyrus SASL distribution available at the time this was written is 2.1.10. We'll step through the process of building the Cyrus SASL library with Kerberos 5 support through the GSSAPI.

The first step, of course, is to acquire the distribution and unpack it. The latest version of Cyrus SASL is available from *ftp://ftp.andrew.cmu.edu/pub/cyrus-mail*. Download the distribution file (*cyrus-sasl-2.1.12.tar.gz* at the time of this writing), uncompress, and untar it.

Building the Distribution

Once the distribution is unpacked, we're ready to configure it for GSSAPI support. The only option required to the configure script to enable GSSAPI support is the enable-gssapi option, which takes one argument: the root directory of your installed Kerberos 5 installation. Of course, additional configure options can be appended for other authentication services that SASL supports.

 Note that Cyrus SASL has several external dependencies, notably a recent vintage database library such as the Berkeley DB or GNU DBM. During build testing of Cyrus SASL on a FreeBSD host, the configure process claimed to find a compatible DB engine, yet the build failed until GDBM was installed. If you encounter build failures, ensure that you have a compatible DB library installed and have provided the appropriate configure flags so that the build system is aware of it.

For our purposes, we'll configure with only GSSAPI support, assuming that our Kerberos 5 distribution and GSSAPI libraries have been installed in */usr/local*:

```
% ./configure  --enable-gssapi=/usr/local
```

Next, we're ready to make the source distribution:

```
% make
```

Cyrus SASL is notoriously difficult to compile. Even if the configure script runs to completion, the make step may fail because of various db library mismatches or strange interactions with the Kerberos 5 distribution. Hopefully, everything compiles well, and if it does, proceed to installation and configuration:

```
# make install
```

SASL Configuration

Cyrus SASL configuration, like PAM, is handled on a per-service basis. Every application that employs SASL for its authentication needs has its own configuration file. These configuration files are located in */usr/lib/sasl2* (or the directory where the plugins are installed) by default, and have the name of *Service.conf*, of which *Service* is the name of the application or service. For example, the configuration file for Sendmail's SASL settings is */usr/lib/sasl2/Sendmail.conf*, and the sample SASL application's configuration file is located at */usr/lib/sasl2/sample.conf*. The service name is defined by the application itself, so the exact name used by a particular application can be gleaned from the source code or the documentation of the application. Other applications mix in SASL configuration directives with the application's own configuration file. In short, the location of the SASL configuration directives for a given application is highly application-dependent, so check the software documentation.

The SASL libraries recognize the following configuration directives. Additional authentication method-specific directives are supported, and documented on the SASL home page. Table 7-2 lists the options that are pertinent to a SASL library configured with GSSAPI support.

Table 7-2. SASL configuration directives

Option	Description	Default
keytab	Location of the Kerberos 5 keytab file for the service's principal.	/etc/krb5.keytab
mech_list	List of the authentication mechanisms this service will use to verify user credentials.	By default, all mechanisms are enabled.
pwcheck_method	The method used to verify plaintext passwords if the PLAIN mechanism is enabled.	auxprop

The SASL libraries can be tested through a sample client and server application located in the sample subdirectory of the source distribution. Before testing, ensure that the machine your sample server resides on has a host principal in the Kerberos database, and the key associated with that principal has been extracted into the system's keytab. When running the server program, ensure that you run it as a user who has access to the system keytab (this usually means root). If you don't feel comfortable running it as root, create a new principal in the Kerberos database, say, sample/hostname@REALM, and extract that to another keytab. Set the KRB5_KTNAME environment variable to point to this new keytab.

The sample server takes several flags. The pertinent flags are -m to define the mechanisms that SASL should use to authenticate the user, and -s to define the service principal that the sample server represents. The service principal should be set to the name portion of the service principal you're using to test (for example sample/hostname@REALM would simply be sample). Run the sample server:

```
# ./server -s host
```

Before starting the client, ensure that you have already acquired a TGT for a principal in your realm. When testing the client, the mechanism can be forced to GSSAPI by using the -m command-line option. The client takes the same two arguments above plus another—the hostname of the server to connect to:

```
% ./client -s host -m GSSAPI freebsd
receiving capability list... recv: {46}
ANONYMOUS PLAIN GSSAPI OTP DIGEST-MD5 CRAM-MD5
ANONYMOUS PLAIN GSSAPI OTP DIGEST-MD5 CRAM-MD5
please enter an authorization id: jgarman
```

The client and server both dump the raw byte contents of the SASL packets to the screen, which while I'm sure is useful to the developers, isn't entirely helpful for anyone else. Either way, don't get too frightened by the sight of this rather verbose debugging information. The client will ask for the authorization id—this is the username that SASL will use to authorize the connection—typically the username portion of the principal that you have a TGT for (see the sidebar "Name Canonicalization and SASL" for more information). If everything works correctly, the last few lines of your client's output will look like this:

```
successful authentication
closing connection
```

If you still have trouble, ensure that the sample server can read the specified keytab, and a key for the service name specified on the command line exists in the keytab.

Name Canonicalization and SASL

Kerberos principal names consist of three major parts: the username, instance, and realm. With these three components, a globally unique name can be constructed. Most applications that use SASL use a traditional single username mechanism for authorization purposes. Therefore, a method is needed to map the three-component Kerberos principal name into a single username for authorization.

By default, SASL will strip off the realm and use the username and instance part together as a username. However, this can cause problems if there is a cross-realm relationship in which users from a foreign realm can acquire tickets for a SASL-protected service; name collisions can result from usernames that exist in both the local and foreign realms.

While SASL does have some support for passing realm information along to the calling application, most applications perform a simple username check. In this case, SASL will only authorize accesses from the local realm, and users coming in through a Kerberos cross-realm trust will be denied access.

Configuring saslauthd

At this point, SASL-enabled applications will be able to use the SASL GSSAPI support to perform native Kerberos 5 authentication. However, there is still a dearth of client applications that are able to perform GSSAPI authentication. Therefore, for backward compatibility with these clients, the saslauthd daemon can be configured to provide password verification services to services that use SASL for authentication services.

The *saslauthd* program is a daemon that runs continuously in the background, listening on a local domain socket for connections from services. When a service receives a connection that wishes to authenticate with a plain text login and password, it sends a message to saslauthd over the local socket, containing the username and password that the user presented for verification. Upon receipt of this information, saslauthd verifies the credentials against the configured authentication source. Through this mechanism, the security-sensitive process of verifying user passwords can be separated out into a small process that can run as root, and free the service itself from requiring superuser privileges just to verify passwords.

One of *saslauthd*'s supported authentication mechanisms is Kerberos 5. When verifying Kerberos passwords, saslauthd takes the username and password passed to it from the requesting service, appends the local realm to the username to form the client principal, and attempts to acquire a TGT for the principal from the local realm's KDC. If the supplied password successfully decrypts the TGT, *saslauthd* then requests the host principal to ensure that the KDC reply is genuine. Because of this check, saslauthd will have to be run with root privileges and the system keytab will have to contain a key for the host principal.

If the host key does not exist in the system keytab, or is not readable by saslauthd, saslauthd will refuse all authentication attempts with a generic error, so this should be one of the first steps taken when troubleshooting saslauthd problems.

To enable *saslauthd*, simply execute it as part of the startup scripts of any host that runs services that use SASL for authentication. You will have to start *saslauthd* as root to read the system keytab, and add a command-line flag to enable the Kerberos 5 mechanism:

```
# saslauthd -a kerberos5
```

Kerberos-Enabled Server Packages

While PAM is a great solution for local login on the system console, the real advantages to using Kerberos are only realized if client/server applications that users interact with are configured for native Kerberos support.

Our users now have Kerberos tickets upon login. The next step is to start adding Kerberos support to the application servers that users access. We want users to enjoy the benefits of a fully-Kerberized environment as much as possible, so I'll focus on enabling native Kerberos support in as many packages that support it, but fall back to the single-login capability provided by other packages that do not have built-in Kerberos support.

We already saw an example of a network protocol with native Kerberos support back in Chapter 4, when we configured the Kerberos telnet server to test our new Kerberos implementation. We're going to take that a step further in this section and examine how to add Kerberos support to other popular network protocols.

Electronic Mail (Cyrus IMAP)

Cyrus IMAP is a part of Project Cyrus, a project developed at Carnegie Mellon University to provide a reliable, scalable electronic mail system for the campus. The Cyrus mail server had, in its original design goals from 1994, many of the same goals of administrators today: the mail service had to scale to thousands of simultaneous readers, it had to support many different clients on different hardware and operating-system platforms, and it had to integrate with the campus-wide authentication system, which happens to be based on Kerberos. Today, Cyrus supports the two major mail access protocols: the Internet Mail Access Protocol (IMAP) and Post Office Protocol (POP). A separate program, a Mail Transfer Agent, handles the task of transferring mail from system to system through the Simple Mail Transfer Protocol (SMTP). Newer mail clients support SMTP authentication, and we'll discuss Kerberos support for MTAs in the next section.

Cyrus IMAP is available from Carnegie Mellon at *http://asg.web.cmu.edu/cyrus/imapd*, and the latest stable version available at the time of this writing is 2.1.12. Cyrus IMAP uses the Cyrus SASL library to handle authentication and session encryption tasks. Therefore, before building Cyrus IMAP, you'll need a working installation of Cyrus SASL.

Building and configuring the distribution

Cyrus IMAP is a complex package and most of the build and configuration options relate to how it handles mail, and not its authentication mechanism. Therefore, we're going to focus on the particular options necessary to enable GSSAPI support in Cyrus IMAP.

After acquiring the source distribution, untar it and the following configure line will configure Cyrus IMAP for GSSAPI and SASL support:

```
% ./configure --enable-gssapi=/usr/local --with-sasl=/usr/local
```

Once the configure step completes, Cyrus IMAP is ready to compile and install:

```
# make && make install
```

Once Cyrus has been installed, it can be configured to work with SASL to provide GSSAPI authentication to clients. The necessary SASL configuration information can be embedded into the *imapd.conf* file; insert sasl_ before every SASL-related configuration directive in *imapd.conf*. For example:

```
sasl_pwcheck_method: saslauthd
sasl_mech_list: gssapi plain pam
```

You'll also need to create a keytab entry for the Cyrus IMAP server, in the form of imap/*hostname*@*REALM* and securely copy it into the IMAP server's filesystem. The keytab should be readable by only the username that Cyrus IMAP runs as (a special user should be created for this purpose, as part of the installation process).

Once the configuration is in place, the Cyrus IMAP daemons can be started with the following command, assuming that the distribution has been installed into the default directory of */usr/cyrus*:

```
# /usr/cyrus/bin/master &
```

At least with the currently available Cyrus IMAP and SASL distribution, specifying the keytab SASL parameter in the /etc/imapd.conf file does not successfully set the keytab for Cyrus IMAP. If you are using a keytab other than the system keytab (which is highly recommended, as the system keytab is readable only by root and Cyrus IMAP runs as a special non-root user), then set the KRB5_KTNAME environment variable to the full path of Cyrus IMAP's keytab before starting Cyrus IMAP. For example (assuming a Bourne shell):

```
# KRB5_KTNAME=/etc/cyrus.keytab
# /usr/cyrus/bin/master &
```

Obviously, details on configuring the mail-handling parameters in Cyrus IMAP is beyond the scope of this book. For further information on configuring Cyrus IMAP, see the documentation included with the distribution.

Testing the authentication

Cyrus IMAP also has a testing program that can be used to ensure the proper operation of the SASL libraries for authentication once the mail system is up and running. The imtest program, which is installed as part of the distribution, logs in to the IMAP server and attempts to authenticate using any of the supported SASL mechanisms.

The only argument that imtest requires is the name of the mail server to contact. If the GSSAPI mechanism has been compiled, and enabled in the server-side *imapd.conf* file, then it should succeed, and a subsequent klist will show that the client has successfully acquired a service ticket. If the authentication fails, check the syslog messages on the server. The most common errors encountered at this stage are related to keytab problems; Cyrus may be looking in the wrong location for the service key, or the permissions may be incorrect on the keytab.

Directory Services (OpenLDAP)

OpenLDAP is an open source implementation of the Lightweight Directory Access Protocol, and is available at its home page at *http://www.openldap.org*. A directory contains information about an organization's resources, typically personnel, but can also contain information about other resources, such as computers, and printers as well. LDAP is extensible through its support for attributes that can hold arbitrary data, such as names, phone numbers, addresses, and photos. Those who are interested in learning more about LDAP and OpenLDAP can refer to *LDAP System Administration* by Gerald Carter (O'Reilly).

To restrict access to this information and to control who can modify the directory, LDAP servers require authentication. OpenLDAP uses the Cyrus SASL library to provide this authentication service. Therefore, before installing OpenLDAP, you will need a working Cyrus SASL installation.

Building, configuring, and testing the distribution

OpenLDAP is a complex package and most of the configuration options are beyond the scope of this book, as they relate to the LDAP functionality rather than the supported authentication methods. The options required to configure OpenLDAP with Kerberos and SASL support are:

```
./configure --with-spasswd --with-cyrus-sasl --with-kerberos
```

More configuration options will probably be required to define the backend database to be used for the LDAP data.

The OpenLDAP server needs a ldap service principal (ldap/hostname.domainname@REALM) created in the Kerberos database. This principal should be created and placed in a keytab that can be read by the OpenLDAP server, slapd.

The ldapsearch command can be used to test the Kerberos authentication. When run, it should output the name of the Kerberos principal that you are authenticated as:

```
% ldapsearch
SASL/GSSAPI authentication started
SASL username: jgarman@WEDGIE.ORG
SASL SSF: 56
SASL installing layers
```

Remote Login (OpenSSH)

OpenSSH is a popular choice for secure, remote access to Unix hosts. The Secure Shell protocol provides secure authentication and session encryption services for remote login. These are the same services that a Kerberized telnet or rlogin provides, but Secure Shell doesn't require a centralized infrastructure, like Kerberos; it only requires users to use one program (the Secure Shell client) to access a SSH server, and finally only communicates on one network port (as opposed to Kerberos, which requires a client to have direct access to both the Kerberos KDC and application server). Therefore, Secure Shell is a popular option for remote access to servers due to its simplicity in operation and small network footprint; its popularity has spawned many interoperable implementations of the protocol for most platforms available today.

OpenSSH is one of these implementations, an open source implementation developed by the OpenBSD group based upon the last unencumbered source code release of the original Secure Shell code.

Secure Shell uses public key encryption methods to perform mutual authentication and negotiation of a symmetric key for session encryption. Since Secure Shell does not require use of a centralized authentication source or signed public keys, it is inherently subject to man-in-the-middle attacks (hence the warnings when connecting to a server for the first time, or when the server's key changes).

Now, with all of that said, how can we use Kerberos with Secure Shell, considering that there is some overlap of functionality between the two? The answer is that

Kerberos can be used for the authentication tasks Secure Shell performs, while Secure Shell provides the session encryption functionality. Therefore, the Kerberos single-sign-on authentication framework can be used for Secure Shell connections as well. Furthermore, a Kerberized Secure Shell server can interoperate with non-Kerberized Secure Shell clients if necessary.

This latter scenario is useful in the example of a Kerberized network located behind a firewall. Remote access to the network can be granted with the same Kerberos username/password pair to remote clients, without requiring clients to install the entire Kerberos distribution on their local systems, by using the Secure Shell password authentication method.

OpenSSH is available from its home page, *http://www.openssh.com*. OpenSSH is available in two versions: the OpenBSD-specific version that is shipped with OpenBSD and the "portable" version that includes support for many popular operating systems. Of course, unless you are running OpenBSD, you'll want to download the latest portable distribution. OpenSSH does ship with Kerberos support included (but not enabled) by default, but it is not sufficient for our use. Simon Wilkinson has developed a set of patches that add GSSAPI support to Secure Shell, and these patches are available at *http://www.sxw.org.uk/computing/patches/openssh.html*. You'll also need a recent version of GNU autoconf; Version 2.52 or greater is required to rebuild the configure script after the GSSAPI patches have been applied. The GSSAPI support also requires that both the server and client be configured for SSH protocol Version 2 support, which is a good idea to require from a security standpoint anyway.

Building the distribution

Once you've retrieved both the OpenSSH distribution as well as the GSSAPI patches, the next step is to apply the patches and configure OpenSSH for GSSAPI support. Assuming that you have downloaded the latest OpenSSH (3.5p1) and GSSAPI patches (the patches are for older OpenSSH, 3.4p1) as of this writing, the OpenSSH distribution has been unpacked, and the GSSAPI patch file is located in the same directory as the OpenSSH *tar* file, the following command will patch OpenSSH:

```
% cd openssh-3.5p1
% patch -p1 -s < ../openssh-3.4p1-gssapi-20020627.diff
1 out of 1 hunks failed--saving rejects to compat.h.rej
```

 The GSSAPI patches for 3.4p1 apply cleanly to OpenSSH 3.5p1 with one exception: the *compat.h* file. OpenSSH 3.5 added the SSH_BUG_PROBE flag, which causes the GSSAPI patches to reject the file.

To remedy this, search for SSH_BUG_K5USER in *compat.h* and edit the file so that it looks like the following:

```
#define SSH_BUG_K5USER    0x00400000
#define SSH_BUG_PROBE     0x00800000
#define SSH_OLD_GSSAPI    0x01000000
```

Once the patch has been applied, `autoreconf` must be run on the distribution to rebuild the configure script to add the GSSAPI configure option:

```
% autoreconf
```

The warnings that `autoreconf` may produce can be safely ignored.

Now we are ready to run the configure script. For our purposes the only option that we need to pass to the configure script is `--with-kerberos5`, to compile in GSSAPI support. This configure option takes one argument, the base directory of the Kerberos 5 and GSSAPI includes and library files. If your environment requires other configure options as well, ensure that those options are appended to the configure script:

```
% ./configure --with-kerberos5=/usr/local
```

If all goes well, then make and install, and you should have a Kerberized Secure Shell server and client ready for use:

```
% make && make install
```

Configuring the distribution

Once the OpenSSH distribution has been installed, the GSSAPI patches add a few options to the *sshd_config* configuration file to control the use of Kerberos authentication. The options in Table 7-3, added to the *sshd_config* file, are enabled by default.

Table 7-3. sshd_config options

Configuration flag	Description
GssapiAuthentication	Specifies whether to enable GSSAPI authentication, through a successful key exchange (in this case Kerberos ticket exchange) or through password authentication. The default is "yes".
GssapiKeyExchange	Specifies whether to enable GSSAPI authentication through key exchange.
PasswordAuthentication	Specifies whether to enable password-based authentication. If PasswordAuthentication is set to "yes", sshd will authenticate passwords against the Kerberos KDC regardless of the value of Gssapi-Authentication.
Protocol	We highly recommend only allowing connections with protocol Version 2 clients. The Secure Shell protocol Version 1 had several vulnerabilities; besides, the GSSAPI patches only function on Version 2.

In addition, the host will need to have a host key in its system keytab. Ensure that a host principal has been created and the keytab for that principal exists in the system keytab. Since all of the GSSAPI-related options default to "on" in the OpenSSH configuration file, the Kerberos single-sign-on should work out of the box. Before testing, ensure that the SSH server host has a valid keytab installed, and ensure that the client has a TGT. If the client still asks for a password when connecting, then starting the SSH server in debug mode (by appending the `-d` parameter to the sshd command line) can help narrow down the problem.

This setup produces an OpenSSH server that can accept three forms of authentication: public key authentication, password-based authentication, and Kerberos authentication. In addition, if your TGT was acquired with the forwardable bit set, then OpenSSH will forward your Kerberos credentials to the target OpenSSH server through the GSSAPI authentication mechanism.

OpenSSH honors the same *.k5login* file that the Kerberized telnet daemon uses for determining authorization of Kerberos principals to Unix usernames. By default, OpenSSH authorizes Kerberos principals in the local realm of the server directly to the same username on the Unix host. To specify additional principals that should be allowed access to a particular Unix username, create a *.k5login* file in the user's home directory. The format of this file is a single principal per line. For example, to grant access to the tdurden user account to the *fgump* and *tdurden* principals in both the WEDGIE.ORG and W2K.WEDGIE.ORG Kerberos realms, the file will contain:

```
tdurden@WEDGIE.ORG
tdurden@W2K.WEDGIE.ORG
fgump@WEDGIE.ORG
fgump@W2K.WEDGIE.ORG
```

Note that if a *.k5login* file exists, the default mapping between the username in the Kerberos realm and the Unix user with the *.k5login* file will no longer exist. Instead, the principal must be explicitly listed in the *.k5login* file.

Kerberos-Enabled Client Packages

To truly use Kerberos as a cross-platform single-sign-on system, Kerberized client software has to be installed as well. A complimentary pair of client and server Kerberized applications must be matched to perform native Kerberos authentication. Applications that use server-side Kerberos password verification will work with unmodified clients, but their use is discouraged as it negates the single-sign-on benefits provided through native Kerberos authentication. This section describes some of the software packages available that provide client-side native Kerberos functionality.

Kerberized Secure Shell Clients

In a previous section, we built OpenSSH with GSSAPI support. This OpenSSH with GSSAPI patches works on many platforms, including all of the common Unix variants, and Mac OS X. However, OpenSSH operates only on the command line, and compiling OpenSSH on Windows can be difficult. A popular, free, and graphical Secure Shell client for Windows is PuTTY, and a company named Certified Security Solutions has developed patches to PuTTY to incorporate GSSAPI authentication support, and provides binaries that are free for noncommercial and internal commercial use.

The modified PuTTY client is available at *http://www.certifiedsecuritysolutions.com/ downloads.html*. Separate distributions are available for Windows 2000 and older Windows operating systems. The distribution for Windows 2000/XP/2003 includes support for the Windows SSPI that can communicate with the GSSAPI-enabled OpenSSH without requiring Kerberos for Windows to be installed on the Windows host.

Reflection X

Reflection X is an X11 server package published by WRQ, Inc. Reflection X allows users on Windows platforms to access X11 applications on Unix hosts. While there are many such packages available, Reflection X has decent Kerberos functionality provided as part of the Security Components. By using the Reflection Security Components, you can set up a cross-platform single-sign-on infrastructure between Windows clients, Windows servers, and Unix servers.

The latest version is WRQ Reflection X 10, and includes support for the latest industry standard X11R6.6 protocol as well as traditional, character-based terminal emulation protocols. For more information on the X server support and terminal emulation features provided by the Reflection X package, visit the WRQ home page at *http://www.wrq.com/*.

To start X11 applications on a Unix server, the X server software running on the Windows host must have a remote login client built in to log into the Unix host, redirect the X11 display to the Windows machine's IP, and then start the X11 application. A diagram of this process is shown in Figure 7-2.

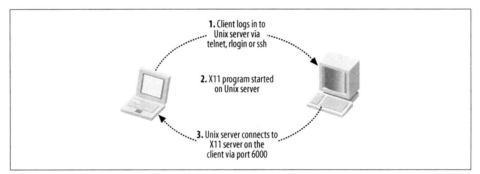

Figure 7-2. Logging into Unix host, redirecting display, and starting application

Most X11 servers for Windows use telnet or rlogin for this process. The downside of using telnet or rlogin to start these X11 applications, of course, is that plain text passwords are sent over the network to log the user into the Unix host. In addition, for convenience, X11 servers will offer to cache the Unix password, so that users do not have to type it in on a regular basis.

Reflection X addresses these security concerns through the Reflection Security Components, which are available for Reflection X customers as a free download from WRQ's web site. The Reflection Security Components include an OpenSSH implementation to launch X11 applications through a Secure Shell connection. More pertinent to our discussion at hand, though, is its support for Kerberized telnet connections to Unix hosts. This support provides for secure authentication, avoiding the problem of sending the user's password over the network in the clear to the telnet server on the Unix host, but it still sends the user's X11 session over the network in the clear. The OpenSSH implementation included in the Security Components uses Secure Shell's X11 tunneling support to provide session encryption for the X11 connections as well, but unfortunately, Reflection's current implementation of Secure Shell only supports password and public key authentication, and does not support GSSAPI authentication.

The Reflection Security Components uses its own custom Kerberos implementation, and does not require MIT's Kerberos for Windows to be installed.

Before starting Reflection X with the security components for the first time, you'll want to set up the Kerberos settings. This procedure will have to be performed for each Windows user who uses Reflection Kerberos to connect to Unix hosts. The application that manages the Reflection Kerberos configuration is named "Kerberos Manager" and can be found in the Utilities subfolder of the WRQ Reflection folder in the Start Menu's Programs folder. When you start the Kerberos Manager for the first time, you'll be greeted with the following initial configuration dialog (Figure 7-3).

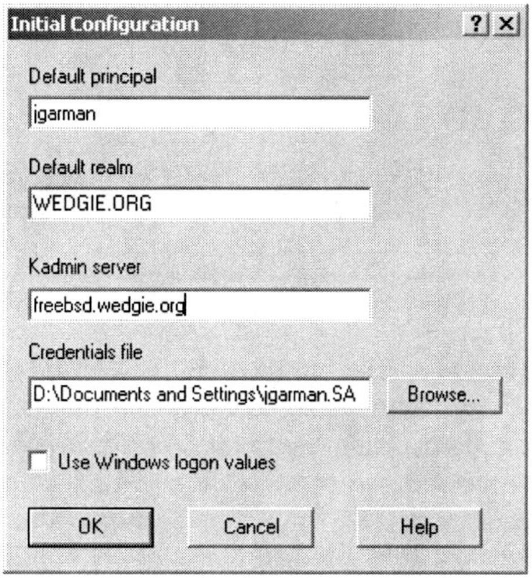

Figure 7-3. Reflection Kerberos initial configuration dialog

The default principal will default to your Windows username; if these differ, change the value to your principal in the Kerberos realm. The default realm should be set to your Kerberos realm, and the kadmin server should be set to your master KDC, or a Windows domain controller, if you're using a Windows machine as your KDC. The credentials file can be left as the default, unless you wish to change where the Reflection applications keep the credential cache.

Once the initial configuration is out of the way, there are a few other configuration parameters that might need adjusting, depending on your realm's set up. The realm configuration parameters can be accessed through the Kerberos Manager program's

Configuration/Configure Realms menu option. That menu option displays the dialog box on the left, as shown in Figure 7-4.

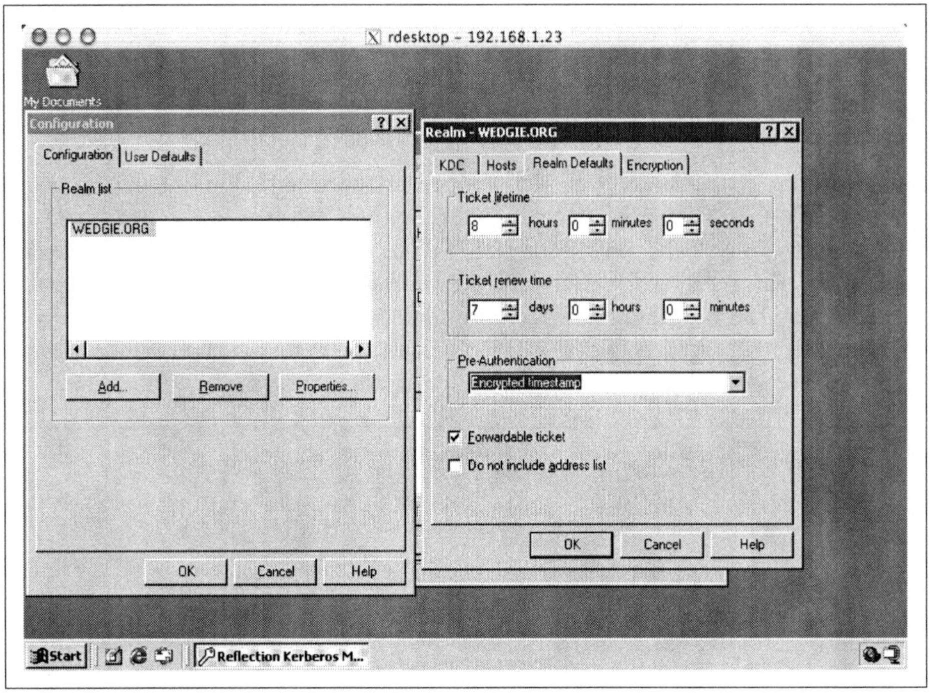

Figure 7-4. Reflection Security Components Kerberos realm configuration

The properties dialog box (displayed on the right) is accessed through the Properties button. Properties such as desired ticket lifetimes and requested ticket flags can be set in this dialog box. A particularly important property that can be changed here is the pre-authentication method, which must be set to Encrypted timestamp if your realm uses pre-authentication. The Reflection Kerberos libraries do not properly respond to the pre-authentication required Kerberos error message, and authentication will fail if the KDC requires pre-authentication.

Once the initial configuration steps are out of the way, a test can be performed by creating a Kerberized telnet connection profile in the terminal emulator. Open the Host → Unix and Digital application under the WRQ Reflection application group. Create a new connection profile by selecting Connection Setup under the Connection menu. Fill in the hostname of the target host running a Kerberized telnet server in the text box. Click the Network radio button in the Connect using group, and the Security button becomes active. Clicking the Security button brings up the security dialog box; inside this dialog box is a Kerberos tab. Ensure the Use Reflection Kerberos is checked, the User ID field is set to your username on the Unix host, and the default principal is correct.

Once all of the settings are in place, click Connect so Reflection will connect to the Unix telnet server, and login via Kerberos. If the authentication is successful, there will be a small yellow key icon on the status bar indicating that the session was authenticated via Kerberos. In addition, if "Encrypt data stream" was checked in the Kerberos options dialog box, a small padlock will also appear in the status bar, indicating that the session contents are also encrypted.

You can check that Reflection successfully acquired an initial TGT and ticket for the host principal by opening the Kerberos Manager application. There should be ticket entries for both the krbtgt principal as well as the host principal. Figure 7-5 shows a successful login to a Unix host and the resulting tickets in the Reflection Kerberos Manager.

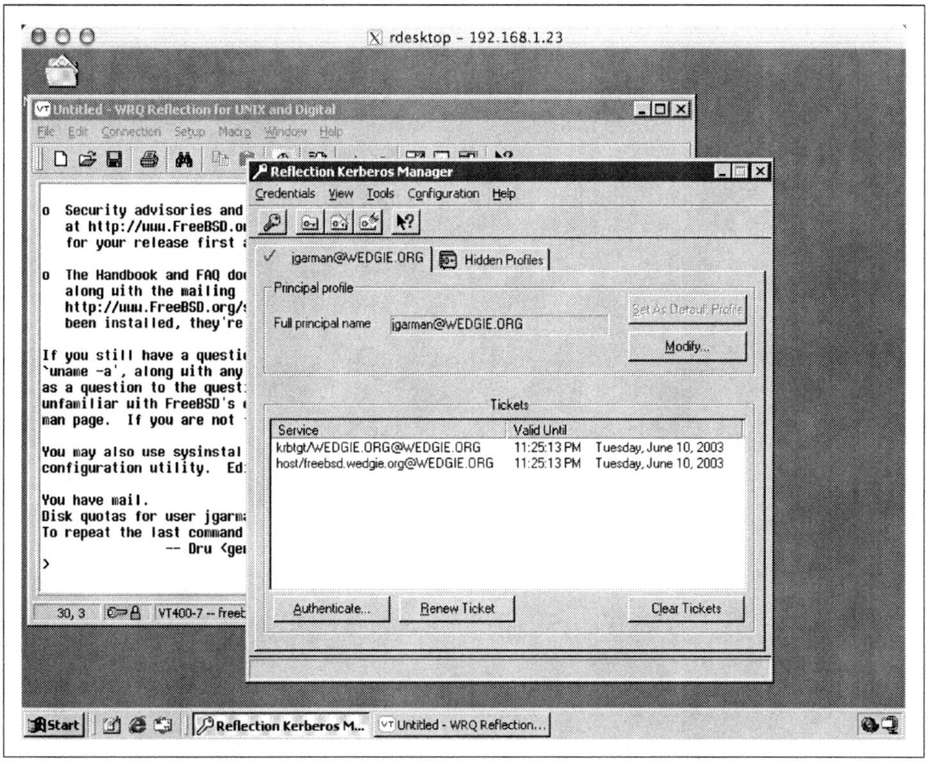

Figure 7-5. Reflection Kerberos ticket manager

When the connection works with the terminal emulator, using the same settings for the X window session options works, too. X client sessions can be created manually through the X Client Manager or the X Client Wizard. Click the Advanced button of a X session property page to find the Kerberos-related settings for X client sessions.

Using existing credential caches with Reflection X

Since the Reflection Security Components includes its own Kerberos implementation, Reflection keeps its credential cache separate from the Windows cache and the MIT credential cache, if MIT Kerberos for Windows is installed. This creates quite a mess of Kerberos credentials, and requires users to login with their username and password multiple times. Thankfully, the Kerberos libraries included with the Reflection Security Components have the ability to import tickets from credential caches created by both the MIT Kerberos libraries as well as the Windows internal credential cache.

The configuration options to toggle this support on and off are found in the Kerberos Manager application. Select the Configure Realms menu item from the Configuration menu, and that will bring up a dialog box listing the names of all the realms Reflection knows about. Select your realm, and click Properties. Under the KDC tab of the Properties dialog box, the two checkboxes at the bottom control whether Reflection will try and copy the TGTs from the Windows and/or MIT credential cache on startup. If the "Use Windows logon credentials" box is disabled, then the currently logged in user was authenticated locally instead of as part of a domain or Kerberos realm. The "Use leash32 cache" checkbox refers to the MIT Kerberos credential cache, and will only be enabled if the Kerberos DLL's included with the MIT Kerberos for Windows distribution are installed in a system-wide location (such as *\WINNT\System32*).

When either checkbox is enabled, Reflection will copy the TGT from the selected cache into its own credential cache when any of the Reflection applications are started. Note that Reflection will only copy the credentials from the source cache upon startup; if the source cache changes (for example, Windows will automatically refresh the TGT before it expires), Reflection will not notice and require the user to re-authenticate directly to Reflection Kerberos.

Electronic Mail

Email is an application users depend on every day. There are several Mail User Agents that include Kerberos support. We'll examine two of these in this section: Qualcomm's Eudora and Apple's Mail.app. Both are modern mail readers that support all of the major electronic mail standards, including POP, IMAP, authenticated SMTP, SSL/TLS encryption, and most importantly, for our discussion, Kerberos support. Microsoft's popular Exchange server and Outlook client will support Kerberos authentication as of Exchange and Outlook 2003.

Qualcomm Eudora

Eudora is a popular email client available for both Windows and Mac OS. It is developed by Qualcomm, and is available at *http://www.eudora.com*. This section discusses how to set up Eudora for Windows to use GSSAPI authentication, and setting up the Macintosh version is very similar.

Before starting, ensure that the MIT Kerberos for Windows distribution has been installed, the Kerberos DLLs are present in the Windows system directory, and a valid *krb5.ini* containing information for your Kerberos realm is also located in the Windows system directory. If either of these are missing or only partially installed, Eudora may fail with no error message when attempting to authenticate to the IMAP server.

When first starting Eudora, you will be presented with a wizard to guide you through the steps of setting up a mail account. Since the wizard has no provisions for enabling Kerberos support, the best option at this point is to choose the "Skip directly to advanced account setup" option. This option drops you into the first tab of the account setup dialog box, as shown in Figure 7-6.

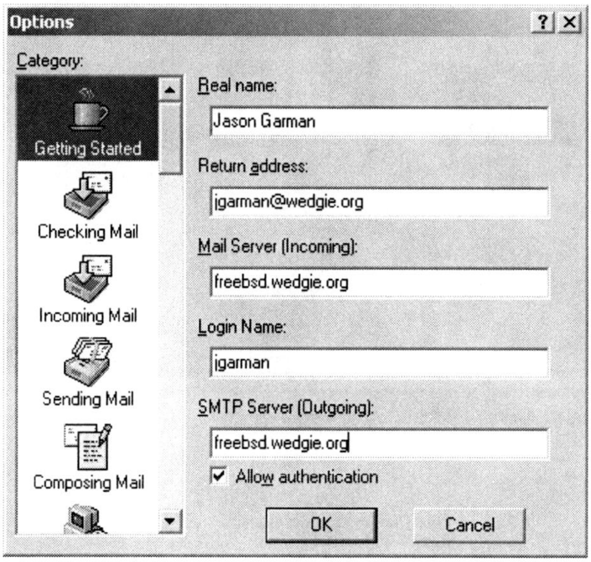

Figure 7-6. Eudora's options dialog

Once the appropriate information regarding the mail servers and usernames have been filled in, go to the Incoming Mail category, and ensure that the authentication style radio button is set to Kerberos (see Figure 7-7). That's the only configuration required to use GSSAPI authentication with IMAP mail servers.

Apple Mail.app

Mail.app integrates directly with the Kerberos infrastructure present in Mac OS X and supports Kerberos authentication for POP, IMAP, and SMTP servers, supporting single-sign-on for all electronic mail–related protocols.

Mail.app is rather easy to set up, and the account information can be accessed through the Accounts pane of the Mail.app Preferences window. When adding or editing an existing account, the sheet shown in Figure 7-8 appears. The Advanced tab is where special authentication options can be chosen for the account, including GSSAPI authentication. To enable Kerberos 5 authentication with a POP or IMAP server is as simple as selecting GSSAPI in the Authentication drop-down box. This has been tested and works at least with the Cyrus IMAP server listed above, but should also interoperate with any server implementation that includes GSSAPI authentication support.

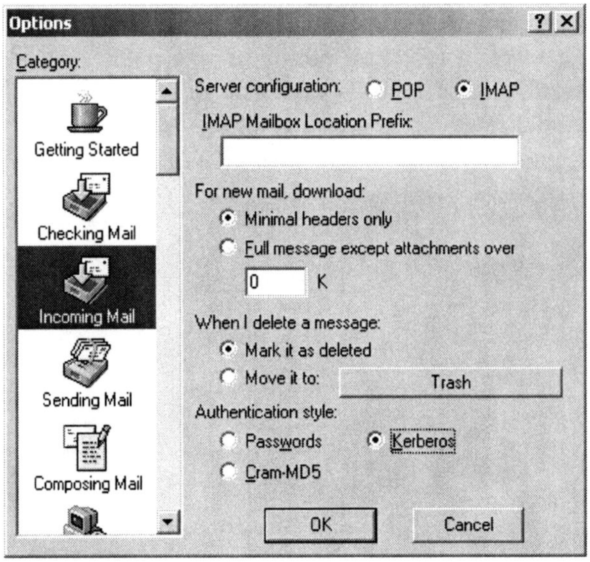

Figure 7-7. Kerberos setting in Eudora's options dialog

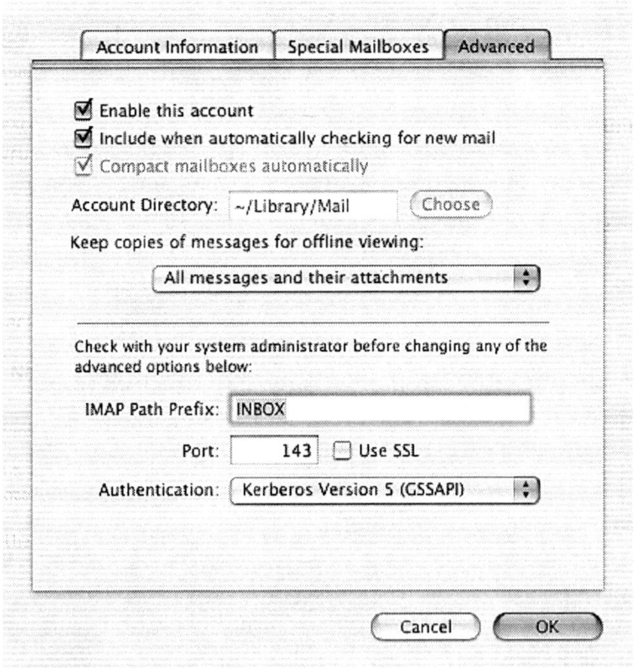

Figure 7-8. GSSAPI option located in Mail.app's Advanced options dialog

More Kerberos-Enabled Packages

While I've tried to present a sample of some of Kerberos-enabled packages, there are still many more applications that support Kerberos authentication. Many applications, like databases, file servers, and print spool software include Kerberos authentication. With the background presented in this chapter, you will be able to enable and configure this support in those products as well.

CHAPTER 8

Advanced Topics

So far, we have covered enough of the Kerberos authentication system to establish useful Kerberos realms and enable Kerberos support in applications to take advantage of a single-sign-on environment. This chapter will prepare you to create networks with multiple Kerberos realms and interoperate between different Kerberos implementations. It also discusses some issues to be aware of when working with multiple Kerberos implementations.

Cross-Realm Authentication

All of the Kerberos discussion so far has assumed that all users and resources on your network are located in a single Kerberos realm. However, what if there are several departments, locations, or other divisions that are under different administrative control, each with their own Kerberos realm? These users want to access not only resources in their local Kerberos realm, but also resources in the other realms as well, with a minimum of hassle. Kerberos cross-realm authentication can solve this problem.

In Kerberos, cross-realm is implemented by sharing an encryption key between two realms. The key that is shared is the Ticket Granting Service principal's key. A typical Ticket Granting Service principal for a single realm looks like:

```
krbtgt/WEDGIE.ORG@WEDGIE.ORG
```

Note that the instance is the same as the realm name. In cross-realm, two principals are created on each participating realm. For two realms, ONE.COM and TWO.COM, these principals would be:

```
krbtgt/TWO.COM@ONE.COM
krbtgt/ONE.COM@TWO.COM
```

These principals have to be created on both realms, and are known as remote Ticket Granting Server principals. The Kerberos trust can be one way or both ways; since there are two separate, shared keys involved, one realm can choose to trust the other realm's tickets, but not the other way around.

When a user who is in the ONE.COM realm wishes to communicate with a Kerberized service in TWO.COM, the client program first requests a ticket for the remote realm's Ticket Granting Server, the *krbtgt/TWO.COM@ONE.COM* principal above. Using that intermediate Ticket Granting Ticket, the client is then able to acquire a service ticket directly for the requested service in the TWO.COM realm. This is called *direct cross-realm trust*, and is the only type of cross-realm trust supported in the older Kerberos 4 protocol. In direct cross-realm trust, every two realms that wish to communicate must share a separate set of keys. Of course, this can get rather unwieldy as the number of shared keys grows exponentially with the increasing number of realms. This can be managed somewhat by building a *certification path* between several realms, a feature introduced with the Kerberos 5 protocol. A certification path defines realms that may be used as intermediaries when acquiring service tickets in foreign realms. Direct cross-realm requires every foreign realm be directly connected, through a shared key, to the local realm, creating a full mesh configuration between the realms. Certification paths allow multiple realms to use another realm as an intermediary, creating hub-and-spoke systems in which multiple realms share a key with a single intermediary realm.

Let's take an example. There are several universities collaborating on a project to produce workable cold fusion together with a fictitious government agency, the National Energy Research Directive (NERD). Obviously, these organizations want to utilize each other's resources, and researchers don't like to memorize numerous logins and passwords, so cross-realm Kerberos is proposed as a solution to the authentication needs of all the organizations involved. However, direct cross-realm between all of these organizations would require approximately n^2 different keys, where n is the number of participating Kerberos realms. This is a management nightmare, especially if, in this example, more universities are added to the project as time goes on. A diagram of these cross-realm relationships in a full mesh configuration is shown in Figure 8-1.

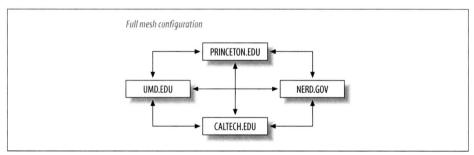

Figure 8-1. Full mesh cross-realm configuration

To solve this problem, each university decides to share a set of cross-realm keys with one organization, namely the NERD government agency. Then, if a set of Kerberos clients and servers wish to communicate between two different universities, NERD can be used as an intermediary realm.

The certification path must be encoded into each client and server's Kerberos configuration in each participating realm. Clients and servers use this information somewhat differently. Clients use the certification path to determine what KDCs to communicate with in order to reach one realm from another. Servers use the certification path to validate that incoming tickets presented for authentication have passed through a satisfactory path, and no untrusted intermediary realms were used to obtain the service ticket. This information is included in the capaths stanza of the */etc/krb5.conf* file. As an example, the above trust relationship would be represented in an MIT-style */etc/krb5.conf* file installed on hosts in the PRINCETON.EDU realm, as follows:

```
[capaths]
    PRINCETON.EDU = {
        CALTECH.EDU = NERD.GOV
        UMD.EDU = NERD.GOV
        NERD.GOV = .
    }

    CALTECH.EDU = {
        PRINCETON.EDU = NERD.GOV
    }
    UMD.EDU = {
        PRINCETON.EDU = NERD.GOV
    }
    NERD.GOV  = {
        PRINCETON.EDU = .
    }
```

The capaths stanza defines the trust relationships necessary to reach every connected Kerberos realm. Inside of the capaths stanza, a key-value pair exists for every participating realm, and the value is an array of more key-value pairs, defining a link in the certification chain.

Each innermost key-value pair defines two realms that are related as a link in a cross-realm trust. The key defines a destination realm in the realm certification path, and the value is either another realm, which is used as an intermediary, or a period (.) that indicates the a cross-realm key is directly shared between the realms defined by the inner key and the outer key.

Figure 8-2 depicts the cross-realm relationship described by the above *krb5.conf* capaths stanza, and shows the certification path that a cross-realm request would take between Princeton and Caltech. Note that since no cross-realm key is directly shared between Princeton and Caltech, the request is routed through the intermediary NERD.GOV realm.

However, this certification path method has its own downside: the distribution of a large amount of configuration information to all machines on all participating realms (not to mention the trouble involved in creating this configuration information in the first place). Therefore, Kerberos 5 also supports *hierarchical trust*.

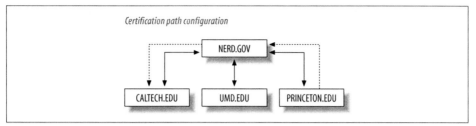

Figure 8-2. Sample cross-realm relationship; the dotted line shows the path a request from Princeton to Caltech would take

With hierarchical trust, all participating realms in the cross-realm trust are subdomains of a larger realm. For example, a company has a Kerberos realm named COMPANY.COM. The company has several offices with their own Kerberos realms, named NEWYORK.COMPANY.COM, PARIS.COMPANY.COM, etc. Each of these realms shares a key with the "parent" realm, COMPANY.COM.

Since NEWYORK.COMPANY.COM trusts the parent, COMPANY.COM (they share a key between them), then NEWYORK.COMPANY.COM implicitly trusts PARIS.COMPANY.COM as well, even though no explicit key is shared between the New York and Paris realms. This is simply a special case of the certification path described above; the common DNS suffix between the two Kerberos realms creates an implicit certification path between all subordinate realms and the parent realm.

Implementing Cross-Realm Relationships

Establishing a cross-realm trust between two Kerberos realms is rather easy. Microsoft's Active Directory will automatically create implicit trusts between member domains in a forest, so no manual configuration is needed. Those administering MIT- or Heimdal-based Kerberos realms will need to manually create the appropriate Ticket Granting Server principals to create the cross-realm trust, and if the trust is not a cross-realm or hierarchical trust, a certification path will need to be defined in each client's */etc/krb5.conf*, as described above.

Each of the two shared keys involved in the cross-realm trust can have a separate secret key associated with it. Currently, the only way to enter a shared key across two MIT or Heimdal Kerberos realms is to use a password, by using the same password for one of the cross-realm principals on both realms. Since these passwords will never have to be used by a human, and the security of the trust depends on the passwords, choose highly secure passwords of at least 16 characters in length that use a combination of printable characters, generated by a good, random password-generator. As an example, let's establish a two-way cross-realm relationship between SAMPLE.COM and EXAMPLE.COM, using MIT Kerberos. First, we must create two secure random passwords—one will be used for the *krbtgt/SAMPLE.COM@EXAMPLE.COM* principal and the other for the *krbtgt/EXAMPLE.COM@SAMPLE.COM* principal. Now we can log into each realm through kadmin and create the principals with the passwords:

```
host.sample.com% kadmin
Authenticating as principal jgarman/admin@SAMPLE.COM with password.
Enter password:
kadmin:  addprinc krbtgt/SAMPLE.COM@EXAMPLE.COM
WARNING: no policy specified for krbtgt/SAMPLE.COM@EXAMPLE.COM; defaulting to no policy
Enter password for principal "krbtgt/SAMPLE.COM@EXAMPLE.COM": abcd
Re-enter password for principal "krbtgt/SAMPLE.COM@EXAMPLE.COM": abcd
Principal "krbtgt/SAMPLE.COM@EXAMPLE.COM" created.
kadmin:  addprinc krbtgt/EXAMPLE.COM@SAMPLE.COM
WARNING: no policy specified for krbtgt/EXAMPLE.COM@SAMPLE.COM; defaulting to no policy
Enter password for principal "krbtgt/EXAMPLE.COM@SAMPLE.COM": defg
Re-enter password for principal "krbtgt/EXAMPLE.COM@SAMPLE.COM": defg
Principal "krbtgt/EXAMPLE.COM@SAMPLE.COM" created.

host.example.com% kadmin
Authenticating as principal jgarman/admin@EXAMPLE.COM with password.
Enter password:
kadmin:  addprinc krbtgt/SAMPLE.COM@EXAMPLE.COM
WARNING: no policy specified for krbtgt/SAMPLE.COM@EXAMPLE.COM; defaulting to no policy
Enter password for principal "krbtgt/SAMPLE.COM@EXAMPLE.COM": abcd
Re-enter password for principal "krbtgt/SAMPLE.COM@EXAMPLE.COM": abcd
Principal "krbtgt/SAMPLE.COM@EXAMPLE.COM" created.
kadmin:  addprinc krbtgt/EXAMPLE.COM@SAMPLE.COM
WARNING: no policy specified for krbtgt/EXAMPLE.COM@SAMPLE.COM; defaulting to no policy
Enter password for principal "krbtgt/EXAMPLE.COM@SAMPLE.COM": defg
Re-enter password for principal "krbtgt/EXAMPLE.COM@SAMPLE.COM": defg
Principal "krbtgt/EXAMPLE.COM@SAMPLE.COM" created.
```

Remember that Access Control Lists will need to be updated so that users from one realm will be able to access resources in the other.

Using Kerberos 4 Services with Kerberos 5

Those who have Kerberos 4 services that need to be integrated into a Kerberos 5 realm need to implement the Kerberos 5-to-4 ticket translator daemon. Both MIT and Heimdal include support for this protocol, the krb524 protocol. As discussed in Chapter 3, the only limit on where the krb524 daemon can run is that the daemon must have access to the service keys for the Kerberos 4–based services for which it translates tickets.

The MIT Kerberos 5 distribution includes a separate krb524 daemon, krb524d. There are two different modes of operation that krb524d supports: master and keytab. The master mode is meant to be run on a KDC in the Kerberos realm, and reads the necessary service keys directly from the Kerberos database. If it is not possible to run the krb524d directly on the KDC, then the second mode of operation can be used: keytab. Keytab mode requires that a Kerberos keytab be installed on the machine running krb524d that includes the service keys for all of the Kerberos 4 services in the realm.

The command-line arguments to krb524d are summarized below:

```
# krb524d
Usage: krb524d [-k[eytab]] [-m[aster] [-r realm]] [-nofork]
```

Either the -k or the -m options are required. The -m option enables the master mode, as described above, where krb524d reads the necessary service keys directly from the Kerberos database on the local disk. The -k option requires an argument, namely, the keytab where the keys are stored for the Kerberos 4 services located in the Kerberos 5 realm.

As an example, let's create a service principal for a popular Kerberos 4–based service, the AFS network filesystem. We first create a service principal for AFS, ensuring that the only encryption type associated with the new principal is single DES. With MIT Kerberos, the kadmin commands to create this principal would be similar to the following:

```
> kadmin
Authenticating as principal jgarman/admin@UNIX.SAMPLE.COM with password.
Enter password:
kadmin:  addprinc -randkey -e des-cbc-crc:v4 afs/unix.sample.com@UNIX.SAMPLE.COM
WARNING: no policy specified for afs/unix.sample.com@UNIX.SAMPLE.COM; defaulting to
no policy
Principal "afs/unix.sample.com@UNIX.SAMPLE.COM" created.
```

After the principal has been created, the keytab can be extracted to a file, which can be placed on the machine running the krb524d daemon.

```
kadmin:  ktadd -k /tmp/afs.keytab -e des-cbc-crc:v4 afs/unix.sample.com@UNIX.SAMPLE.COM
Entry for principal afs/unix.sample.com@UNIX.SAMPLE.COM with kvno 3, encryption type
DES cbc mode with CRC-32 added to keytab WRFILE:/tmp/afs.keytab.
```

Heimdal Kerberos also includes the Kerberos 5-to-4 ticket translator daemon, but it is integrated with the rest of the KDC and does not require running a separate daemon.

Windows Issues

While the Windows implementation of Kerberos is compatible with the specifications in RFC 1510, the Microsoft implementation of Kerberos varies significantly enough from the MIT and Heimdal implementations to warrant its own explanation. In order to provide the additional functionality required for the Windows Active Directory, as well as backwards compatibility with older Windows NT workstations, the Windows Kerberos environment differs in several important areas from its Unix counterpart.

Encryption Algorithm Support

The primary encryption type used in Windows is based on the RC4 stream cipher, with an MD5-HMAC algorithm used for the checksum field. This encryption type is referred to as RC4-HMAC, and has a variable key length to support both weaker, "export" quality key lengths, as well as stronger 128-bit key lengths.

The reasoning behind this decision by Microsoft is two-fold: first, for compatibility with older Windows NT domains; and second, for political reasons. During the initial design of Windows 2000, neither DES nor triple DES were approved for export from the United States. Microsoft wanted to encourage deployment of Windows 2000; therefore, the RC4-HMAC cipher was chosen as the default Kerberos encryption type since it is the same cipher used to generate the older NT4 password hashes. This way, when an older NT4 domain is migrated to an Active Directory domain, the users' passwords continue to work without manual intervention.

Microsoft did add DES support to Windows 2000 before its release, and users created in a Windows Active Directory have both RC4 and DES encryption keys associated with their account. However, there are two situations when a DES key is not available for an account in the Active Directory. The first situation is the one discussed above, in which an NT4 domain is converted into a Windows Active Directory domain. Since the hashing algorithm only works one way, there is no way for Windows to convert the existing users' RC4 encryption keys into DES keys. The second special-case situation is when a new Windows 2000 domain is created. As part of the domain creation procedure, an Administrator account is created as the new Domain Administrator. This account only has an RC4 key when it is initially created.

In order to add DES keys to users' accounts in both of the above situations, simply change the user's password. When a user's password is changed, the KDC will generate both RC4 and DES encryption keys for that user.

Note that even without the "Use DES encryption types for this account" checkbox checked for a user, the DES keys do exist in the Active Directory database (subject to the limitations of the previous two scenarios), but are not used by the KDC when responding to ticket requests unless the checkbox is activated.

A better solution to this is for other Kerberos implementations to adopt the RC4-HMAC encryption type into their code as well. Heimdal has recently added this support to its distribution, and MIT has incorporated full RC4-HMAC support for its Kerberos 5 1.3 release. With RC4 encryption–type support, interoperability between Unix and Windows Kerberos realms can occur without downgrading the encryption keys used to single DES.

Also note that Windows does not support salts other than the standard Kerberos 5 salt. If you have a Unix KDC that has encryption keys with other salts (such as Kerberos 4 salt or AFS salt) for interoperability with older clients, then you may have issues when attempting to interoperate with Windows. Careful reordering of the encryption types in the configuration file of the Unix KDC can help alleviate this problem, but it is recommended to use only Kerberos 5 salt and encryption types when interoperating with Windows.

Cached Login Credentials

Many Windows machines are mobile, and do not have a fixed network connection. For example, laptops can spend most of their time disconnected from a network; yet, end users expect the ability to log into their own computers, even when no network connection is present. Traditionally, systems that require successful Kerberos authentication for local access, as Active Directory does, require a stable network connection to operate, since communication with the KDC is required to authorize logon. Microsoft provides for disconnected login to domain accounts through a cached credentials feature.

When a user logs into a Windows 2000, XP, or 2003 host, the Local Security Authority (LSA) derives a password verifier and saves this verifier into the local machine's registry. Later, if the user is disconnected from the network or the domain controller is otherwise unavailable, the local system will authorize access if the username and password match the saved credentials stored on the local disk.

The cached credentials are stored in the local machine's registry inside of the HKEY_LOCAL_MACHINE\Security\Cache key, which contains sub-keys NL$1 to NL$10. The last 10 users' login username and password verifier are stored as the values of each of these keys.

Notice that I have been referring to a *password verifier*, and not password or password hash. The password verifier is a hash of the password hash, so the password verifier cannot be used to derive either the original password or a password hash. The verifier therefore contains just enough data that it is able for the local login process to take in a password, run a hashing algorithm over it twice, and compare to the verifier.

 For security reasons, Windows restricts access to this registry key to the local SYSTEM account. To view these keys as Administrator, launch the regedt32 application, navigate to HKEY_LOCAL_MACHINE\Security, and select Security → Permissions. Set the checkbox for read permission for the Administrators group.

Unfortunately, certain situations cause Windows to provide no indication to the end user when the system authenticates the user through a cached credential verifier. When a user is verified against a password verifier located in the cache, the login process cannot acquire any initial tickets for the user. While Windows will notice when a Windows domain controller becomes available again and transparently acquire tickets, cached login credentials can be particularly problematic when Windows is set up to authenticate against a non-Microsoft KDC, either directly or through a cross-realm trust with a Windows domain.

Disabling the cached credentials feature

The drawback, of course, to disabling the cached credentials feature is that if the machine loses its network connection and can no longer reach the domain controller, any local login requests to that domain will fail. The number of cached logins can be forced to zero by using a Domain Security Policy. Set "Number of previous logins to cache (in case domain controller is not available)," which can be found under Computer Configuration → Security Settings → Local Policies → Security Options, to zero. This change affects the CachedLogonsCount registry key on each member machine in the domain. This registry value can be found inside the registry key HKLM\SOFTWARE\Microsoft\Windows NT\CurrentVersion\WinLogon.

Windows Active Directory Authorization Field

The initial announcement by Microsoft that Windows 2000 would use Kerberos as its authentication system has produced mixed feelings in the security community. On one hand, observers lauded Microsoft for choosing a standardized Internet protocol for its security needs, opening the door for cross-platform authentication between Windows and other operating systems. However, concerned readers posted messages on discussion sites such as Slashdot implying that Microsoft was planning to "embrace and extend" the standard Kerberos protocol for their own gain.

It certainly didn't help when Microsoft announced that Windows 2000 domain controllers would add a proprietary Privilege Access Certificate (PAC) to tickets returned by the KDC, and that a reimplementation of the Windows domain controller functionality would have to create valid PAC structures. Adding fuel to the fire, Microsoft has only released the full specifications to the PAC as a Windows executable file, requiring readers to accept a restrictive license that grants the right to review the specification only for security reasons, and specifically forbids the creation of software that implements the specification as described in the document. Readers who wish to download the full specification from Microsoft (and permanently give up their rights to develop Kerberos software relating to the information contained therein) can do so at *http://www.microsoft.com/Downloads/details.aspx?displaylang=en&FamilyID=BF61D972-5086-49FB-A79C-53A5FD27A092*.

In 2002, Microsoft released a summary of the Windows 2000 PAC specification, which is available at *http://msdn.microsoft.com/library/default.asp?url=/library/en-us/dnkerb/html/MSDN_PAC.asp*, and also submitted an Internet Draft to the IETF, currently available at *http://www.ietf.org/internet-drafts/draft-brezak-win2k-krb-authz-01.txt*.

The PAC is generated by the KDC during the Authentication Server exchange and contains authorization data about the client, including the SID (a unique numeric identifier for users and groups) associated with the user who requested the ticket and any groups that the user is a member of. This data is encrypted to ensure integrity and authenticity, so Windows services can trust the information to make authorization decisions based on the contents of service tickets presented for validation. This authorization data is also available by performing LDAP queries against the Active Directory servers, but is included here as an optimization, to reduce the number of round-trips between clients and the Domain Controllers. However, most Windows-based services will not perform this extra step if the authorization field is missing from tickets presented by clients, refusing access to those clients.

In general, non-Microsoft Kerberos clients will ignore the PAC field included with tickets issued by a Microsoft KDC. There is, however, one case where some interoperability problems may arise: if a user is a member of a large number of groups, then the PAC might grow large enough that the KDC reply does not fit in a single UDP packet. If this happens, the Windows KDC asks the client to retry the request using TCP. Earlier versions of MIT Kerberos 5 (before 1.3) and some other Kerberos implementations cannot retry with TCP, and will fail.

Windows and Unix Interoperability

In the previous chapters, we focused mostly on the design and implementation of a homogenous Kerberos network. However, the true allure of moving to a Kerberos-based authentication scheme network-wide is to enable centralized authentication, and more importantly, single-sign-on across all platforms. Cross-platform single-sign-on is considered to be a panacea of network authentication, and even with Kerberos, can be very difficult to achieve because of the wide variation between Kerberos implementations. The end objective is for users to have only one set of credentials, a username/password pair that will enable them to access all network resources regardless of the platforms these services may reside on.

These interoperability scenarios are also addressed in a Microsoft document, the Step-by-Step Guide to Kerberos 5 Interoperability, available at *http://www.microsoft.com/windows2000/techinfo/planning/security/kerbsteps.asp*.

Using a Windows Domain Controller as a KDC for Unix Clients

Using a Windows domain controller as a KDC for non-Microsoft platforms is trivial to set up; as long as the users have DES keys enabled in Active Directory, they will be able to kinit to the Windows domain controller without a problem. The only difference is in administration; you'll be using MMC to create and modify Kerberos users in this case. Since Microsoft does not implement a kadmin interface similar to MIT or Heimdal's, creating keytabs for Unix services when using a Windows domain controller is a bit different than the process of generating keytabs from Unix KDCs.

Creating Unix keytabs from a Windows domain controller

When using a Windows domain controller as the KDC for a mixed platform Kerberos environment, a method is required to extract keys from the Windows KDC into keytab entries for Unix hosts and services. The kadmin programs that are included with the MIT and Heimdal Kerberos distributions do not work with

Windows domain controllers since Microsoft uses its own administration protocol for communication with the KDC. Instead, Microsoft includes a program to create a keytab file with a specified password (run through the Kerberos 5 string2key function to create the appropriate DES key).

This program, ktpass, is not installed by default. If your domain controller does not have a ktpass program installed, it can be found in the *support/tool* subdirectory of the Windows 2000 Server installation CD.

First, a user account for the service must be created in the Active Directory. Since Active Directory does not handle Kerberos-style username and instance principal formats, this username cannot be the desired principal name (as Windows does not allow the "/" character in usernames, along with most other special characters). Instead, this name can be any valid Windows username, and will be mapped to the principal name later. It is recommended that these accounts be placed in a separate OU to distinguish them from other user accounts in the domain.

For example, for the host principal *host/unix.wedgie.org@W2K.WEDGIE.ORG*, an AD account named *unixhost* is created in the Unix services Organizational Unit. Figure 8-3 shows the new user wizard for this principal.

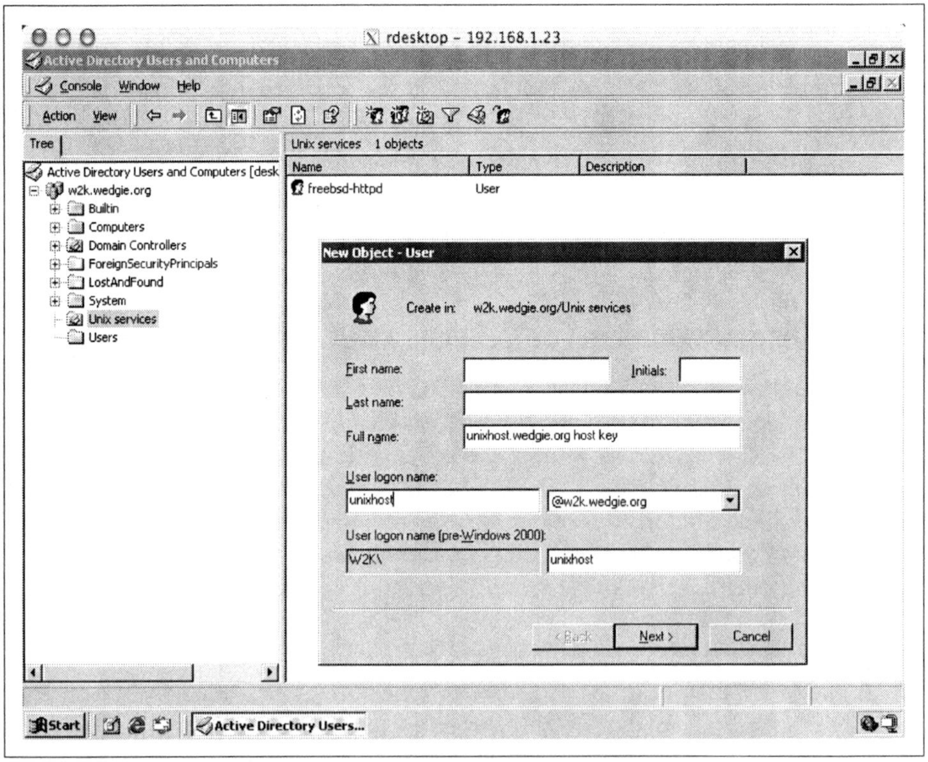

Figure 8-3. Creating a new user for a Unix service principal in Active Directory

Ensure that the password can never change on this user account by selecting the "Password never expires" and "User cannot change password" options on the next screen of the wizard.

After the user account for the Unix service has been created, the ktpass program will handle the tasks of producing the appropriate mapping between username and principal name in the Active Directory database, setting the user to accept DES encryption types, and creating a keytab file that can be imported into the Unix host's keytab. The ktpass program accepts the /? argument to get help on its parameters, and the most commonly used parameters are listed below:

Table 8-1. Common ktpass parameters

Parameter	Arguments	Description
-out	Filename of keytab	Designates the file the new keytab will be written to.
-princ	Kerberos principal name	Designates the principal name of the service that this keytab is for.
-pass	Password or "*" to prompt for password	The password associated with the username must be given, either as an argument to ktpass, or, if the argument to the pass parameter is "*", ktpass will prompt for the password on the console. This password must match the password for the username in AD; otherwise, ktpass will write out a keytab with the incorrect encryption key.
-mapuse	Username in AD	Designates that the username provided as an argument to this parameter is to be mapped to the Kerberos principal designated by the princ argument.

A keytab for the example host principal can be generated with ktpass through the following command:

```
D:\Documents and Settings\Administrator.DESKTOP.000>ktpass -out unixhost.keytab -princ
host/unix.wedgie.org@W2K.WEDGIE.ORG -pass * -mapuser unixhost
Successfully mapped host/unix.wedgie.org to unixhost.
Type the password for host/unix.wedgie.org:
Key created.
Output keytab to unixhost.keytab:

Keytab version: 0x502
keysize 59 host/unix.wedgie.org@W2K.WEDGIE.ORG ptype 1 (KRB5_NT_PRINCIPAL) vno 1
etype 0x1 (DES-CBC-CRC) keylength 8 (0x973ec2ab52f48343)
Account has been set for DES-only encryption.
```

After generating a keytab entry with ktpass, it must be securely copied over to the Unix host and installed in the appropriate keytab file. This can be done either by copying the keytab onto a floppy and physically moving the file to the Unix host, or through another encrypted channel, such as Secure Shell.

Using a Non-Microsoft KDC for Windows Clients

This section describes the two methods by which a Windows network can authenticate against a non-Microsoft KDC. The first option, cross-realm trust between a Windows domain and a non-Microsoft KDC, is best used when there's an extensive network of Windows machines that requires centralized administration and already has a Windows domain established. The second option is best applied to networks that have few Windows machines that are not already members of a Windows domain. These scenarios are useful when a large, non-Microsoft Kerberos realm has been installed, and moving the users to a new Active Directory domain would be difficult.

Each user who will access the Windows box or domain must still be created either in the Active Directory (for the cross-realm trust option) or on the local Windows machine (for the standalone Windows machine option). This is done so that a SID is created for authorization purposes for users authenticated through the non-Microsoft Kerberos realm. Mappings will be set up in either case to associate principals in the Kerberos database with these Windows usernames. Windows will still require these users in the AD database or local security database to have valid passwords, and these passwords must be secure, as they can be used to bypass the non-Microsoft Kerberos realm and login directly to the Windows machine.

The interoperability presented here only functions for Windows services that use Kerberos authentication. There are several applications, notably Microsoft Exchange (2000 and below), that still use the older NTLM-style authentication that Windows provides. Since these applications do not use the Microsoft Kerberos implementation for authentication, there's no way to make them authenticate against a non-Microsoft source. The application has to be rewritten to use Kerberos authentication. In addition, as discussed earlier in the section on the PAC, some Windows services will not accept tickets that do not have a PAC generated by a Windows domain controller. Also, older Microsoft operating systems, released before Windows 2000, XP, and 2003, cannot participate in Kerberos realms, even if they are part of a Windows domain, as those older operating systems do not include Kerberos support. If compatibility with older Windows operating systems or applications that utilize NTLM authentication is required, the passwords in the Windows domain or local security database must be synchronized with the Kerberos realm through external means.

Cross-realm trust

If there is already an existing Windows domain, then a cross-realm trust between that domain and the Unix-based Kerberos realm is the best option for authenticating users against a non-Microsoft KDC. A cross-realm trust is established between the Windows domain and the non-Microsoft Kerberos realm, so that users who provide their Kerberos credentials are authorized for access to resources inside of the Windows domain. In addition, since the Windows domain still exists, the administration advantages, such as centralized administration, login scripts, and more that come with establishing a Windows domain still function.

Each Windows machine in the Windows domain participating in the cross-realm trust must have the appropriate values inserted into its registry. The ksetup tool (see the sidebar "The Microsoft ksetup Tool") is a command-line utility that inserts the appropriate entries into the registry. Each KDC for the non-Windows domain must be specified with the ksetup tool:

```
D:\>ksetup /addkdc WEDGIE.ORG freebsd.wedgie.org
```

If your realm has more than one KDC, the command can be repeated with each KDC's DNS name. Define your non-Windows KDCs through ksetup on your domain controller as well. Each machine needs to be rebooted for the registry entries to take effect.

The Microsoft ksetup Tool

The ksetup utility is a program that establishes a few entries in the Windows registry describing the non-Windows Kerberos realm and KDCs. The registry entries that ksetup modifies can be found in *HKLM\SYSTEM\CurrentControlSet\Control\Lsa\ Kerberos\Domains*, which can be compared to the */etc/krb5.conf* file on an MIT or Heimdal Kerberos client host. Whenever a Windows machine participates in a non-Microsoft Kerberos realm, either through cross-realm trust with a Windows domain, or directly with the non-Microsoft KDCs, ksetup is used to create the appropriate configuration entries in the registry. Unfortunately, ksetup is not installed by default with Windows, but you can find a copy in the *support\tool* subdirectory of the Windows 2000 Server installation CD.

Note that whenever any Kerberos settings are changed, either directly through the registry entry above or through the ksetup tool, the machine will need to be rebooted for the changes to take effect.

The ksetup tool recognizes the following flags:

/SetDomain
> This flag designates the non-Microsoft Kerberos realm that the Windows machine will be communicating with.

/MapUser
> This flag creates a user mapping between usernames in the local Windows user database and principal names in the Kerberos realm. MapUser takes two parameters: the first parameter is a Kerberos principal name, and the second parameter is the local username on the Windows host that the principal will be authorized as. An asterisk can be used in either field to match all possible principal names and usernames, respectively. For example /MapUser * * will map all Kerberos principals with the corresponding username on the Windows machine or domain.

/AddKdc
> This flag creates a mapping between Kerberos realm names and a KDC that serves the realm. This flag can be specified multiple times in different ksetup commands in order to select multiple KDCs per realm.

/AddKpasswd
> This flag creates a mapping between a Kerberos realm and the master KDC that is used to change user passwords in the realm.

/SetMachPassword
> This flag sets the password on the host key for the Windows machine. The required argument to this flag is the password associated with the Windows machine's host principal in the Unix KDC's database.

The next step is to establish the cross-realm trust between the Windows domain and the non-Microsoft Kerberos realm. A random password must be chosen for the cross-realm Ticket Granting Server key, and this password will have to be provided to kadmin on the Unix side, and Active Directory on the Windows side. On a Unix host, use kadmin to generate the cross-realm krbtgt keys.

For an example Windows domain of W2K.WEDGIE.ORG, and a Kerberos realm of WEDGIE.ORG, the *krbtgt/W2K.WEDGIE.ORG@WEDGIE.ORG* principal will have to be added to the WEDGIE.ORG realm to provide the one-way trust required for Windows users logging into the WEDGIE.ORG realm to gain access to Windows resources in the W2K domain. If you wish to create a two-way trust, then the principal for the opposite direction, *krbtgt/WEDGIE.ORG@W2K.WEDGIE.ORG*, will also have to be created. These principals can have different passwords associated with them. We'll create both principals here:

```
% kadmin
Authenticating as principal jgarman/admin@WEDGIE.ORG with password.
Enter password:
kadmin:  addprinc -e des:normal krbtgt/W2K.WEDGIE.ORG@WEDGIE.ORG
WARNING: no policy specified for krbtgt/W2K.WEDGIE.ORG@WEDGIE.ORG; defaulting to no
policy
Enter password for principal "krbtgt/W2K.WEDGIE.ORG@WEDGIE.ORG":
Re-enter password for principal "krbtgt/W2K.WEDGIE.ORG@WEDGIE.ORG":
Principal "krbtgt/W2K.WEDGIE.ORG@WEDGIE.ORG" created.
kadmin:  addprinc -e des:normal krbtgt/WEDGIE.ORG@W2K.WEDGIE.ORG
WARNING: no policy specified for krbtgt/WEDGIE.ORG@W2K.WEDGIE.ORG; defaulting to no
policy
Enter password for principal " krbtgt/WEDGIE.ORG@W2K.WEDGIE.ORG ":
Re-enter password for principal " krbtgt/WEDGIE.ORG@W2K.WEDGIE.ORG ":
Principal " krbtgt/WEDGIE.ORG@W2K.WEDGIE.ORG " created.
```

Now the trust has to be established on the Windows side. Log into an account with Domain Administrator privileges and open Active Directory Domains and Trusts. Right-click on the Windows domain in the left-hand tree view, and select Properties. Select the Trusts tab in the Properties dialog and click Add in "Domains trusted by this domain group" at the top. Your screen should look similar to Figure 8-4.

In our example, the Windows domain is W2K.WEDGIE.ORG and the Unix-based Kerberos realm is WEDGIE.ORG. When setting the password under the "Domains trusted by this domain" on the Active Directory server, use the password associated with the *krbtgt/W2K.WEDGIE.ORG@WEDGIE.ORG* principal created above. Similarly, when setting the password under the "Domains that trust this domain," you must use the password associated with the *krbtgt/WEDGIE.ORG@W2K.WEDGIE.ORG* principal.

Enter the appropriate realm and password in the dialog box, and click OK. An error dialog, pictured in Figure 8-5, will appear.

Click OK on this error dialog, and the realm will now appear in the top listbox. This process establishes the one-way trust from the non-Microsoft Kerberos realm to the

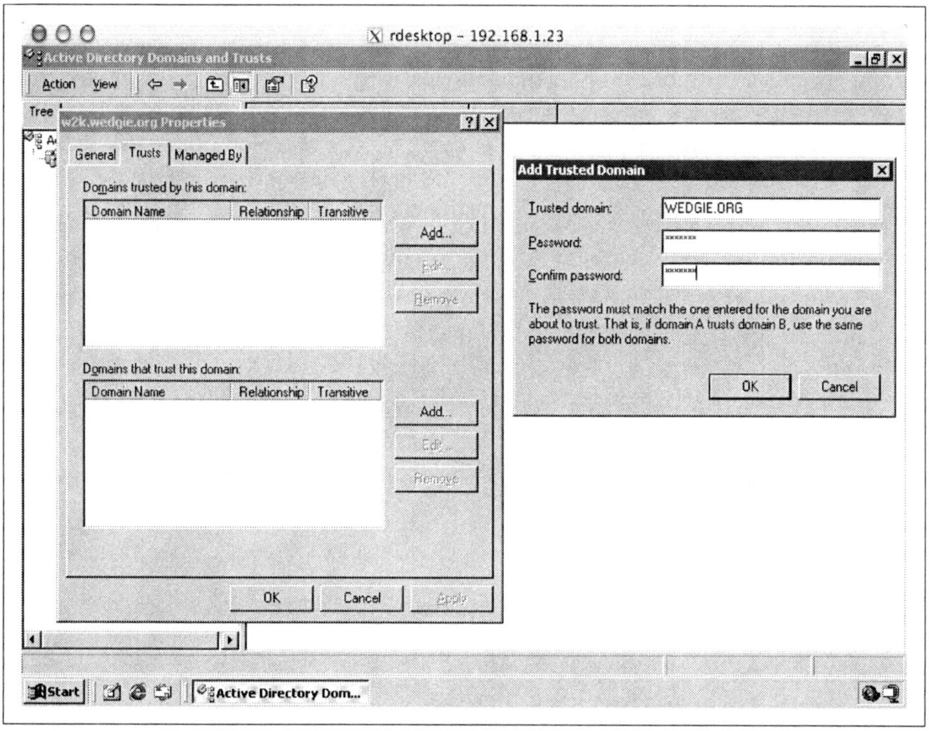

Figure 8-4. Establishing cross-realm trusts between Active Directory and a non-Microsoft Kerberos realm

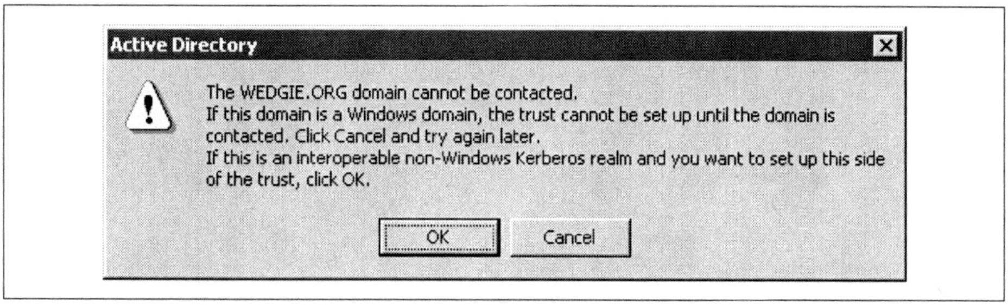

Figure 8-5. Warning message generated when establishing a cross-realm trust between Active Directory and a non-Microsoft Kerberos realm

Windows domain. If you want the trust to operate both ways, repeat the process by clicking the Add button in the Domains that trust this domain group, and ensure that both krbtgt principals were created in kadmin earlier.

Also, this trust can be marked as transitive; that is, child domain members can also authenticate against the non-Microsoft Kerberos realm.

```
D:\>netdom trust W2K.WEDGIE.ORG /Domain:WEDGIE.ORG /Transitive:yes
```

Finally, username mappings must be established between Kerberos principals in the non-Microsoft KDC and usernames that exist in the Windows Active Directory. This mapping forms an authorization relationship between a Kerberos principal in the non-Microsoft Kerberos realm and a user identity in the Microsoft Active Directory. The process is performed through the Active Directory Users and Computers tool. The following procedure is used to map a Kerberos principal to a Windows username:

1. Open the Active Directory Users and Computers tool, which is located under the Administrative Tools folder of Programs in the Start Menu.

2. Ensure that the Advanced Features menu item is checked in the View menu. This step will enable the Name Mappings contextual menu item that we'll use in a bit.

3. Locate the Windows account to which the Kerberos principal should be authorized. Right-click on the username and select Name Mappings.

4. Select the Kerberos Names mapping tab, and you should see the screen pictured in Figure 8-6.

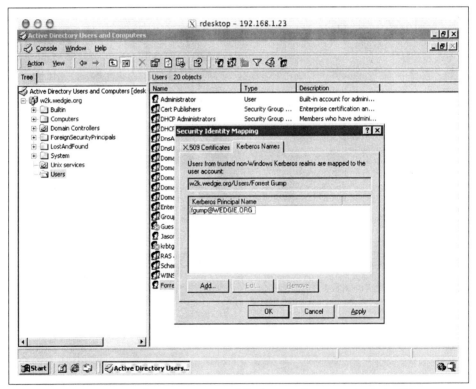

Figure 8-6. Mapping principals in a non-Microsoft Kerberos realm to users in Active Directory

5. Click Add and specify the name of the Kerberos principal in the non-Microsoft Kerberos realm. Click OK.

Now, when the user logs in to Windows with the username and password associated with the Kerberos principal, and the non-Microsoft Kerberos realm showing in the "Log on to" drop-down box, the user is authorized as the selected Windows username in the Active Directory.

Standalone Windows machine

It is also possible to set up standalone Windows clients that are not part of a Windows domain to authenticate directly against a Unix-based KDC. For authorization purposes, user entries will still have to be created, only they'll be created in the local user database in this case, since there is no Windows domain involved. Then information describing the Kerberos realm and KDCs will be input into a Microsoft tool named ksetup, and finally, user mapping will be established between Kerberos principals and the local usernames on the Windows machine. The command-line parameters for ksetup are covered in the sidebar, "The Microsoft ksetup Tool."

The first task when adding a standalone Windows machine to a Kerberos realm is to create a host key for the Windows machine on the KDC. The encryption type of this key must be single DES. In addition, since the key is set on the Windows host through a password specified on the command line, the administrator must generate a random password manually for this purpose.

For example, the following commands create a principal for the Windows host *desktop.w2k.wedgie.org*, using an MIT KDC:

```
> kadmin
Authenticating as principal jgarman/admin@WEDGIE.ORG with password.
Enter password:
kadmin:  addprinc -e des:normal host/desktop.w2k.wedgie.org@WEDGIE.ORG
WARNING: no policy specified for host/desktop.w2k.wedgie.org@WEDGIE.ORG; defaulting
to no policy
Enter password for principal "host/desktop.w2k.wedgie.org@WEDGIE.ORG":
Re-enter password for principal "host/desktop.w2k.wedgie.org@WEDGIE.ORG":
Principal "host/desktop.w2k.wedgie.org@WEDGIE.ORG" created.
```

Now the information about the non-Windows Kerberos realm must be set up on the Windows host; this is accomplished through the ksetup utility. While Windows systems have no problems using DNS to find the appropriate Domain Controllers for Active Directory domains, they cannot use DNS to find the addresses of the KDCs for non-Windows Kerberos realms.

For our example, the following commands will have to be entered on the Windows host to create the appropriate configuration:

```
D:\>ksetup /setdomain WEDGIE.ORG
D:\>ksetup /addkdc WEDGIE.ORG freebsd.wedgie.org
D:\>ksetup /addkdc WEDGIE.ORG slave.wedgie.org
D:\>ksetup /addkpasswd WEDGIE.ORG freebsd.wedgie.org
D:\>ksetup /setmachpassword host principal's password
```

These commands create the configuration entries in the Windows host's registry for the WEDGIE.ORG Kerberos realm. The registry entries function similarly to the *krb5.ini* file used by MIT Kerberos to define the KDC information for Kerberos realms. In addition, the machine password set here must correspond to the host principal password set earlier in kadmin.

Next, mappings must be established between Kerberos principal names and local user names on the Windows host. These mappings are used for authorization purposes during the login process. The mappings are created with the ksetup tool's `MapUser` command-line argument.

The `ksetup` command can map a particular Kerberos principal to a given Windows username by explicitly specifying their identities in the mapuser command:

```
D:\>ksetup /mapuser fgump@WEDGIE.ORG guest
```

This command maps the Kerberos principal *fgump@WEDGIE.ORG* to the Windows username guest. As you can see, the principal name and Windows username do not have to match. A shortcut is available to map all Kerberos principals in a realm to the same-named counterpart in the Windows user database. This can be specified by using an asterisk for both parameters of the `MapUser` argument. For example:

```
D:\>ksetup /mapuser * *
```

If there is a Kerberos principal with a user component of *fgump*, and a Windows user named *fgump*, the mapping will authorize the user to login to the *fgump* Windows account via his Kerberos credentials in the non-Microsoft Kerberos realm.

## CHAPTER 9

Case Study

In the previous eight chapters, we examined the technical details behind the Kerberos system, and how to implement Kerberos in your network. Now, in this chapter, we will take a step back and examine a hypothetical organization that wants to implement a network-wide single-sign-on solution. This organization has chosen to use Kerberos. We describe the decision process as the necessary Kerberos realms are created and implemented. The example includes many of the decision processes that apply to organizations implementing Kerberos in their own networks.

The Organization

The fictitious organization that we'll use for our example is the Sample Internet Service Provider, a prominent provider of local dial-up, T1, and DSL service in the Anytown area. The Sample ISP has an internal network with two major divisions in its IT organization. One division of the IT organization provides end user support and services to the Windows desktops and servers. This department administers the company email server, which runs Microsoft Exchange, and has a Windows 2000 Active Directory system already in place to handle user logins on the Windows network.

The second IT department administers the backend Unix systems, most notably a large bank of web-hosting machines running Linux and Apache. In addition, the Sample ISP has a small testing and staging laboratory where new software is tested before deployment. The Unix systems currently do not have a centralized authentication system in place; there is a mishmash of /etc/passwd files, htpasswd files, and password hashes stored in a MySQL database that handle the current authentication needs.

The current setup has some serious problems from a manageability standpoint. Adding or removing users on the Unix machines is a tedious process that involves logging into each machine separately and adding or removing an entry from the local machine's /etc/passwd file. In addition, the lack of synchronization between the Unix machines means that users have separate passwords for each machine they have access to. As a result, the Sample ISP has many stale *passwd* files on its machines, some containing entries for users who should no longer have access.

To solve the authentication problems, an infrastructure should be established that centralizes the administration of the user authentication information. In addition to centralizing the authentication information for the Unix systems, management has decided to establish a cross-platform single-sign-on system so that staff can login once via their desktop Windows systems and then be able to transparently authenticate to any other system, whether Windows- or Unix-based. Of course, Kerberos is chosen to provide this capability. More specifically, Kerberos v5, as it is the latest revision of the Kerberos protocol and provides compatibility with the existing Windows 2000 Active Directory setup.

Right now, the only applications that the Sample ISP is planning to kerberize are remote login to the Unix machines as well as some X-Windows applications that the support and network operations staff run on a regular basis.

Planning

The first step is a planning stage. Here we evaluate the current setup and the requirements that the new Kerberos realms need to fulfill, and balance those against the cost constraints involved with the project. During this planning stage, we will sketch out the new Kerberos realm structure, define what set of users each Kerberos realm will contain, and finally, prepare the necessary systems to install the Kerberos KDC software.

Planning the Kerberos Realms

The first decision to make when implementing Kerberos is whether there will be multiple Kerberos realms, and if so, what their relationship to each other will be. We've decided to split the organization into three realms to enforce the separation between the three functions of the ISP, namely, the production/business operations, the Unix servers involved in the customer support and hosting functions, and the lab, which is isolated from everything else.

In this case, one realm is already established: the Windows Active Directory domain. This domain was established as SAMPLE.COM, which is also the ISP's DNS domain name. There are two more realms that we will establish as part of this example, named UNIX.SAMPLE.COM and LABS.SAMPLE.COM. We will create them as subdomains of the existing SAMPLE.COM realm to make the cross-realm relationships easier—the hierarchical realm structure creates an implicit certification path for cross-realm authentication, as we saw in Chapter 8.

With the realm names out of the way, we need to establish trust relationships between the realms, if any. Remember that a trust relationship between realms does not automatically provide access to resources in one realm from the trusted realm.

However, with that limitation in mind, it is still important to create a layered approach to security, and we want to restrict the trust relationships of the Kerberos realms as much as possible. While this does force users who wish to use resources in both realms to login to both realms, it enforces the administrative and security separation between the Kerberos realms.

Considering the above, we'll separate the LABS.SAMPLE.COM realm from the production SAMPLE.COM and UNIX.SAMPLE.COM realms, to enforce the separation of the testing environment in the labs realm from the production realms. A two-way cross-realm trust is established between the two production realms, SAMPLE.COM and UNIX.SAMPLE.COM, in order to enable sharing of resources between the two realms with one set of credentials. Figure 9-1 depicts the Kerberos realms that are involved, and the trust relationships between them.

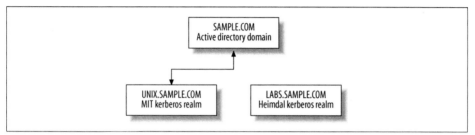

Figure 9-1. Sample ISP's Kerberos realm layout

Existing Network Layout

With the conceptual model in mind, let's go a little deeper and examine the hosts that are members of each Kerberos realm. Since this is an example, we'll keep it simple and limit the number of machines to make things easy to follow. Figure 9-2 shows the hosts involved in our sample network, their IP addresses, and what Kerberos realm each host belongs to.

Our existing network has been assigned the 192.168.0.0/16 network block, and is divided into several subnets to separate out the production network, customer hosting network, and lab networks. In the production network, 192.168.1.0/24, there is a Microsoft Active Directory server for the SAMPLE.COM domain that also serves as the Exchange server, known as *exchange.sample.com*. A Windows desktop machine is a member of the SAMPLE.COM domain, with a DNS name of *desktop.sample.com*. At the conclusion of this example, it should be possible for technical support personnel to login to the Windows desktop machine and transparently access their accounts on the Unix servers in the *hosting.sample.com* domain.

Also notable in the production network are several Unix hosts that will be part of the UNIX.SAMPLE.COM realm. The host *dns.sample.com* handles DNS for the Sample ISP, as well as providing a stratum-2 NTP service for the rest of the Sample ISP network. We'll use it as our time-synchronization source for Kerberos.

Next, the customer web-hosting subnet at 192.168.2.0/24 contains several Unix-based web servers that will be members of the new UNIX.SAMPLE.COM Kerberos realm. These servers all have DNS suffixes of *hosting.sample.com*, indicating that they are part of the customer subnet.

Note that there are Unix servers scattered about both the customer subnet and production subnet. While these Unix servers are all part of the UNIX.SAMPLE.COM Kerberos realm, they have differing DNS suffixes, and as such, some special care needs to be taken when creating our *krb5.conf* file. Namely, the domain_realm stanza will need to have explicit entries to map these hostnames to the correct Kerberos realm. This problem could have been avoided by changing the hostnames of the systems in the UNIX.SAMPLE.COM realm to have a DNS domain suffix of *unix.sample.com*, but there could be instances where this is not practical, as other software may depend on the existence of the current hostname.

Finally, the lab subnet at 192.168.3.0/24 contains the separate lab machines used for testing. This network is kept separate from the other two in order to prevent any experimental applications running on the network from interfering with the production systems located on the other two networks.

Kerberos KDC Planning

With the Kerberos realms mapped out, now we can begin planning the implementation details for each of our new realms. Figure 9-2 shows some planning activity. In that figure, there are two KDCs (unixkdc1 and unixkdc2) for the UNIX.SAMPLE.COM realm, and they are located in the production subnet. A conscious decision was made to replicate the data located in this important realm onto two machines, to ensure high availability. In addition, because of the sensitive nature of the data located on these servers, they are separated from the customer hosting network, presumably behind a restrictive firewall that prevents attackers from gaining access to the KDCs from the hosting network, in the case one of the customer hosting machines is compromised.

Similar reasoning is used for the LABS.SAMPLE.COM Kerberos KDC placement. Only one KDC is deemed necessary for the labs realm, as it is used for experimental purposes and not for production. The KDC is placed inside the lab network to further isolate the lab environment from the rest of the network.

Next, the hardware and operating system need to be selected for these new Kerberos realms. A powerful machine is not required; the number of principals that will be located in either of these 2 realms is not great, probably under 100. Therefore, a mid-range, Intel-based machine running a free operating system, such as Linux or FreeBSD, fits the bill perfectly. We use FreeBSD for our examples, but any operating system will do.

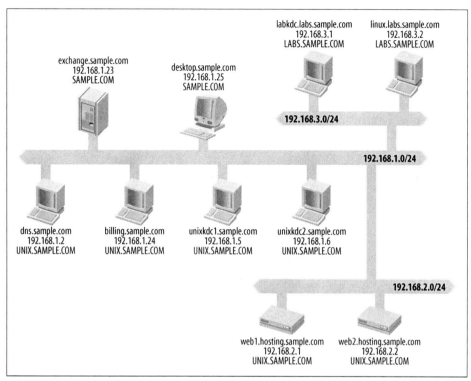

Figure 9-2. Sample ISP's network layout

Since this is an example, we will use two different Kerberos implementations for UNIX.SAMPLE.COM and LABS.SAMPLE.COM. The first, UNIX.SAMPLE.COM, will use the MIT Kerberos 5 implementation, while LABS.SAMPLE.COM will use the Heimdal Kerberos implementation. This is somewhat of an arbitrary decision, as any of the available Kerberos KDCs would work fine in this circumstance. Continuing with the software decisions, we must decide what additional services, if any, to run on the KDC machines. OpenSSH is a good choice to provide remote access for management purposes, but no other services are installed in order to ensure the security of the KDCs.

Disk layout and backup strategy are important to consider during planning. As these machines will contain data (the Kerberos database) that is not easily replaceable and needs to be always available, it is a good idea to place the Kerberos software and database on a separate, hardware, RAID-mirrored disk set. This RAID1 disk will contain only the Kerberos software and database, and will be backed up on a regular basis. Placing the Kerberos software along with the database on this separate disk has the advantage that the backup image can be restored to a spare machine and service restored quickly, as the entire Kerberos KDC is self-contained within the backup image. Reestablishing the Kerberos authentication service would take significantly more time if the Kerberos software had to be restored from a separate backup, or recompiled and reinstalled from scratch.

Another idea, which can be more practical in today's world of large, hard disk platters, is to place everything on one mirrored disk set. Partitions should be established on the disk to ensure that logs and other temporary space do not fill up the entire disk and affect operations of the Kerberos server. The server can be imaged with software such as Symantec's Ghost for Intel-based systems, and periodic dumps can be made of the Kerberos database directory. In either of these techniques, a cold spare can be brought online quickly by restoring the image onto the cold spare system. We'll use this latter technique in our example.

Finally, there are some Kerberos-specific parameters that can be tweaked when installing new Kerberos realms. These include the maximum ticket lifetime, the maximum renewable ticket lifetime, and the option to allow forwardable/addressless tickets. In this example, we won't need to tweak any of these parameters; if you want to adjust the default lifetime parameters, you can use settings in MIT's *kdc.conf* file, or you can specify different settings in response to prompts when Heimdal initializes the realm. The remaining properties can be set on a per-principal basis through kadmin. See the Appendix for details.

Implementation

Now we can start creating the two new Kerberos realms. Before we begin, we must establish the prerequisites that must be satisfied before implementation of the new realms can start. The first prerequisite is a DNS server with functioning forward and reverse DNS zones for the *sample.com* DNS domain. In our example, the service is hosted through the existing Active Directory domain, and appropriate DNS records have been added to the zone files already for all of the machines in our sample network.

The second prerequisite is that all machines have NTP installed and configured. The Windows domain will perform time synchronization against the domain controllers, but NTP must be manually installed and configured on the Unix machines. Before the Kerberos realms is implemented as described below, these two services must be functioning correctly.

Implementing UNIX.SAMPLE.COM

We'll start with UNIX.SAMPLE.COM. Both KDCs, unixkdc1.sample.com and *unixkdc2.sample.com*, have a fresh installation of the latest FreeBSD distribution. Two 18GB hot-swappable SCSI disks have been installed into each machine, and each box has a hardware RAID card set up to do mirroring across the installed drives. The partition layout looks like Table 9-1.

Table 9-1. Partition table for Unix hosts

Mount point	Description	Size
/	Root drive, includes all operating system programs and data	5GB
/krb5	Kerberos database and software	4GB
/var	Log files	5GB
/tmp	Temporary files	2GB
swap	Kernel swap space	1GB

This layout gives ample room for Kerberos database growth, while enforcing the separation between the critical Kerberos database data and any log files or temporary files. A partition layout such as the one above ensures that these log files cannot fill up the entire disk, which may cause the operating system or Kerberos software to malfunction or, worse, corrupt the Kerberos database.

Building and installing the Kerberos KDC software

The first task to perform when implementing a new Kerberos realm is, of course, installing the Kerberos KDC software. We'll be following the steps outlined in Chapter 4 to build our MIT Kerberos 5 KDC.

Grab the MIT Kerberos 5 distribution from *http://web.mit.edu/kerberos/www*. Once the distribution is downloaded and uncompressed, we can begin configuring and compiling it for our uses. We will compile the MIT Kerberos code with a prefix of */krb5*. In our case, there's no reason to compile in the Kerberos 4 compatibility code, so we will explicitly specify this on the configure line:

```
> ./configure --prefix=/krb5 --without-krb4
creating cache ./config.cache
checking for C compiler... cc
checking for gcc... cc
checking whether the C compiler (cc  ) works... yes
checking whether the C compiler (cc  ) is a cross-compiler... no
checking whether we are using GNU C... yes
...
```

Assuming the configure step went well, it's now time to make the distribution and install it:

```
# gmake && gmake install
# mkdir /krb5/var
# mkdir /krb5/var/krb5kdc
# chown root /krb5/var/krb5kdc
# chmod 700 /krb5/var/krb5kdc
```

Note that we use gmake as we're building on FreeBSD. Other operating systems such as Linux that use GNU Make by default can simply use "make" instead. Note that the software must be placed on both KDCs, and (assuming that both KDCs are running the same operating system and processor platform) this can be accomplished by simply *taring* up the */krb5* directory on one and placing it on the other. Even though we haven't created the realm yet and the */krb5/var/krb5kdc* directory is currently empty, when mirroring the Kerberos software between the two machines, do not copy the Kerberos databases. The slave replication script that we'll put in place below will handle replicating the Kerberos database between the master and slave KDCs, and manually copying the Kerberos database located in the */krb5/var/krb5kdc* directory from one to the other can corrupt it.

Once the software has been installed, it's time to create a *kdc.conf* file to be installed on both KDCs. This file must be placed in the */krb5/var/krb5kdc* directory on each KDC. While this file is not strictly necessary, it is still a good idea to spell out the intended configuration, which in this case includes the directories where the KDC database are located as well as the default ticket lifetimes and encryption types.

```
[kdcdefaults]
    kdc_ports = 88

[realms]
    UNIX.SAMPLE.COM = {
        database_name = /krb5/var/krb5kdc/principal
        admin_keytab = /krb5/var/krb5kdc/kadm5.keytab
        acl_file = /krb5/var/krb5kdc/kadm5.acl
        dict_file = /krb5/var/krb5kdc/kadm5.dict
        key_stash_file = /krb5/var/krb5kdc/.k5.UNIX.SAMPLE.COM
        kadmind_port = 749
        max_life = 10h 0m 0s
        max_renewable_life = 7d 0h 0m 0s
        master_key_type = des3-hmac-sha1
        supported_enctypes = des3-hmac-sha1:normal des-cbc-crc:normal
    }
```

Realm configuration files

With this file in place, we can now create the *krb5.conf* file that will be used for every host in the UNIX.SAMPLE.COM Kerberos realm. Note the additional entries in the domain_realm stanza, as there is no *unix.sample.com* DNS domain that contains all of the hosts in the UNIX.SAMPLE.COM Kerberos realm. As a result, the mapping between DNS names and the corresponding Kerberos realm must be specified explicitly.

```
[libdefaults]
        default_realm = UNIX.SAMPLE.COM

[realms]
        UNIX.SAMPLE.COM = {
                kdc = unixkdc1.sample.com:88
                kdc = unixkdc2.sample.com:88
```

```
                     admin_server = unixkdc1.sample.com
            };

            SAMPLE.COM = {
                     kdc = exchange.sample.com:88
            };

      [domain_realm]
            .sample.com = SAMPLE.COM
            sample.com = SAMPLE.COM
            .hosting.sample.com = UNIX.SAMPLE.COM
            hosting.sample.com = UNIX.SAMPLE.COM
            dns.sample.com = UNIX.SAMPLE.COM
            billing.sample.com = UNIX.SAMPLE.COM
            unixkdc1.sample.com = UNIX.SAMPLE.COM
            unixkdc2.sample.com = UNIX.SAMPLE.COM

      [logging]
            kdc = FILE:/var/log/kdc.log
            admin_server = FILE:/var/log/kadmin.log
```

This file is installed on all machines that are members of the UNIX.SAMPLE.COM
Kerberos realm. The logging stanza is only important for the KDC machines, but will
do no harm if it is included with the *krb5.conf* file installed on other machines as well.

Creating the realm

Now we're ready to initialize and create the first principals in our new realm. First,
initialize the Kerberos database:

```
unixkdc1# /krb5/sbin/kdb5_util create -s
Initializing database '/krb5/var/krb5kdc/principal' for realm 'UNIX.SAMPLE.COM',
master key name 'K/M@UNIX.SAMPLE.COM'
You will be prompted for the database Master Password.
It is important that you NOT FORGET this password.
Enter KDC database master key:
Re-enter KDC database master key to verify:
```

We also have to set up the administrative interface. First, we'll create an administrative user principal:

```
unixkdc1# /krb5/sbin/kadmin.local
Authenticating as principal jgarman/admin@UNIX.SAMPLE.COM with password.
kadmin.local: addprinc jgarman
WARNING: no policy specified for jgarman@UNIX.SAMPLE.COM; defaulting to no policy
Enter password for principal "jgarman@UNIX.SAMPLE.COM":
Re-enter password for principal "jgarman@UNIX.SAMPLE.COM":
Principal "jgarman@UNIX.SAMPLE.COM" created.

kadmin.local:  addprinc jgarman/admin
WARNING: no policy specified for jgarman/admin@UNIX.SAMPLE.COM; defaulting to no
policy
Enter password for principal "jgarman/admin@UNIX.SAMPLE.COM":
Re-enter password for principal "jgarman/admin@UNIX.SAMPLE.COM":
Principal "jgarman/admin@UNIX.SAMPLE.COM" created.
```

While we're already in kadmin, we might as well also set up the principals required to perform kadmin tasks over the network. We'll create the two principals needed for this task, kadmin/admin and kadmin/changepw:

```
kadmin.local: ktadd -k /krb5/var/krb5kdc/kadm5.keytab kadmin/admin kadmin/changepw
Entry for principal kadmin/admin with kvno 3, encryption type Triple DES cbc mode
with HMAC/sha1 added to keytab WRFILE:/krb5/var/krb5kdc/kadm5.keytab.
Entry for principal kadmin/admin with kvno 3, encryption type DES cbc mode with CRC-
32 added to keytab WRFILE:/krb5/var/krb5kdc/kadm5.keytab.
Entry for principal kadmin/changepw with kvno 3, encryption type Triple DES cbc mode
with HMAC/sha1 added to keytab WRFILE:/krb5/var/krb5kdc/kadm5.keytab.
Entry for principal kadmin/changepw with kvno 3, encryption type DES cbc mode with
CRC-32 added to keytab WRFILE:/krb5/var/krb5kdc/kadm5.keytab.
```

Also, we can create the host principals for the machines in our new realm. We won't show them all, but here's the kadmin commands to add host principals for our master and slave KDCs to the Kerberos database:

```
kadmin.local:  addprinc -randkey host/unixkdc1.sample.com
WARNING: no policy specified for host/unixkdc1.sample.com@UNIX.SAMPLE.COM; defaulting
to no policy
Principal "host/unixkdc1.sample.com@UNIX.SAMPLE.COM" created.
kadmin.local:  addprinc -randkey host/unixkdc2.sample.com
WARNING: no policy specified for host/unixkdc2.sample.com@UNIX.SAMPLE.COM; defaulting
to no policy
Principal "host/unixkdc2.sample.com@UNIX.SAMPLE.COM" created.
```

While we're in kadmin and logged into the master KDC as root, we can extract the host key for the master KDC and place it in the system keytab. We'll do the same for the other machines in the realm later.

```
kadmin.local: ktadd host/unixkdc1.sample.com
Entry for principal host/unixkdc1.sample.com with kvno 3, encryption type Triple DES
cbc mode with HMAC/sha1 added to keytab WRFILE:/etc/krb5.keytab.
Entry for principal host/unixkdc1.sample.com with kvno 3, encryption type DES cbc
mode with CRC-32 added to keytab WRFILE:/etc/krb5.keytab.
```

Once the basic principals for our realm are in place, we can also exit kadmin and create an administrative ACL file that grants *jgarman/admin@UNIX.SAMPLE.COM* permission to modify the Kerberos database. Our new */krb5/var/krb5kdc/kadm5.acl* file on unixkdc1 simply has one line in it:

```
jgarman/admin@UNIX.SAMPLE.COM              *
```

Now we can start up the Kerberos KDC and kadmin servers:

```
unixkdc1# /krb5/sbin/krb5kdc
unixkdc1# /krb5/sbin/kadmind
```

Setting up slave replication

Now that the master Kerberos KDC is up and running, we can begin setting up our slave KDC for database replication. The first task is to ensure that the Kerberos binaries have been successfully copied over or rebuilt from source on the slave machine, as discussed above in the installation section for the master KDC. Once the Kerberos binaries are in place, the keytab for the slave machine's host key can be extracted from the Kerberos database through kadmin:

```
unixkdc2# /krb5/sbin/kadmin
Authenticating as principal jgarman/admin@UNIX.SAMPLE.COM with password.
Enter password:
kadmin:  ktadd host/unixkdc2.sample.com
Entry for principal host/unixkdc2.sample.com with kvno 3, encryption type Triple DES
cbc mode with HMAC/sha1 added to keytab WRFILE:/etc/krb5.keytab.
Entry for principal host/unixkdc2.sample.com with kvno 3, encryption type DES cbc
mode with CRC-32 added to keytab WRFILE:/etc/krb5.keytab.
```

Next, we create the *kpropd.acl* file in the */krb5/var/krb5kdc* directory that will list all of the host principals of the participating KDCs in our realm. For our example, the *kpropd.acl* file will contain the following entries:

```
host/unixkdc1.sample.com@UNIX.SAMPLE.COM
host/unixkdc2.sample.com@UNIX.SAMPLE.COM
```

Now we can place an entry in the slave KDC's *inetd.conf* file to enable the Kerberos database propagation service. First, the following line needs to be placed in the slave's */etc/services* file:

```
krb5_prop  754/tcp
```

Then we can place the following line into the slave's */etc/inetd.conf* to enable the service.

```
krb5_prop  stream tcp nowait  root /krb5/sbin/kpropd kpropd
```

After restarting inetd on unixkdc2, we can perform a quick test to ensure that the database propagation works. Log into unixkdc1 and issue the kprop command:

```
unixkdc1# /krb5/sbin/kdb5_util dump /krb5/var/krb5kdc/slavedump
unixkdc1# /krb5/sbin/kprop -f /krb5/var/krb5kdc/slavedump unixkdc2.sample.com
Database propagation to unixkdc2.sample.com: SUCCEEDED
```

On unixkdc2, you'll have to re-enter the Kerberos master key first entered when the Kerberos database was initialized. Since the replicated database is encrypted with the Kerberos master key, the slave needs the master key to decrypt and load the replicated database.

```
unixkdc2# /krb5/sbin/kdb5_util stash
kdb5_util: Cannot find/read stored master key while reading master key
kdb5_util: Warning: proceeding without master key
Enter KDC database master key:
```

Finally, a script such as the one shown in Chapter 4, at the end of the "Adding slave KDCs" section for MIT Kerberos, can be used to automate the task of replicating the master KDC database to the slave.

Once the database has been propagated to unixkdc2, the KDC service can be started on unixkdc2 as well:

```
unixkdc2# /krb5/sbin/krb5kdc
```

Installing the Kerberos software on client and application servers

The MIT Kerberos 5 distribution needs to be installed on the rest of the machines in the UNIX.SAMPLE.COM realm. The same configuration and installation instructions given above for the KDC software will make the Kerberos client libraries and utilities as well. Log into each Kerberos client and application server, and make the Kerberos software:

```
> ./configure --prefix=/krb5 --without-krb4
creating cache ./config.cache
checking for C compiler... cc
checking for gcc... cc
checking whether the C compiler (cc ) works... yes
checking whether the C compiler (cc ) is a cross-compiler... no
checking whether we are using GNU C... yes
...
> su
Password:
# gmake && gmake install
```

Copy the *krb5.conf* file listed above in the Realm Configuration Files section above into the */etc* directory on the target machine. Then you'll be able to use kadmin to login remotely to the Kerberos database, create a principal for this machine, and extract the host key to the machine's keytab. As an example, for *www1.hosting.sample.com*, the commands would look like the following:

```
www1# /krb5/sbin/kadmin
Authenticating as principal jgarman/admin@UNIX.SAMPLE.COM with password.
Enter password:
kadmin:  addprinc -randkey host/www1.hosting.sample.com
WARNING: no policy specified for host/www1.hosting.sample.com@UNIX.SAMPLE.COM;
defaulting to no policy
Principal "host/www1.hosting.sample.com@UNIX.SAMPLE.COM" created.
kadmin: ktadd host/www1.hosting.sample.com
Entry for principal host/www1.hosting.sample.com with kvno 3, encryption type Triple
DES cbc mode with HMAC/sha1 added to keytab WRFILE:/etc/krb5.keytab.
Entry for principal host/www1.hosting.sample.com with kvno 3, encryption type DES cbc
mode with CRC-32 added to keytab WRFILE:/etc/krb5.keytab.
```

Once the host key has been extracted into a keyfile, the Kerberized telnet daemon can be enabled by adding the Kerberized telnet daemon to the host's *inetd.conf* file. Any telnet service lines in the */etc/inetd.conf* file should be changed to the following, assuming that the Kerberos distribution was installed in */krb5*:

```
telnet stream tcp nowait root /krb5/sbin/telnetd telnetd
```

After the *inetd.conf* file has been modified, inetd must be restarted for the changes to take effect.

Before testing the Kerberos telnet functionality, remember that each user's *.k5login* file, located in their home directory, must contain the names of the Kerberos principals authorized to that user's account. For example, with a Unix username of *tdurden* and two principals tdurden@SAMPLE.COM and tdurden@UNIX.SAMPLE.COM, the *.k5login* file must contain both principal names, otherwise the Kerberos login program will refuse authorization for the cross-realm principal, tdurden@SAMPLE.COM.

Establishing Cross-Realm Relationships with SAMPLE.COM

We must establish a cross-realm trust between the UNIX.SAMPLE.COM realm and the Active Directory domain SAMPLE.COM. This trust will be used so that users in the SAMPLE.COM Active Directory domain can transparently log into machines located in the UNIX.SAMPLE.COM Kerberos realm. We'll be following the instructions outlined in Chapter 8 to establish a cross-realm trust between a Unix-based Kerberos realm and a Windows domain.

First, we'll create the appropriate cross-realm principals on the Unix KDC:

```
unixkdc1# /krb5/sbin/kadmin
Authenticating as principal jgarman/admin@UNIX.SAMPLE.COM with password.
Enter password:
kadmin:  addprinc -e des:normal krbtgt/SAMPLE.COM@UNIX.SAMPLE.COM
WARNING: no policy specified for krbtgt/SAMPLE.COM@UNIX.SAMPLE.COM; defaulting to no
policy
Enter password for principal "krbtgt/SAMPLE.COM@UNIX.SAMPLE.COM":
Re-enter password for principal "krbtgt/SAMPLE.COM@UNIX.SAMPLE.COM":
Principal "krbtgt/SAMPLE.COM@UNIX.SAMPLE.COM" created.

kadmin:  addprinc -e des:normal krbtgt/UNIX.SAMPLE.COM@SAMPLE.COM
WARNING: no policy specified for krbtgt/UNIX.SAMPLE.COM@SAMPLE.COM; defaulting to no
policy
Enter password for principal "krbtgt/UNIX.SAMPLE.COM@SAMPLE.COM":
Re-enter password for principal "krbtgt/UNIX.SAMPLE.COM@SAMPLE.COM":
Principal "krbtgt/UNIX.SAMPLE.COM@SAMPLE.COM" created.
```

Remember the passwords given here; we'll be entering them in on the Windows side next. After logging in under a Domain Administrator account on a machine in the SAMPLE.COM domain, start the Active Directory Domains and Trusts tool, right click on the SAMPLE.COM domain in the tree view on the left, and select Properties. After selecting the Trusts tab and clicking the Add button in the Domains trusted by this domain group, the window pictured in Figure 9-3 appears.

Here, you'll enter the password associated with the *krbtgt/SAMPLE.COM@UNIX. SAMPLE.COM* principal. Repeat the process for "Domains that trust this domain". At this point, you can click Add, and enter the password that is associated with the *krbtgt/UNIX.SAMPLE.COM@SAMPLE.COM* principal.

Implementing LABS.SAMPLE.COM

The next realm, LABS.SAMPLE.COM, is much simpler: there is no cross-realm relationship and only a single KDC, with no database replication. Once again, we'll go through the process of installing and configuring the KDC and Kerberos client utilities for this realm; however, this time we'll use the Heimdal Kerberos distribution.

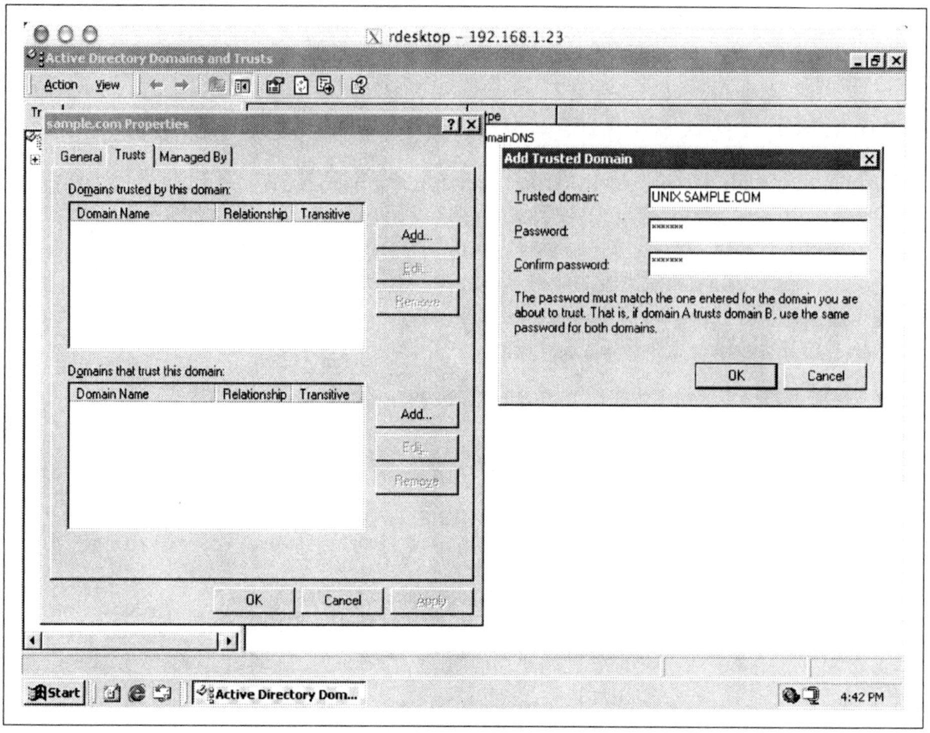

Figure 9-3. Establishing cross-realm relationship between UNIX.SAMPLE.COM and SAMPLE.COM

The disk layout for the KDC of the LABS.SAMPLE.COM realm is similar to the disk layout used earlier for UNIX.SAMPLE.COM's KDCs (Table 9-2).

Table 9-2. Partition table for LABS.SAMPLE.COM

Mount point	Description	Size
/	Root drive, includes all operating system programs and data	5GB
/usr/heimdal	Kerberos database and software	4GB
/var	Log files	5GB
/tmp	Temporary files	2GB
swap	Kernel swap space	1GB

Building and installing the Kerberos KDC software

We'll follow the steps outlined in Chapter 4 to build our Heimdal Kerberos KDC. Grab the Heimdal Kerberos distribution from *http://www.pdc.kth.se/heimdal*. Once the distribution is downloaded and uncompressed, we can begin configuring and compiling it. We compile the Heimdal Kerberos code with a prefix of */usr/heimdal*, and place the Kerberos database in */usr/heimdal/db*.

```
> ./configure --prefix=/usr/heimdal
checking for gcc... gcc
```

```
checking for C compiler default output... a.out
checking whether the C compiler works... yes
checking whether we are cross compiling... no
checking for suffix of executables...
checking for suffix of object files... o
...
```

Assuming the configure step went well, it's now time to make the distribution and install it:

```
# make && make install
# mkdir /usr/heimdal/db
# chown root /usr/heimdal/db
# chmod 700 /usr/heimdal/db
# ln -s /usr/heimdal/db /var/heimdal
```

We've created a symbolic link from */var/heimdal* to the location we'd like to keep our Kerberos database, */usr/heimdal/db*. This avoids the problem of the */var* partition filling up with log files and possibly corrupting or otherwise interfering with the proper operation of the Kerberos KDC.

Realm configuration files

Before we can continue with initializing the LABS.SAMPLE.COM Kerberos database, we need to create an */etc/krb5.conf* file that will be installed on each machine in the LABS.SAMPLE.COM realm, including the KDC.

```
[libdefaults]
        default_realm = LABS.SAMPLE.COM

[realms]
        LABS.SAMPLE.COM = {
                kdc = labkdc.labs.sample.com:88
                admin_server = labkdc.labs.sample.com
        };

[domain_realm]
        .labs.sample.com = LABS.SAMPLE.COM
        labs.sample.com = LABS.SAMPLE.COM

[logging]
        kdc = FILE:/var/log/kdc.log
        admin_server = FILE:/var/log/kadmin.log
```

Creating the realm

With the *krb5.conf* file in place, we can continue on to initializing the Kerberos database and populating the realm with administrative principals. First, we establish a stash file where the master key for the Kerberos database will be stored:

```
labkdc# /usr/heimdal/sbin/kstash
Master key:
Verifying password - Master key:
/usr/heimdal/sbin/kstash: writing key to `/var/heimdal/m-key'
```

Now, we can initialize the realm, using the local kadmin interface:

```
labkdc# /usr/heimdal/sbin/kadmin -l
kadmin> init LABS.SAMPLE.COM
Realm max ticket life [unlimited]:1d
Realm max renewable ticket life [unlimited]:1w
```

We have decided to make the maximum ticket lifetime 24 hours, and the maximum renewable ticket lifetime one week. These parameters can of course be adjusted.

While still inside of kadmin, we can create our administrative user and give him permissions to modify the Kerberos database through kadmin. First, we'll create the administrative user principals:

```
kadmin> add jgarman
Max ticket life [1 day]:
Max renewable life [1 week]:
Principal expiration time [never]:
Password expiration time [never]:
Attributes []:
jgarman@LABS.SAMPLE.COM's Password:
Verifying password - jgarman@LABS.SAMPLE.COM's Password:

kadmin> add jgarman/admin
Max ticket life [1 day]:
Max renewable life [1 week]:
Principal expiration time [never]:
Password expiration time [never]:
Attributes []:
jgarman/admin@LABS.SAMPLE.COM's Password:
Verifying password - jgarman/admin@LABS.SAMPLE.COM's Password:
```

Now, we'll have to give jgarman/admin@LABS.SAMPLE.COM administrative rights on the Kerberos database. All we need to do is place the following line in the */usr/heimdal/db/kadmind.acl* file:

```
jgarman/admin@LABS.SAMPLE.COM  all
```

This entry will grant jgarman/admin@LABS.SAMPLE.COM all administrative rights to all principals in the Kerberos database. Now we can start the KDC to finish the installation.

```
labkdc# /usr/heimdal/libexec/kdc &
labkdc# /usr/heimdal/libexec/kadmind &
```

Installing the Kerberos software on client and application servers

The Heimdal Kerberos distribution needs to be installed on the rest of the machines in the LABS.SAMPLE.COM realm. The same configuration and installation instructions given above for the KDC software will make the Kerberos client libraries and utilities as well. Log into each Kerberos client and application server, and make the Kerberos software:

```
> ./configure --prefix=/usr/heimdal
checking for gcc... gcc
```

```
checking for C compiler default output... a.out
checking whether the C compiler works... yes
checking whether we are cross compiling... no
checking for suffix of executables...
checking for suffix of object files... o
...
> su
Password:
# make && make install
```

Copy the *krb5.conf* file listed above in the "Realm configuration files" section into the */etc* directory on the target machine. Then you'll be able to use Heimdal's ktutil program to login remotely to the Kerberos database, create a principal for this machine, and extract the host key to the machine's keytab. The commands to extract a host key for linux.labs.sample.com are:

```
linux# /usr/heimdal/sbin/ktutil get host/linux.labs.sample.com
jgarman/admin@LABS.SAMPLE.COM's Password:
```

Once the host key has been extracted onto a keyfile on a host, the Kerberized telnet daemon can be enabled on the host. This is done simply by adding the Kerberized telnet daemon to the *inetd.conf* file on the host, as seen in Chapter 4. Assuming that the Kerberos distribution was installed in */usr/heimdal*, any telnet service lines in the */etc/inetd.conf* file should be changed to:

```
telnet stream tcp nowait root /usr/heimdal/libexec/telnetd telnetd
```

After the *inetd.conf* file has been modified, inetd must be restarted for the changes to take effect.

Configuring Applications

Now that all of the realms have been set up and the cross-realm keys have been established between UNIX.SAMPLE.COM and SAMPLE.COM, we can configure Reflection X for transparent login to the Unix hosts from the Windows domain.

We'll start by adding a user principal to the Active Directory domain with which we can do some tests along the way. Ensure that the principal has the "Use DES encryption types for this account" checkbox checked, as shown in Figure 9-4.

Now we continue to configure WRQ Reflection X to use Kerberos authentication for its telnet connections to the Unix hosts. These telnet sessions will then start X11 client programs that will display back on the Windows host. To do this, you'll need a copy of Reflection X and the freely downloadable Reflection Security Components. More information on Reflection X can be found in Chapter 7 and at the WRQ home page at *http://www.wrq.com*.

Now we need to set up our first user's Reflection Security Components. Start the Kerberos Manager application, which can be found inside the Utilities subfolder of the WRQ Reflection folder in the Start Menu's Programs folder. When Kerberos Manager is started for the first time by a user, it opens the Initial Configuration dialog box pictured in Figure 9-5.

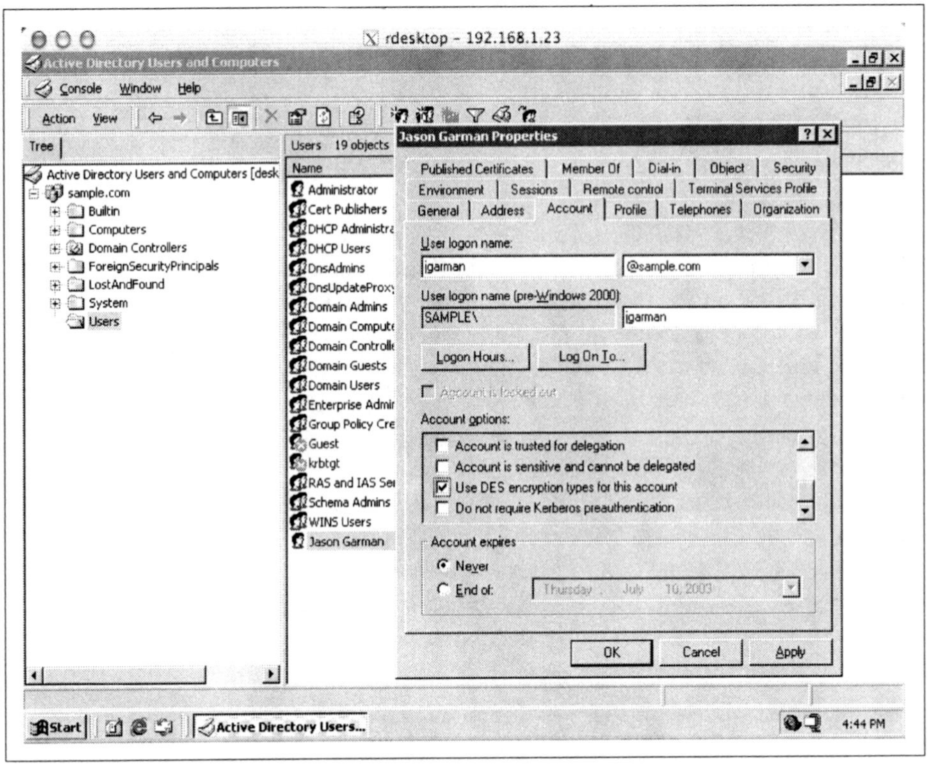

Figure 9-4. Setting the DES encryption checkbox in the jgarman user's properties dialog box

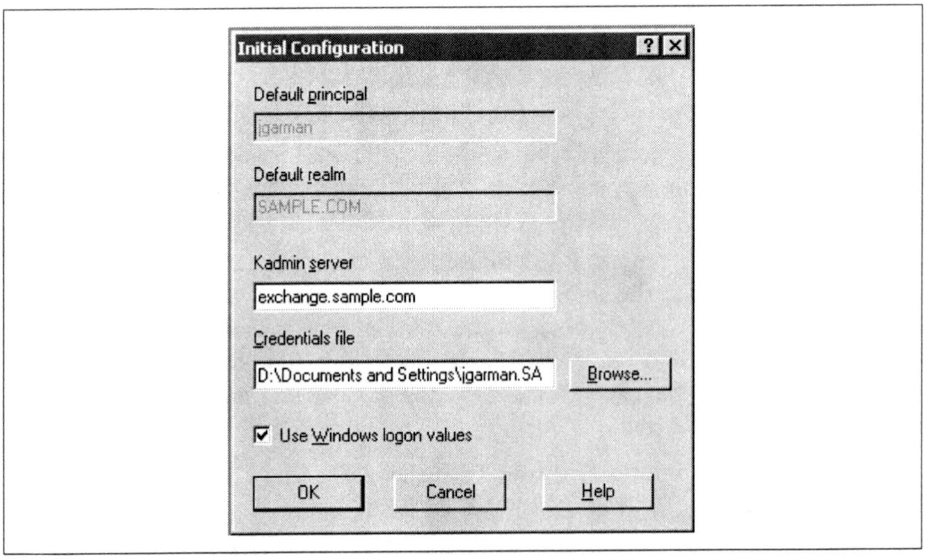

Figure 9-5. Reflection Kerberos initial configuration window

Note that since we're using the credentials associated with the user's Windows domain login, we can check the "Use Windows logon values" checkbox, which fills in the first two text boxes for us. The kadmin server should be set to one of the domain controllers for SAMPLE.COM, in this case *exchange.sample.com*. Once this configuration is complete, the next step is to use the Kerberos Manager to add the configuration information for UNIX.SAMPLE.COM. The same information that is encoded in the Unix systems' */etc/krb5.conf* file must be entered into Reflection Security Components, namely the addresses of the KDCs for the realm and the DNS names of the various machines in the realm.

The realm configuration parameters can be accessed through the Kerberos Manager program's Configuration/Configure Realms menu option. That menu option displays the list of currently configured realms. We'll add the UNIX.SAMPLE.COM realm to this list by clicking the Add button. Enter the realm name, UNIX.SAMPLE.COM, and one of the KDCs, *unixkdc1.sample.com*, in the dialog box. UNIX.SAMPLE.COM will be listed in the left-hand list box; click on it and then on the Properties button. We'll use the properties dialog box to set the KDCs and DNS name to realm mappings for the UNIX.SAMPLE.COM realm.

The KDC tab controls the list of KDCs for the realm. Switch to that tab, and enter the information for the second KDC, *unixkdc2.sample.com*. The result is Figure 9-6.

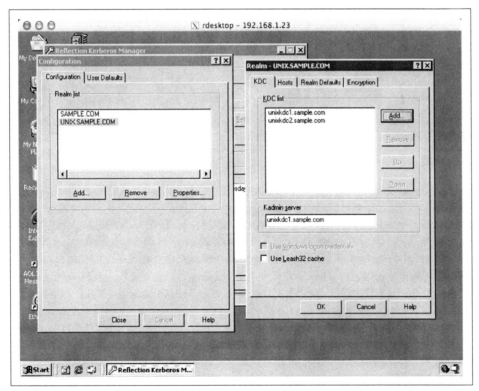

Figure 9-6. Creating the UNIX.SAMPLE.COM realm configuration in Reflection Kerberos

Ensure that the kadmin server is the master KDC, *unixkdc1.sample.com*, as the slave KDC does not run the kadmin service.

Next, enter in the DNS names of all the hosts in this realm under the hosts tab. Just as in the */etc/krb5.conf* file, names prefixed with a period match all names within the DNS domain specified. The hosts tab for our example should look like Figure 9-7.

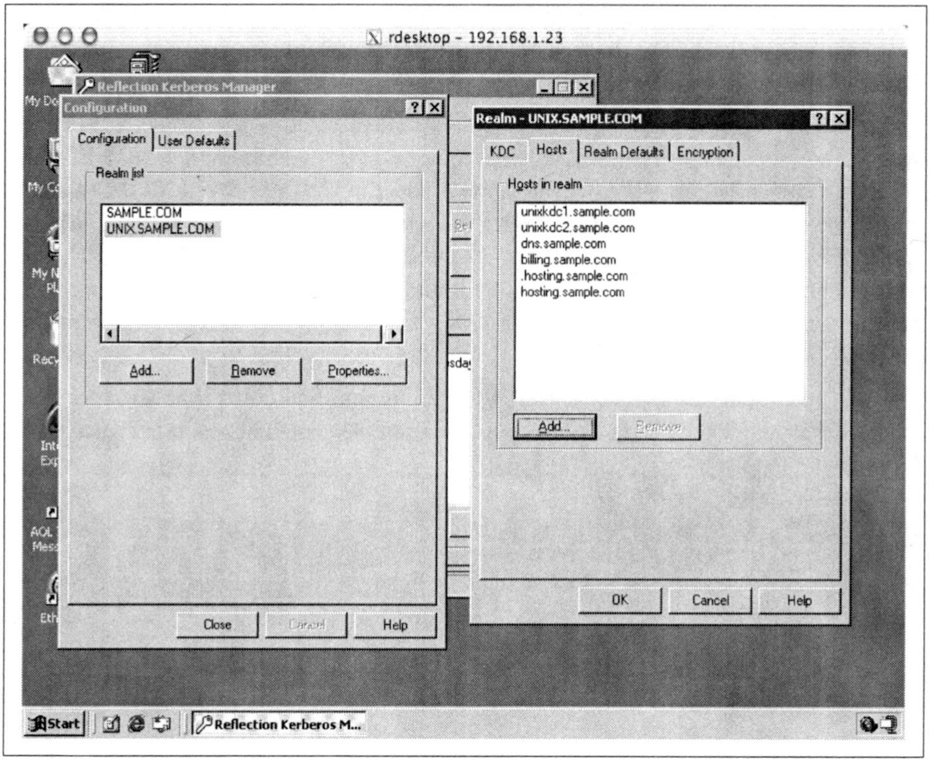

Figure 9-7. Creating the hostname to realm mapping for UNIX.SAMPLE.COM

You could enter information for LABS.SAMPLE.COM here as well if you wish to use Kerberos to log into the lab machines through Reflection X as well. Since there is no cross-realm key shared between SAMPLE.COM and LABS.SAMPLE.COM, you'll have to log into the LABS.SAMPLE.COM Kerberos realm through Reflection X, as it cannot use the domain credentials to authenticate you to the labs Kerberos realm.

Once the Kerberos realm setup is finished, host connections can be established to each of the machines in UNIX.SAMPLE.COM. Since Reflection uses the TGT acquired by Windows during the login process, and cross-realm relationships have been established between the Active Directory domain and the UNIX.SAMPLE.COM Kerberos realm, Reflection uses your existing Kerberos credentials to acquire tickets for the Unix host and log into it. This is just one example of a Kerberized application that can take advantage of the Kerberos infrastructure. As needs grow, more applications can be made Kerberos-aware to extend the usefulness of the single-sign-on Kerberos system.

## CHAPTER 10

Kerberos Futures

Kerberos is constantly evolving to integrate new technologies and thwart new threats. As a result, the Kerberos working group has developed several extensions to the base Kerberos 5 protocol to provide the necessary capabilities to continue using Kerberos in the future. These protocol extensions are currently available as Internet Drafts from the IETF. The principal draft is the Kerberos Clarifications, which will replace the current RFC 1510 as the authoritative document for Kerberos protocol implementers. While the Kerberos Clarifications is true to its name and, for the most part, simply provides a more concise and clear description of the current protocol, it also contains new recommendations and small protocol changes that result from years of practical implementation experience and security reviews. Other related draft documents describe more dramatic protocol extensions that are optional.

The current home page of the Kerberos Clarifications is the Kerberos page at the USC Center for Computer Systems Security, located at *http://www.kerberos.isi.edu*. Additionally, current Internet Drafts can be downloaded from the IETF home page at *http://www.ietf.org*. The index to the current Internet Drafts issued by the Kerberos working group is located at *http://www.ietf.org/ids.by.wg/krb-wg.html*. Readers interested in a more technical discussion of these proposals are encouraged to read the Internet Drafts published at the IETF and USC Kerberos sites.

Public Key Extensions

Kerberos was designed when public key encryption was still in its infancy. Public key algorithms were not widely in use at the time, the technology was heavily patented by RSA Security, Inc., and the computing power commonly available at the time was not sufficient to sustain a large public key infrastructure. Today, these factors have changed: the patents on the popular RSA public key algorithm have expired, opening the door to royalty-free implementations of RSA, and Moore's law of exponential growth in computing speed has provided more than enough computing power to handle the large calculations involved in public key cryptography. The development and wide deployment of the Secure Sockets Layer (SSL) and its successor, Transport Layer Security (TLS), which use public key cryptography primarily for securing communication with web sites, have proven that public key cryptography is useful and can be trusted for secure systems.

The question is, then, what benefits can the introduction of public key cryptography bring to Kerberos? To answer this question, we need a clear understanding of what makes public key cryptography different from traditional, private key cryptography.

Public Key Cryptography

Traditional cryptographic systems require the sender and recipient to share a common secret key to communicate securely. The sender uses the secret key to encrypt messages to the recipient, and the recipient uses the same secret key to decrypt the incoming message. This is known as *symmetric*, or *private key cryptography*, and is the type of cryptography used by the Kerberos protocol. The problem, of course, is how the two parties agree on and communicate the secret key. This problem is generally known as *key management*, and is a crucial factor in the practical operation of any encryption scheme. Key management affects all encryption algorithms, regardless of their strength, and a compromised key in a relatively weak cryptosystem has exactly the same consequences as a compromised key in a relatively strong cryptosystem—namely, that all communications using that key are now easily decrypted by an attacker. Implementers of private key cryptosystems typically address the key distribution issue by using some form of personal contact between sender and recipient prior to the first message exchange to establish a secret key; for example, users requesting access to a Kerberos-protected network may have to apply for an account and receive an initial password from a system administrator in person. This process becomes unwieldy in a large environment; however, a different type of cryptographic algorithm provides another approach to the problem of key management.

Public key, or *asymmetric key cryptography* splits the encryption key into two parts. Each user in a public key system generates a key pair, consisting of a private key and public key. These two keys are mathematically linked so that messages are encrypted with one key and decrypted with the other. Furthermore, deriving one half of the key given the other half is mathematically very difficult, and the difficulty of performing this operation determines the relative strength of public key encryption algorithms.

The two parts of the encryption key are termed the *private key* and the *public key*. The private key is kept secret, and the public key is widely distributed to everyone that you wish to communicate with. When someone wants to send you an encrypted message, he encrypts the message with your public key. Once encrypted, the only person who can decrypt the message is the person who holds the other half of the key—the private key—which is securely stored on your computer. This demonstrates the advantage of key distribution that public key cryptography has over symmetric cryptography. Each participant simply publishes her public key, and we no longer have to worry about key distribution.

In addition to encryption, public key cryptography also provides a method for electronically signing messages. This is accomplished by simply reversing the keys involved in the encryption and decryption process. To sign a message, the sender encrypts it with his private key, and to ensure its authenticity, the recipient can decrypt it with the sender's public key. If the message is decrypted successfully with the public key of the sender, then the recipient is assured of the identity of the sender, as only the sender could have encrypted the message with his private key.

With all of these advantages over symmetric key cryptography, there must be some downsides to the use of public key cryptography. As it turns out, there are a few disadvantages of public key algorithms, but with some extra work, they can be overcome. The first issue with public key cryptography is its speed. Current public key algorithms require mathematical operations on numbers hundreds of digits long, which, even with today's processing power, can present a large performance penalty when encrypting large amounts of data. The second problem is related to the very issue that public key cryptography purports to solve: the problem of key distribution. The issue at hand is, while everyone can publish their own public key, and others can encrypt messages intended for a particular recipient with that person's published public key, how does the sender know that someone's published public key is *really* his public key?

Combining public key and symmetric key ciphers

To solve the first problem, we need to combine the power and flexibility of public key cryptography with the speed of symmetric key cryptography. Today's security products and protocols, such as PGP and SSL, use a hybrid approach that combines the use of both. First, a public key algorithm is used to encrypt a small amount of data, namely, an encryption key. This encryption key is then used to encrypt the remainder of the message using a traditional symmetric key algorithm. Through this approach, we combine the key management advantages of public key cryptography yet use a symmetric key cipher to encrypt the bulk of the message, leveraging the better speed of the symmetric key cipher.

This combination of methods does not lessen the strength of the resulting cipher. Instead, it uses each type of encryption's strength to its advantage. Since conventional symmetric key cryptography is much more efficient than public key algorithms, the use of symmetric key algorithms provide the speed and low CPU usage required for encrypting and decrypting large amounts of data. The public key algorithms excel at easy key distribution and so they are used to negotiate a secret key to be used for the subsequent symmetric key algorithms.

Public key cryptography key distribution

It turns out that the public key's principal strength (the ease of key distribution) is also its Achilles's heel. Since anyone can publish a public key, nothing stops an attacker from creating a key pair, keeping the private key, and publishing the public key under someone else's name. When someone encrypts a message in what she thinks is the victim's public key, the attacker is able to decrypt and read it instead. Furthermore, if the attacker has the intended recipient's real public key, the attacker can re-encrypt the message with the correct key and forward it on to the recipient without the recipient being aware that the message was intercepted.

This is a man-in-the-middle attack, similar to the man-in-the-middle attacks that we examined in Chapter 6. To prevent this attack, let's say that the original sender now signs his message, in addition to encrypting it, before sending the message to the recipient. This seems to solve the attack above, as now the attacker can't re-sign the message when forwarding it on to the recipient. But the problem still exists, only in reverse: how does the recipient know the true sender's public key? Furthermore, the most common implementation of public key cryptography in use on the Internet today, SSL, does not require the use of mutual authentication, as most users do not have a key pair.

One solution to this problem is called *key certification*. Before someone publishes their public key, he sends it to a Certification Authority (CA) whose job is to ensure that the person is genuinely who he says he is. The CA then signs the person's public key, which functions as a seal ensuring that the key does, in fact, belong to the person. The public key, along with the signature from the CA, and some identifying information such as the person's name, are all combined into one file, called a *certificate*. Of course this requires centralized control to determine the validity of signature requests and sign valid requests. This system of a centralized certificate signing authority is also referred to as a Public Key Infrastructure, or PKI.

Another, more decentralized approach, is taken by the package Pretty Good Privacy (PGP). In PGP, users generate their own key pair and have the public key signed by people they personally know. Multiple people can sign a single key, indicating that each signer vouches for the authenticity of the target's key.

Initial Authentication (PKINIT)

One situation where public key cryptography can benefit the Kerberos protocol is in the initial Authentication Server exchange. Instead of sharing a secret key between the client and KDC, the client possesses a public key pair that is signed by a Certification Authority, which is used to authenticate to the realm.

The key certification method described in the previous section may seem similar to the trusted third party system employed by Kerberos, and, in fact, it is very similar—with one important distinction. The difference is that while both Kerberos and public key certificate authorities employ a trusted third-party model, the trusted third-party is only involved in the public key method when signing the public keys. The rest of the time, the certification authority operates *offline*; that is, it doesn't have to be actively involved every time an authentication request is made.

The typical use of PKINIT is to provide each user in the Kerberos realm a signed public key certificate. Each user on their workstation generates a public/private key pair, and the public key is presented to a Certification Authority for validation. Once the key is signed, the certificate is returned to the user and stored on the local hard drive.

The only change to the Kerberos protocol is in the initial Authentication Server message exchange between the authentication client and the KDC. In the traditional symmetric key Kerberos protocol, the client requests a TGT from the KDC, and the KDC responds with a TGT encrypted with the user's secret key. If the realm requires pre-authentication, the user must supply a timestamp encrypted with the user's secret password (or other authenticator) to the KDC, providing reasonable proof that the client is genuine.

PKINIT extends the Kerberos protocol by using the pre-authentication field to house a public key certificate instead. When a user wishes to authenticate to a KDC that supports PKINIT, the user places his certificate in the pre-authentication field of the AS request. The KDC receives the request and returns the validated TGT encrypted with the public key contained within the user's public key certificate.

Of course, we don't want to simply issue everyone who has a public key pair a valid TGT to use our Kerberos network. Therefore, the KDC will validate the signature included in the user's certificate to ensure that a trusted Certification Authority signed the user's key. In addition, the client can validate the KDC's certificate included in its reply to the client, and determine whether it deems the KDC trustworthy or not. Once the initial AS request/response is finished, the remaining Kerberos protocol exchanges are unchanged. The TGT contains a conventional symmetric session key that can then be used to obtain tickets for further Kerberos resources.

Cross-Realm (PKCROSS)

PKCROSS simplifies the management of cross-realm relationships between Kerberos realms. Traditional cross-realm relationships in Kerberos require the participating realms to share secret keys, which imposes the key management problems inherent in symmetric key cryptography. Namely, secret keys must somehow be securely transmitted to each of the participating Kerberos KDCs. PKCROSS uses public key cryptography to eliminate the need for KDCs to share secret keys and allows for more scalable Kerberos cross-realm relationships.

From a client's perspective, communicating with two realms that use PKCROSS for cross-realm communication is exactly the same as communicating with two realms that use traditional Kerberos cross-realm shared keys. The operation of PKCROSS is entirely transparent to end users.

The PKCROSS extensions, instead, define a communication between the two KDCs involved in the cross-realm relationship. This is a major departure from traditional Kerberos protocols; no other Kerberos protocol exchange occurs between a KDC and another KDC. However, in this case, the direct KDC-to-KDC communication represents an elegant solution to public key cross-realm authentication. This way, Kerberos clients do not have to support public key encryption in order to communicate with realms that use PKCROSS for cross-realm authentication.

When a client requests a cross-realm TGT for two realms that support PKCROSS, the local KDC acts as a Kerberos client and requests a special cross-realm TGT from the remote realm's KDC. This process works much like the PKINIT process, except the role of client is played by the local realm's KDC.

Smart Cards

Traditionally, Kerberos has relied solely on one of the three factors of authentication, namely, something you know. As discussed early on in Chapter 2, the security of authentication systems can be greatly enhanced by requiring more than one factor to grant authentication. Smart cards provide another factor (what you have), and some Kerberos implementations support the use of smart cards for initial authentication.

The use of smart cards solves one of the most problematic issues with Kerberos; namely its dependence on users to choose (and remember) good passwords. Traditionally, the user's long-term key is a password, which is something the user must choose and memorize. The human brain is notoriously poor at producing and consequently remembering random sequences, so passwords are typically something easily remembered by the user. As a consequence, passwords have low entropy, and most fall to dictionary attacks. The use of pre-authentication in the initial Authentication Server exchange mitigates this risk somewhat, but a determined attacker who can sniff Kerberos protocol exchanges over the network can still obtain encrypted material on which to perform a dictionary attack.

In addition, smart cards limit the exposure of the sensitive cryptographic keys used throughout the Kerberos protocol. Secret keys stored on machine hard disks, such as keytab files, are vulnerable to attack. Even though filesystem protection is designed to prevent unauthorized users from reading sensitive files, software bugs persist that, when exploited, provide attackers with administrative access to the entire computer, including any encryption keys stored within.

Smart cards solve this problem by storing the key material internally on the smart card itself, and never allowing the key material to leave the smart card. Instead, the smart card has enough processing power to perform the cryptographic functions necessary to generate and respond to Kerberos authentication messages. Storing the key material on the smart card and securing the smart card from unauthorized access means that an attacker who has control over the user's workstation can never retrieve the encryption keys stored inside of the smartcard. This also mitigates Trojan horse techniques, where a program masquerading as the Kerberos login program acquires unwitting users' passwords.

Since a smart card is a physical device, it needs an interface to the host computer—the smart card reader. Smart card readers can connect to the host computer through several physical means, including serial, USB, and for laptops, PCMCIA slots. Because of the requirement for specialized hardware connected to the host machine, smart cards are currently only practically deployable in an organization's network.

Attacks on smart cards are difficult, as they are small physical devices designed to resist attack. It requires a determined and well-funded adversary to carry out an attack on a smart card. Analyses of the smart card's power usage and timing have been developed that greatly reduce the search space of possible encryption keys during a brute-force attack on a key stored inside of a smart card. Since the amount of calculations needed to perform encryption algorithms depends on the size and content of the encryption key, these attacks analyze the minute differences in power and time as the smart card performs these operations on various data. Determined attackers can narrow down the possible encryption keys based on this analysis and on detailed knowledge of the algorithms involved.

Incidentally, the timing attack has been demonstrated as a useful against on traditional software-based encryption software as well; a security advisory issued in 2003 warned users that the popular OpenSSL software package exposes timing information that may be enough for an adversary to derive the private encryption keys on a server. This goes to show that you can never be paranoid enough when implementing cryptographic systems.

Smart Cards and the Kerberos Protocol

Smart cards are typically deployed as part of a Public Key Infrastructure. When a new user is enabled, a public key pair is generated for the user, the public key is signed by the certificate authority, and the resulting key pair and certificate are placed onto the smart card's memory. The smart card is then issued to the user.

When the user uses a smart card to authenticate to a Kerberos realm, he inserts the smart card into the smart card reader connected to his computer. The computer prompts the user for a PIN, which is then sent to the smart card. The PIN unlocks the portion of the memory that houses the user's public key pair, to lessen the damage if the smart card is lost or stolen. Once the card has been unlocked in this way, PKINIT is used to obtain initial tickets for the user. The only difference is that the actual decryption of the initial AS response from the KDC is performed on the smart card itself, so that the public key pair is never directly accessible to the host computer.

Better Encryption

The art and algorithms of cryptography are always evolving, driven by the explosive growth in computer power and cryptographic theory. Increasing computer power provides a dual driving force for emerging cryptographic algorithms: first, it obsoletes older algorithms and short key lengths as they fall to practical brute-force attacks. A 56-bit single DES key can be brute forced by a network of commodity computers in less than a week, and that time is decreasing rapidly. Conversely, the increase in computing power makes possible the complex calculations of even more sophisticated algorithms and longer key lengths necessary to secure information from prying eyes. Theory drives the development of cryptographic algorithms as well, providing new ways to protect data as well as techniques to crack codes.

Because Kerberos is a system that depends heavily on cryptography, it is crucial that these new encryption methods are implemented in the Kerberos protocol. The Kerberos 5 protocol was designed to be extendable and support multiple encryption types; however, currently the only interoperable encryption type available across Kerberos implementations is single DES. Thankfully, the upcoming release of MIT Kerberos 1.3 will provide wider support for the RC4-HMAC encryption type first introduced by Microsoft for use in Windows 2000's Kerberos service.

For further growth, there are proposed Internet Drafts that specify more, stronger encryption options for future implementations of the Kerberos protocol. The new NIST encryption standard, the Advanced Encryption Standard or AES, is one of the encryption algorithms that is proposed for future implementations of the Kerberos protocol. AES will replace the decades-old DES encryption algorithm as the federal standard for encrypting sensitive but unclassified information. The algorithm for AES, Rijndael, was chosen in 2000 among a field of algorithms submitted by civilian cryptographers from around the world. Rijndael is a block cipher that boasts a variable key size, providing protection against brute force attacks in the foreseeable future.

The latest Kerberos Clarifications require that new Kerberos implementations support AES encryption types, greatly increasing the cryptographic security of future Kerberos implementations. The Kerberos Clarifications have demoted the current single DES encryption type to optional ("SHOULD support") status, due to its small fixed key size. The use of stronger cryptographic algorithms in the future will continue to protect Kerberos from brute-force attacks.

Kerberos Referrals

As originally implemented in MIT Kerberos 5, each Kerberos client requires detailed configuration information about all realms the client participates in. With Unix clients, the information is coded in the */etc/krb5.conf* file. This file must be kept up to date and distributed to all clients, which, in large and complex network environments, can quickly become an unwieldy and unmanageable task. Furthermore, machines that are not centrally managed or mobile machines such as laptops are even more problematic, as distributing changes to the Kerberos configuration files to these machines is nearly impossible.

Microsoft recognized the need for a new method for handling this configuration information in a centralized place when it implemented Kerberos in its Windows 2000 operating system, and created a system by which the KDC can provide clients correct replies, even when queries are misdirected or malformed. Through this mechanism, clients only require minimal configuration, enough to find their local Kerberos realm, and all queries are directed to the local KDC, even cross-realm queries destined for a foreign Kerberos realm. The Kerberos support in Microsoft's Windows 2000 and later operating systems includes support for—and, indeed, depends on—the functioning of Kerberos referrals for Windows domain operations.

There are three classes of information that the Microsoft implementation of Kerberos referrals handles for Kerberos clients: user and service principal name canonicalization through the AS and TGS exchanges respectively, and cross-realm trust relationships. Extensions to the Kerberos protocol are used to provide this capability and retain backwards compatibility with implementations that do not understand Kerberos referrals.

But first, what is *name canonicalization?* Both people and hosts can be known by several names, such as in the case of hostname aliases or multihomed hosts. Each user can have several names associated with him as well, such as his email address or his Kerberos principal name. Since Kerberos associates a single principal with a single key, it is required that these names be changed into a normalized format and name, so that there is a single Kerberos principal that refers uniquely to a given user or host. For example, a host with several IP addresses and several hostnames must be assigned a single "official" hostname. This hostname is referred to as the host's *canonical* hostname. Kerberos referrals move the burden of name canonicalization from the client and DNS to the KDC.

User Principal Canonicalization

KDC-side user principal canonicalization provides for both user and administrator convenience. Similar to passwords, users want to remember only one identifying principal. For example, a user's email address may be different than his Kerberos principal name. Furthermore, the Kerberos principal name associated with the user may change if he moves between departments, while his email address stays the same.

Therefore, Kerberos referrals provide a new field in the AS exchange for clients to send an alternative name when acquiring the initial TGT. When the KDC receives an AS request with this field filled in, the KDC will search a directory to map the user name given to a principal that exists in the local Kerberos database. If the user does not exist in the local realm, the KDC may instead use the cross-realm referral mechanism, described below, to refer the client to the correct realm.

Service Principal Canonicalization

Service name canonicalization is a hard problem to solve on the client side. There are several solutions that are commonly used for service name canonicalization in current implementations. The first technique employed is to simply take the network name given by the user verbatim, and shift it to lowercase. The service name and the lowercased hostname are concatenated to form the service principal that the client requests from the KDC. This method has a major drawback: many users may use a short hostname or host alias when entering in host names, when the service principal is generated using the fully qualified domain name of the host name. When these names are used in the TGS request to the KDC, then the KDC may not be able to find the service principal, as the hostname given by the user may not be the same as the hostname component of the service principal in the Kerberos database.

The second canonicalization technique uses the DNS. The Kerberos libraries take the hostname given by the user, perform a DNS lookup to get the host's IP address, and perform a reverse lookup on the IP address to get the host's primary DNS fully-qualified domain name. This technique solves the problem of a host that has several DNS aliases, but does not solve the problem of a multihomed host that has several IP addresses, each with a different hostname. While this behavior of assigning multiple hostnames to the different interfaces of a multihomed machine is discouraged in the Host Requirements RFC, it is still common in many network layouts. Furthermore, DNS lookups are not secure, and it is possible that a user may acquire tickets for a service he did not intend to communicate with. The Kerberos Clarifications require that future Kerberos implementations not use the DNS for service name canonicalization for this reason.

KDC-side service principal canonicalization can solve these problems. The KDC maintains a mapping between the host aliases and the canonical hostname used in the Kerberos service principals for that host. When Kerberos clients request a service principal through the TGS exchange, the client sets a canonicalize bit in the TGS request, signaling the KDC that it is permitted to return a ticket for a service name other than the one requested. The KDC looks up the service name in its Kerberos database, and returns a different principal name than the one requested if it recognizes that the client has requested a principal with a hostname other than the canonical hostname.

Cross-Realm Referrals

All of the above also ties into the cross-realm referral capability provided by Kerberos referrals. Traditionally, clients are required to track the mapping of DNS domain names to Kerberos realm names as well as the certification and trust relationships between multiple realms. These mappings exist in the domain_realm and capaths stanzas of the MIT and Heimdal *krb5.conf* configuration file. The client is responsible for determining the realm that each service it requests a ticket for belongs to, and if necessary, requesting all of the required tickets along the certification path between the client and the service the client wishes to reach. In the case that both client and service are located in the same realm, this is a trivial task since the client can ask its KDC directly for tickets for the service. However, when client and service are located in different realms, the client must request cross-realm tickets from all intermediary Kerberos realms between itself and the destination service.

With Kerberos referrals, the client simply asks its local KDC for tickets to all services, regardless of whether the service is in the local realm or in a remote realm. When the KDC receives a ticket request, the KDC checks to see if the service exists in the local realm. If so, it returns a ticket as usual; if it does not find the service, it will instead return a cross-realm ticket to the next realm in the certification path. The client will then use this cross-realm ticket and contact the KDC in the next realm in the path, asking for the target service. This process repeats until either the client receives a ticket for the target service from a KDC serving the service's realm, or an error is returned because either there is no path to the target realm, or the target realm doesn't have an entry in its Kerberos database for the target service.

Web Services

Web services are an important new technology, and are used extensively in new frameworks such as Microsoft's .Net. Web services facilitate the transfer of structured data across networks by defining a standardized transport mechanism (for example, SOAP over HTTP). While the explosion of the World Wide Web was due to the large amount of human-readable content available through HTML pages, the development of more complex systems requires a standard by which applications can communicate directly with one another over the web. Web services seek to use the power of the web to provide language- and platform-neutral communication methods that can link applications across many different organizations.

However, current web services typically do not provide secure authentication and encryption support. Many web services that require access control use the authentication and security mechanisms of the underlying protocol (HTTP)—for example, by using Basic Authentication for access control and SSL-encrypted HTTP (HTTPS) for transport. This solution does not scale well, and if the HTTP server is decoupled from the web service, it presents a problem where authentication information for the web service must be kept synchronized with the HTTP server.

To address these shortcomings, the WS-Security specification is under development by IBM, Microsoft, and VeriSign. The WS-Security specification defines a set of

SOAP extensions that can be used to provide confidentiality and integrity services to web services. WS-Security defines a set of SOAP messages that can encapsulate generic security token objects and associate these security tokens with specific SOAP messages. Therefore, WS-Security is not tied to one particular algorithm or security system, and indeed can be used with security and authentication protocols such as SSL, X.509 (for public key certificates), and Kerberos.

While WS-Security specifies a standardized format for the transmission and encoding of security tokens and encrypted messages, it does not cover the messages needed to perform the actual authentication or key exchange required to establish secure communications. Instead, the WS-Security proposal delegates this task to the individual security mechanism used in the communications. In the case of Kerberos, the traditional Kerberos protocol is used to establish identity and generate a session key that then can be used by applications that use WS-Security to protect SOAP message exchanges.

Work on WS-Security is ongoing, and general information on WS-Security can be found on Microsoft's MSDN site at *http://msdn.microsoft.com/library/default.asp?url=/ library/en-us/dnwssecur/html/securitywhitepaper.asp*. The full WS-Security specification can be found at IBM's DeveloperWorks web site at *http://www-106.ibm.com/ developerworks/webservices/library/ws-secure/*.

Appendix: Administration Reference

Each of the KDC implementations covered in this book has different administrative interfaces. We've already seen the basics of each administrative interface when we set up the KDC, but this section provides an in-depth reference on the various commands available to Kerberos administrators.

MIT

In MIT Kerberos 5, Kerberos database tasks are performed by the kadmind daemon. Normally, this daemon is run on KDC startup when the main Kerberos daemon, krb5kdc, is started. The kadmind daemon listens for client requests on TCP port 749. The client, kadmin, can be run on any machine that is able to communicate with the KDC. It is recommended that a firewall be used to limit network access to port 749 to restrict unauthorized users from connecting to the administrative daemon.

The kadmin client uses configuration from *etc/krb5.conf* to locate the master KDC that runs the kadmind server. It will use the value of the admin_server parameter located in the realm that the client is a member of. If you compiled with DNS support (the default), it will also attempt to use DNS to locate the admin server service. If these methods fail, kadmin will give up attempting to look for a server, and exit with an error message. You can manually specify a realm name and server address with the -r and -s options, respectively.

After a connection has been established between the kadmin client and the kadmind server, the client performs mutual authentication with the administration server, using a temporary credential cache to acquire tickets to authenticate with the server, for security reasons.

Note that a MIT kadmin client is required to communicate with an MIT kadmind server. You cannot use Heimdal kadmin to administer an MIT KDC.

There is also a fail-safe copy of kadmin named kadmin.local that accesses the Kerberos database directly on the KDC. To run kadmin.local, you must be root on the master KDC. The commands available in kadmin.local are the same as the commands available in kadmin.

Connecting to kadmin

You do not need any special privileges on the client machine to use kadmin; all you need is the password to a principal that has privileges enabled in the kadmin ACL file.

```
% /usr/local/sbin/kadmin
Authenticating as principal jgarman/admin@WEDGIE.ORG with password.
Enter password:
kadmin:
```

Inside of kadmin, a list of available commands is always available through the "?" command.

The fail-safe copy of kadmin, *kadmin.local*, requires root privileges to run. You have to be root on the master KDC to run *kadmin.local* because it modifies the Kerberos database directly. As such, running *kadmin.local* does not require any Kerberos daemons to be running, and in fact it is most commonly used to set up the initial Kerberos principals when establishing a new realm. Starting *kadmin.local* is very similar to starting kadmin:

```
# /usr/local/sbin/kadmin.local
Authenticating as principal jgarman/admin@WEDGIE.ORG with password.
kadmin.local:
```

---

listprincs   Listing principals

listprincs *[glob-pattern]*

Aliases   list_principals, get_principals, getprincs

The listprincs command lists the principals currently residing in the Kerberos database. Without parameters, listprincs lists all principals. An optional glob-pattern can be used to limit the output to a particular subset of principals.

The output of listprincs is terse; each line of output contains the principal name and nothing more. For more information about a principal or set of principals, see the getprinc command.

The listprincs command requires that the user have L permissions on the principals that they are listing.

Examples

```
kadmin:  listprincs
K/M@WEDGIE.ORG
jdoe/admin@WEDGIE.ORG
jdoe@WEDGIE.ORG
jgarman/admin@WEDGIE.ORG
kadmin/admin@WEDGIE.ORG
```

kadmin/changepw@WEDGIE.ORG
kadmin/history@WEDGIE.ORG
krbtgt/WEDGIE.ORG@WEDGIE.ORG

getprinc

getprinc *principal-name*

Aliases

get_principal

The getprinc command retrieves detailed information about a principal from the Kerberos database. The getprinc command requires one parameter, a principal name that matches one principal that exists in the Kerberos database.

getprinc requires that users have I permissions on the principals that they are retrieving information on.

Examples

```
kadmin:  getprinc jgarman/admin
Principal: jgarman/admin@WEDGIE.ORG
Expiration date: [never]
Last password change: Wed Nov 13 00:38:06 GMT 2002
Password expiration date: [none]
Maximum ticket life: 0 days 10:00:00
Maximum renewable life: 0 days 00:00:00
Last modified: Wed Nov 13 00:38:06 GMT 2002 (kadmind@WEDGIE.ORG)
Last successful authentication: [never]
Last failed authentication: [never]
Failed password attempts: 0
Number of keys: 2
Key: vno 5, Triple DES cbc mode with HMAC/sha1, no salt
Key: vno 5, DES cbc mode with CRC-32, no salt
Attributes:
Policy: [none]
```

The output contains the following fields:

Expiration date
> This is the date and time at which the principal will no longer be able to acquire tickets. It can be set per-principal or as part of a policy.

Last password change
> This is the date that the principal's password was last changed, either through kpasswd or through a change password command executed by an administrator. Will show [never] if the principal's password has never been reset.

Password expiration date
> This is the date when the principal's password expires. Password expiration dates can be set per-principal or as part of a policy. If this principal's password never expires, [none] will be shown in this field.

Maximum ticket life and Maximum renewable life
> These fields show the maximum lifetime of tickets that can be issued on behalf of this principal.

Last modified

This field shows the time that any of the principal's data was last modified, and what principal made the change. If a principal's password is changed through kpasswd, the modification appears to come from the special principal kadmind. If a modification is made from inside the administrative interface, the administrator's principal is shown in this field. In the above case, jgarman/admin's password was last modified on November 13, 2002 through kpasswd.

Last successful authentication, Last failed authentication, and Failed password attempts

Unfortunately, these fields always show [never]. While all of the other updates to a principal's information, such as password changes or policy changes, must be made through the master KDC, any KDC (master or slave) can perform authentication. There is currently no way for a slave KDC to report back to the master KDC that an authentication has occurred, so the MIT code disables these fields.

Number of keys (and Key listing)

This field enumerates the different key encryption types and salts that are associated with this principal. This field can help troubleshoot problems that may occur when trying to interoperate between Kerberos implementations that support different key types.

Attributes

This field enumerates special attributes that are associated with principals. Typical user principals will not have any attributes, but some attributes can be useful for security purposes. MIT sets the DISALLOW_TGT_BASED attributes on the kadmin/ changepw and kadmin/admin principals to prevent the KDC from issuing TGTs for these principals. In addition, MIT sets the DISALLOW_ALL_TIX on the master key's principal, K/M, to prevent any tickets (including service tickets) to be issued for it. A full list of attributes can be found in the next section, Adding a Principal.

Policy

This field lists the policy that this principal is subject to. Policies are discussed in more detail in Chapter 6.

---

addprinc
Adding a principal

addprinc *[-expire expiredate] [-pwexpire pwexpiredate] [-maxlife maxtixlife]*
 [-kvno kvno] [-policy policyname] [-randkey] [-pw password] [-maxrenewlife
 maxrenewlife] [-e keysaltlist] [(+/-)attribute] principal-name

Aliases   add_principal, ank

The addprinc command adds a new principal into the Kerberos database. This command requires one argument, the name of the new principal to add. The command also recognizes several optional arguments that specify policy information the new principal should be subject to. More information about password policies is available in Chapter 6.

Other options include the randkey option, which adds the principal with a random key. This option is good to use for services that require secure keys that don't have to be memorized by a human. If the principal needs to have a special key encryption type or salt, it can

---

be specified with the -e option. Following is a full list of all of the options available to addprinc:

-expire expiredate

This option sets an expiry date for the principal. After the date specified, tickets will no longer be issued for the principal, and requests by the principal to obtain service tickets will not be honored.

-pwexpire pwexpiredate

This option sets the password expiry date for the principal.

-maxlife maxtixlife

This option sets the maximum lifetime of tickets issued for the principal.

-kvno kvno

This option sets the key version number for the principal's key to kvno. Unless you need to override the default for some reason, this option is not recommended.

-policy policyname

This option sets the principal's policy to policyname. Policies are discussed in more detail in Chapter 6.

-randkey

This option gives the new principal a random encryption key, instead of prompting the administrator for a password.

-pw password

This option sets the principal's password to password instead of prompting on the terminal for one.

-maxrenewlife maxrenewlife

This option sets the maximum renewable lifetime of tickets issued for the principal.

-e keysaltlist

This option forces the key encryption type and salts generated for the principal to those listed in keysaltlist. If more than one encryption type and salt type are desired, then keysaltlist should be a space-separated list of encryption type:salt pairs enclosed by quotation marks.

The following attributes can be set on a new principal. An attribute can be prefixed by either a plus (+) or a minus (–) sign, denoting whether to enable or disable that attribute.

allow_postdated

This attribute allows the issuance of postdated tickets for the principal. By default, the KDC will issue postdated tickets for a new principal.

allow_forwardable

This attribute allows the issuance of forwardable tickets for the principal. By default, the KDC will issue forwardable tickets for a new principal.

allow_renewable

This attribute allows the issuance of renewable tickets for the principal. By default, the KDC will issue renewable tickets for a new principal.

allow_proxiable

This attribute allows the issuance of proxiable tickets for the principal. By default, the KDC will issue proxiable tickets for a new principal.

allow_dup_skey

This attribute allows the KDC to issue this principal tickets containing the session key of another user. This functionality is used during User-to-User authentication. By default, this attribute is enabled.

requires_preauth

This attribute requires pre-authentication to be performed before tickets will be issued on this principal's behalf. Pre-authentication is discussed in more detail in Chapter 6. By default, principals do not have to pre-authenticate.

requires_hwauth

This attribute requires hardware pre-authentication to be performed before tickets will be issued on this principal's behalf. By default, principals do not have to use hardware pre-authentication.

allow_svr

This attribute allows the KDC to issue service tickets for this principal. By default, the KDC will issue service tickets for every principal.

allow_tgs_req

This attribute allows the KDC to issue Ticket Granting Tickets for this principal. By default, the KDC will issue a TGT to any requesting principal.

allow_tix

This attribute allows the KDC to issue tickets for this principal. Disabling this attribute disallows the issuance of any ticket for or on behalf of this principal. By default, this attribute is enabled.

needchange

This attribute forces a password change when the principal next requests a ticket. Once the password is successfully changed, this attribute is cleared. By default, this attribute is disabled.

password_changing_service

This attribute is set on the principals used for password changing (for example, kadmin/changepw). You should never have to use this attribute; it is only included here for completeness.

The addprinc command requires that the administrator have A permissions on the principal he is adding.

Example

```
kadmin: ank -randkey -allow_tgs_req host/desktop.wedgie.org
WARNING: no policy specified for host/desktop.wedgie.org@WEDGIE.ORG; defaulting to no
policy
Principal "host/desktop.wedgie.org@WEDGIE.ORG" created.
```

This example creates a host principal for *desktop.wedgie.org* with a random key and marks it so that no TGTs can be issued for it.

modprinc

modprinc *[-expire expiredate] [-pwexpire pwexpiredate] [-maxlife maxtixlife]*
  [-kvno kvno] [-policy policyname] [-clearpolicy] [(+/-)attribute] principal-name

Aliases
          modify_principal

The modprinc command modifies selected attributes of the principal. It accepts most of the arguments that are accepted by addprinc, and adds one: clearpolicy. The optional clearpolicy argument removes all policies that are currently applied to the principal given. For more information on the optional arguments accepted by modprinc, see the previous section on addprinc.

The modprinc command requires that the administrator have M permissions on the principal she is modifying.

Example

```
kadmin:  modprinc -clearpolicy jdoe/admin
Principal "jdoe/admin@WEDGIE.ORG" modified.
```

cpw

cpw *principal-name*

Aliases
          change_password

The cpw command changes the password associated with the principal given as an argument.

The cpw command requires that the administrator have C permissions on the principal whose password he is changing.

Example

```
kadmin:  cpw jgarman/admin
Enter password for principal "jgarman/admin":
Re-enter password for principal "jgarman/admin":
Password for "jgarman/admin@WEDGIE.ORG" changed.
```

delprinc

delprinc *principal-name*

Aliases
          delete_principal

The delprinc command deletes a principal from the Kerberos database. Note that deleting a principal does not automatically delete it from access control lists in which it appears. If a principal is added with the same name as one that is deleted, the new principal inherits all of the privileges of the old principal.

The delprinc command requires that the administrator have the D permission on the principal he is deleting.

Example

```
kadmin: delprinc jdoe
Are you sure you want to delete the principal "jdoe@WEDGIE.ORG"? (yes/no): yes
Principal "jdoe@WEDGIE.ORG" deleted.
Make sure that you have removed this principal from all ACLs before reusing.
```

ktadd

Adding keys into keytabs

ktadd [-k keytab] [-e keysaltlist] principal-name | -glob glob-pattern

Aliases   xst

The ktadd command creates a random key for a principal or set of principals in the Kerberos database, and returns those keys to the client so that they can be saved into a keytab file on the client machine. This command is used to create keytabs for service and host principals in a Kerberos realm.

Note that ktadd does not extract the current key from the Kerberos database; it instead creates a new, random key and returns it, incrementing the key version number to indicate that a new key has been generated. This is a deliberate design decision, as it prevents a rogue administrator from simply dumping the entire Kerberos database through kadmin. It also means that the old keys or passwords assigned to this principal will no longer be valid once ktadd is run on the principal, and you cannot run ktadd from more than one system on the same principal since they will receive different keys.

Optional parameters include -k to specify the path to the keytab file to append to; the default is the system keytab file in /etc/krb5.keytab. You can also specify the -e option to indicate the list of encryption keys and salts to use when creating and extracting the new key.

The ktadd command requires that the administrator have I and C permissions on the principals that she is adding to the keytab.

Example

```
kadmin:  ktadd -k /tmp/key host/slave.wedgie.org@WEDGIE.ORG
Entry for principal host/slave.wedgie.org with kvno 3, encryption type Triple DES cbc
mode with HMAC/sha1 added to keytab WRFILE:/tmp/key.
Entry for principal host/slave.wedgie.org with kvno 3, encryption type DES cbc mode
with CRC-32 added to keytab WRFILE:/tmp/key.
```

Ktutil

The ktutil program is a small utility program that allows administrators to manipulate keytab files. Ktutil is the recommended way to append keytabs to one another and delete entries from existing keytabs. The ktutil program requires no arguments, but will require enough privileges to read and write the appropriate keytabs. Typically, this means that you must run ktutil as root.

The ktutil utility starts with an empty keylist. Keys are added to the keylist as keytab files are read in, and keys can be deleted from the keylist. When the keylist is ready, it can be written out to a new keytab file, or appended to an existing one. A synopsis of the commands follows.

clear
Clear keylist

clear

This command clears the current keylist held in memory. It does not affect the contents of any keytab files that may have previously been read into ktutil.

list
List entries in keylist

list [-e] [-t] [-k]

Aliases   l

The list command displays the principals whose keys are stored in the keylist. By default, the list command will dump the key version number and the principal of each entry in the keylist, along with a numerical identifier referred to as the "slot" that can be used as input to the delete command to uniquely identify a particular entry.

Each of the optional arguments adds additional information to the keylist display. The -e argument also dumps the encryption type of every entry in the keylist. The -t argument dumps the timestamp of when the key was added into the keytab, and the -k argument dumps the hexadecimal encryption key itself.

Example

```
ktutil: l -e
slot KVNO Principal
---- ---- ----------------------------------------------------------------
   1    3     host/freebsd.wedgie.org@WEDGIE.ORG (Triple DES cbc mode with HMAC/sha1)
   2    3     host/freebsd.wedgie.org@WEDGIE.ORG (DES cbc mode with CRC-32)
   3    3     ldap/freebsd.wedgie.org@WEDGIE.ORG (Triple DES cbc mode with HMAC/sha1)
   4    3     ldap/freebsd.wedgie.org@WEDGIE.ORG (DES cbc mode with CRC-32)
```

rkt
Read keytab

rkt keytab-file

The rkt command reads the contents of a keytab file and appends the keys in the keytab to the keylist. The original keytab file is unchanged.

addent

addent *(-key | -password) -p principal -k kvno -e enctype*

The addent command adds an entry to the keylist manually. All parameters to addent are required. The encryption key associated with the new entry can be specified either by a hexadecimal key or by a password that is run through string2key to produce an encryption key. Ktadmin will prompt for the key or password.

The second parameter specifies that principal that is to be added to the keylist. If no realm is specified with the principal name, the default realm is assumed. The remaining parameters specify the key version number and encryption type to be associated with this entry.

Example

To create a new keylist entry for the principal blah@WEDGIE.ORG, with a key version number of 1 and using a DES key derived from a password string:

```
ktutil:  addent -password -p blah@WEDGIE.ORG -k 1 -e des
Password for blah@WEDGIE.ORG:
```

delent

delent *slot-no*

The delent command deletes an entry from the internal keylist. The entry to be deleted is specified by the slot number that it occupies, which can be determined from the output of the list command.

wkt

wkt *keytab-file*

The wkt command writes the contents of the keylist into a keytab file. The wkt command can be rather confusing. Instead of overwriting the contents of the keytab file if it already exists, the wkt command will append the contents of the keylist to the existing keytab file. Therefore, if you want to delete an entry from the system keytab file, you must read it in, delete the offending entry, use the wkt command to write it to a new file, then replace the system keytab file with the new keytab file. If you instead use wkt to write the keylist to the system keytab directly, it will append the keylist to the existing keytab, creating a mess of duplicate entries.

Heimdal

In Heimdal Kerberos, Kerberos database tasks are performed by the kadmind daemon. Normally this daemon is run on KDC startup when the main Kerberos daemon, kdc, is started. The kadmind daemon listens for client requests on TCP port

749. The client, kadmin, can be run on any machine that is able to communicate with the KDC. It is recommended that a firewall be used to limit network access to port 749 to restrict unauthorized users from connecting to the administrative daemon.

Heimdal uses the */etc/krb5.conf* configuration file to locate the master KDC running the kadmind server. The value of the admin_server parameter listed in the realm that the client is a member of is used as the server to connect to. If this parameter does not exist, or the administration server is not running on that server, then kadmin will exit with an error message. You can manually specify a realm and kadmind server by using the -r and -a command-line options, respectively.

After a connection has been established between the kadmin client and the kadmind server, the client performs mutual authentication with the administration server, using a temporary credential cache to acquire tickets to authenticate with the server for security reasons.

Note that a Heimdal kadmin client is required to communicate with a Heimdal kadmind server. You cannot use MIT kadmin to administer a Heimdal KDC.

Heimdal also contains a fail-safe method for editing the Kerberos database. By logging into the master KDC directly as root, and using the -l option to kadmin, you can edit the Kerberos database directly on disk without communicating over the network.

Connecting to kadmin

The Heimdal kadmin program is used to connect to the Heimdal kadmind server. To connect to a remote kadmind server over the network, you do not have to have any special privileges on your local machine, but you do have to login with a principal that has privileges defined in the *kadmind.acl* file.

```
% /usr/heimdal/sbin/kadmin
kadmin>
```

Note that kadmin will not ask for your credentials until after you've submitted your first command.

---

list Listing principals

list *glob-pattern*

The list command lists the principals currently residing in the Kerberos database. Without parameters, list will list all principals. A glob-pattern is a required parameter to list; the asterisk (*) can be used to list all principals in the database.

The output of list is terse; each line of output contains the principal name and nothing more. For more information about a principal or set of principals, see the get command.

The list command requires that the user have list permissions on the principals that they are listing.

Example

```
kadmin> list *
  jdoe@WEDGIE.ORG
  default@WEDGIE.ORG
  jgarman@WEDGIE.ORG
  jdoe/admin@WEDGIE.ORG
  kadmin/admin@WEDGIE.ORG
  kadmin/hprop@WEDGIE.ORG
  jgarman/admin@WEDGIE.ORG
  kadmin/changepw@WEDGIE.ORG
  krbtgt/WEDGIE.ORG@WEDGIE.ORG
  changepw/kerberos@WEDGIE.ORG
```

---

get   Getting detailed principal information

get *glob-pattern*

Aliases   get_entry

The get command retrieves detailed information about a principal from the Kerberos database. The get command requires one parameter, a glob pattern that matches one or more principals that exist in the Kerberos database.

The get command requires that the user have get permissions on the principals that they are retrieving information on.

Examples

```
kadmin> get jgarman*
              Principal: jgarman@WEDGIE.ORG
      Principal expires: never
       Password expires: never
   Last password change: never
         Max ticket life: 1 day
      Max renewable life: 1 week
                   Kvno: 2
                  Mkvno: 0
                 Policy: none
   Last successful login: never
      Last failed login: never
      Failed login count: 0
          Last modified: 2002-11-10 23:54:58 UTC
               Modifier: jgarman/admin@WEDGIE.ORG
             Attributes:
Keytypes(salttype[(salt-value)]): des3-cbc-sha1(pw-salt), des-cbc-md5(pw-salt), des-
cbc-md4(pw-salt), des-cbc-crc(pw-salt)

              Principal: jgarman/admin@WEDGIE.ORG
      Principal expires: never
       Password expires: never
   Last password change: never
         Max ticket life: 1 day
      Max renewable life: 1 week
```

```
                   Kvno: 1
                  Mkvno: 0
                 Policy: none
  Last successful login: never
      Last failed login: never
     Failed login count: 0
          Last modified: 2002-10-25 03:02:55 UTC
               Modifier: kadmin/admin@WEDGIE.ORG
             Attributes:
Keytypes(salttype[(salt-value)]): des3-cbc-sha1(pw-salt), des-cbc-md5(pw-salt), des-
cbc-md4(pw-salt), des-cbc-crc(pw-salt)
```

The output contains the following fields:

Principal expires

> This field lists the date and time at which the principal expires. At this time, the principal will no longer be valid either as a client or server principal, and no tickets will be issued for it.

Password expires

> This field lists the date and time at which the principal's password (or key) expires. The next time the principal requests a Ticket Granting Ticket as part of its login process, it will be required to change its password.

Last password change

> This field lists the date and time at which the principal's password was last changed, either by the user or by a Kerberos administrator.

Max ticket life and Max renewable life

> These fields list the maximum lifetime of tickets issued on behalf of this principal.

Kvno

> This field lists the key version number of the principal; typically, the key version number is incremented every time the key of that principal changes.

Mkvno

> This field lists the master key version number of the principal. The master key can be changed on a regular basis, and this field lists which master key this principal is currently using.

Policy

> This field lists the password policy that the principal is subject to. More information about password policies can be found in Chapter 6.

Last successful login, Last failed login, and Failed login count

> Unfortunately, these fields will always show never (or zero). The reason for this is that while all of the other updates to a principal's information, such as password changes or policy changes, must be made through the master KDC, any KDC (master or slave) can perform authentication. There is currently no way for a slave KDC to report back to the master KDC that an authentication has occurred, so the Heimdal code disables these fields.

Last modified and Modifier

> These fields report the last time any attribute of this principal was modified, and the principal that performed the modification. Newly created principals will have a modifier of kadmin/admin, and any other modifications will contain the users' principal (if

the user changes their own password) or an administrators' principal (if an administrator changes an attribute of the principal).

Attributes

This field enumerates special attributes that are associated with principals. Typical user principals will not have any attributes, but some attributes can be useful for security purposes. A full list of attributes can be found in the next section.

Keytypes

This field enumerates all of the key encryption types and salts that are stored for the principal. This field can help troubleshoot problems that may occur when trying to interoperate between Kerberos implementations that support different key types.

---

add
Adding a principal

```
add [--random-key] [--random-password] [--password=password] [--key=hexkey]
   [--max-ticket-life=lifetime] [--max-renewable-life=lifetime]
   [--attributes=attributes] [--expiration-time=time] [--pw-expiration-time=time]
   [--use-defaults] principal-name
```

Aliases   add_new_key, ank

The add command adds a new principal into the Kerberos database. This command requires one argument, the name of the new principal to add, and also recognizes several optional arguments that specify policy information the new principal should be subject to. More information about password policies is available in Chapter 6.

Other options include the random-key option that adds the principal with a random key. This option is good to use for services that require secure keys that don't have to be memorized by a human. Following is a full list of all of the options available to addprinc:

--expiration-time=expiredate

This option sets an expiry date for the principal. After the date specified, tickets will no longer be issued for the principal, and requests by the principal to obtain service tickets will not be honored.

--pw-expiration-time=pwexpiredate

This option sets the password expiry date for the principal.

--max-ticket-life=maxtixlife

This option sets the maximum lifetime of tickets issued for the principal.

--password=password

This option sets the principal's password to the argument given, instead of prompting on the terminal for one. This option is useful when invoking kadmin through a script.

-policy policyname

This option sets the principal's policy to policyname. Policies are discussed in more detail in Chapter 6.

--random-key and --random-password

This option gives the new principal a random encryption key, instead of prompting the administrator for a password. The --random-password parameter is similar, but instead of creating a DES key directly, it creates a random password which is then run through string2key and can handle multiple encryption types.

-max-renewable-life=maxrenewlife

This option sets the maximum renewable lifetime of tickets issued for the principal.

--attributes=attributelist

This option gives the newly created principal the attributes listed in attributelist. A complete list of attributes is provided below.

Every principal can have one or more attributes associated with it. Most of the time, you won't need to specify any attributes; however, here is a list of the attributes available in Heimdal and possible scenarios in which they may be useful. Note that to unset any of the following attributes, prepend the attribute with a minus sign (–). For example, to unset the `disallow-all-tix` attribute, use `--attributes=-disallow-all-tix`. Multiple attributes can be listed by separating them with commas.

disallow-postdated

This attribute disallows the issuance of postdated tickets for the principal. By default, the KDC will issue postdated tickets for a new principal.

disallow-forwardable

This attribute disallows the issuance of forwardable tickets for the principal. By default, the KDC will issue forwardable tickets for a new principal.

disallow-renewable

This attribute disallows the issuance of renewable tickets for the principal. By default, the KDC will issue renewable tickets for a new principal.

disallow-proxiable

This attribute disallows the issuance of proxiable tickets for the principal. By default, the KDC will issue proxiable tickets for a new principal.

disallow-dup-skey

This attribute disallows the KDC to issue this principal tickets containing the session key of another user. This functionality is used during User-to-User authentication. By default, the KDC will issue tickets containing the session key of another user for User-to-User authentication.

requires-pre-auth

This attribute requires pre-authentication to be performed before tickets will be issued on this principal's behalf. Pre-authentication is discussed in more detail in Chapter 6. By default, principals do not have to pre-authenticate.

requires-hw-auth

This attribute requires hardware pre-authentication to be performed before tickets will be issued on this principal's behalf. By default, principals do not have to use hardware pre-authentication.

disallow-svr

This attribute disallows the KDC to issue service tickets for this principal. By default, the KDC will issue service tickets for every principal.

disallow-all-tix

Setting this attribute will cause the KDC to deny issuing any tickets for the principal. Enabling this attribute disallows the issuance of any ticket for or on behalf of this principal. By default, this attribute is disabled and the KDC will issue tickets for and on behalf of the principal.

modify

```
modify [--max-ticket-life=lifetime] [--max-renewable-life=lifetime]
  [--attributes=attributes] [--expiration-time=time] [--pw-expiration-time=time]
  [--kvno=kvno] [-policy policyname] principal-name
```

The modify command modifies selected attributes of the principal. It accepts most of the arguments that are accepted by add, and adds one: kvno. The optional kvno argument changes the key version number listed on the principal. You should never have to change the key version number manually, but it can come in handy in some unusual circumstances. For more information on the optional arguments accepted by modify, see the previous section on add.

The modify command requires that the administrator have modify permissions on the principal she is modifying.

Note that when modifying a principal's attributes, the attributes given will replace any attributes already set on the principal.

Example

```
kadmin> modify --attributes=requires-pre-auth jgarman
```

cpw

```
cpw [--random-key] [--random-password] [--password=password] [--key=hexkey]
  principal-name
```

Aliases   passwd

The cpw command changes the password of the principal-name given as an argument. Without arguments, cpw will prompt for a new password on the terminal. The other arguments have the same meaning as in the add command.

The cpw command requires that the administrator have change-password (or cpw) permissions on the principal she is modifying.

Example

```
kadmin> cpw jgarman
jgarman@WEDGIE.ORG's Password:
Verifying password - jgarman@WEDGIE.ORG's Password:
```

delete

```
delete principal-name
```

The delete command deletes a principal from the Kerberos database. Note that deleting a principal does not automatically delete it from various access control lists that the principal may be listed on. If a principal is readded with the same name as one that is deleted, then the new principal will inherit all of the privileges of the old principal.

The delete command requires that the administrator have delete permission on the principal he is deleting.

Example

```
kadmin> delete jgarman
kadmin>
```

ext_keytab Adding keys into keytabs

ext_keytab [-k keytab] glob-pattern ...

Aliases   ext

The ext_keytab command creates a random key for a principal or set of principals in the Kerberos database, and returns those keys to the client so that they can be saved into a keytab file on the client machine. This command is used to create keytabs for service and host principals in a Kerberos realm.

Note that ext_keytab will not extract the current key from the Kerberos database; it instead creates a new, random key and return it, incrementing the key version number to indicate that a new key has been generated. This is a deliberate design decision, as it prevents a rogue administrator from simply dumping the entire Kerberos database through kadmin. It also means that the old keys or passwords assigned to this principal will no longer be valid once ext_keytab is run on the principal, and you cannot run ext_keytab from more than one system on the same principal since they will receive different keys.

The only optional parameter that ext_keytab understands is -k to place the key into a different keytab than the default, */etc/krb5.keytab*. Any number of principal names or glob patterns matching principals can follow the command; all of the principals that match the list given will be appended to the keytab file.

The ext_keytab command requires that the administrator have get privileges on the principal(s) he is extracting.

Example

```
kadmin> ext_keytab -k /tmp/hostkey host/desktop.wedgie.org
kadmin>
```

Ktutil

The ktutil program is a small utility program that allows administrators to manipulate keytab files. Ktutil is the recommended way to append keytabs to one another and delete entries from existing keytabs. The ktutil program requires no arguments, but will require enough privileges to read and write the appropriate keytabs. Typically, this means that you must run ktutil as root.

The Heimdal ktutil program operates differently from the MIT ktutil program. Heimdal ktutil is entirely command-line driven, and not interactive like MIT ktutil. The command-line option that is most commonly used is the `--keytab` or `-k` option, which specifies what keytab that the current command should operate on. By default, the ktutil command operates on the system keytab. It is located in */etc/krb5.keytab*.

list

```
list [--keys] [--timestamp]
```

The `list` command displays the principals whose keys are stored in the keytab. By default, the `list` command will dump the key version number, the encryption type, and the principal of each entry in the keytab.

Each of the optional arguments adds additional information to the keytab display. The `--timestamp` argument dumps the timestamp of when the key was added into the keytab, and the `--keys` argument dumps the hexadecimal encryption key itself.

Example

```
% ktutil --keytab=/tmp/one.key list --timestamp
Vno  Type        Principal          Date
   3 des-cbc-md5 jgarman@WEDGIE.ORG 2003-04-23
   5 des-cbc-md5 jgarman@WEDGIE.ORG 2003-04-23
```

add
Create key manually

```
add [-p principal] [-V kvno] [-e enctype] [-w password]
```

The `add` command adds an entry to the keytab manually. Any parameters not specified on the command line will be prompted for interactively. If no realm is specified with the principal name, the default realm is assumed. The remaining parameters specify the key version number and encryption type to be associated with this entry.

Example

Here's how to create a new keylist entry for the principal blah@WEDGIE.ORG with a key version number of 1, using a DES key derived from a password string:

```
% ktutil --keytab=/tmp/two.key add -p blah@WEDGIE.ORG -V 1 -e des-cbc-crc
Password:
Verifying password - Password:
```

remove
Delete entry from keytab

```
remove -p principal | -V kvno | -e enctype
```

The `remove` command removes an entry from the keytab. Entries to be removed can be specified by one or more of three parameters: the principal, the key version number, or the encryption type. At least one of these must be specified on the command line.

Example

```
% ktutil --keytab=/tmp/one.key remove -p jgarman@WEDGIE.ORG
```

get   Extract

get *principal*

The get command creates a keytab for a given service principal, and creates the principal if it doesn't already exist. A new key is generated for the given principal, and that key is placed both in the keytab and the Kerberos database. This command is most often used to create service keytabs.

Example

```
% ktutil --keytab=/tmp/one.key get host/kerberos.wedgie.org@WEDGIE.ORG
```

Windows Domain Controllers

Administering a Windows domain controller is dramatically different than the other KDCs that we've discussed here. MIT and Heimdal both have similar command line based administration tools, while Windows' administration tools are integrated into a the larger Microsoft Active Directory.

Behind the scenes, Active Directory uses an LDAP server as the data store for the Kerberos database. All of the user information as well as each principal's secret key are held inside the Active Directory Domain Controller's LDAP server. Microsoft provides graphical applications that can query and modify data contained within the LDAP server, and we'll examine these applications from a Kerberos-centric view. We won't cover Windows-specific features.

Typically, administrators administer Windows domain controllers through the Microsoft Management Console (MMC) interface. We discuss the necessary commands to perform the same tasks that we have covered for the Unix KDCs. Note that the administration protocol used by Windows is dramatically different from either MIT or Heimdal's kadmin protocols. It is not possible to administer a Windows domain controller through an MIT or Heimdal kadmin.

To access MMC, you must have domain administrator credentials. Login as the domain Administrator user (or another user that is a member of the Enterprise Administrators group). Go to Start → Run, and type mmc. This will bring up the Microsoft Management Console application. Choose Console → Add/Remove Snap In... and click Add. Choose Active Directory Users and Computers from the list, and click Add, then Close. Click OK to close the Add/Remove Snap In... dialog. Now you'll have a screen that looks similar to Figure A-1.

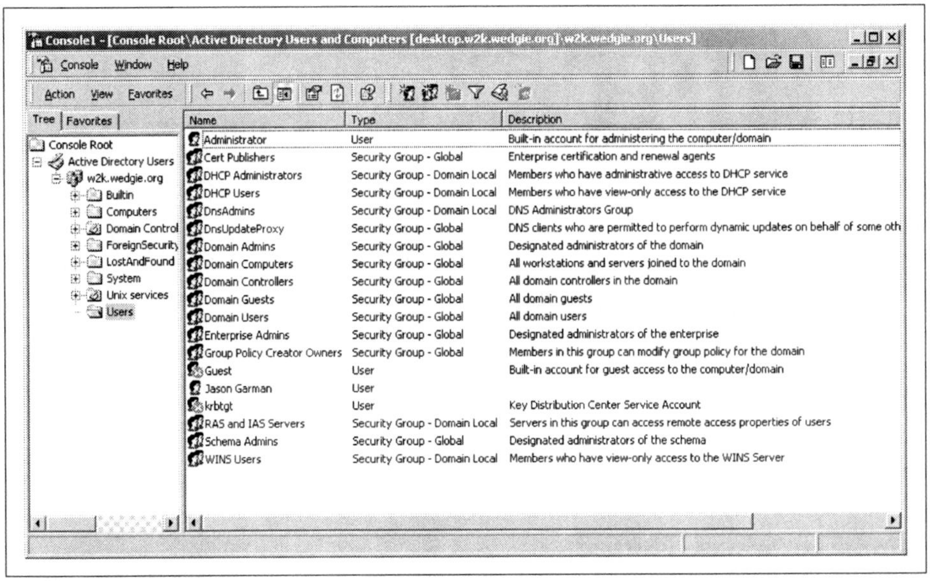

Figure A-1. Listing the users in an Active Directory domain

This window is the equivalent to listing the available principals in a Unix KDC. Every User object is mapped to a Kerberos principal, and any OU (Organizational Unit, represented as folders underneath the domain) can contain User objects. The username portion of the Kerberos principal is made up of the user logon name, which can be viewed in the Account tab of the object properties page. To access the properties of a particular object, double-click on it. The Account tab in the properties page is depicted in Figure A-2.

The properties page is equivalent to the get or getprinc commands in Unix KDC kadmin utilities. This properties page contains all of the relevant Kerberos-related information about the selected principal, as well as a lot of extraneous Windows-related properties that we won't worry about.

These two windows are the main interfaces that you'll use to administer your Windows domain controller.

Adding a principal

To add a principal into a Windows domain controller, simply right click on the OU that you wish the user to be a member of (for example, Users) and choose New → User. Windows will bring up a New User wizard, shown in Figure A-3.

The new principal for this user is shown as the User logon name text box. The pre-Windows 2000 logon name is only used for NTLM authentication and not for Kerberos, so it can be ignored. The next page asks for a password and has a few options regarding password expiration and account expiration. The last page is simply a

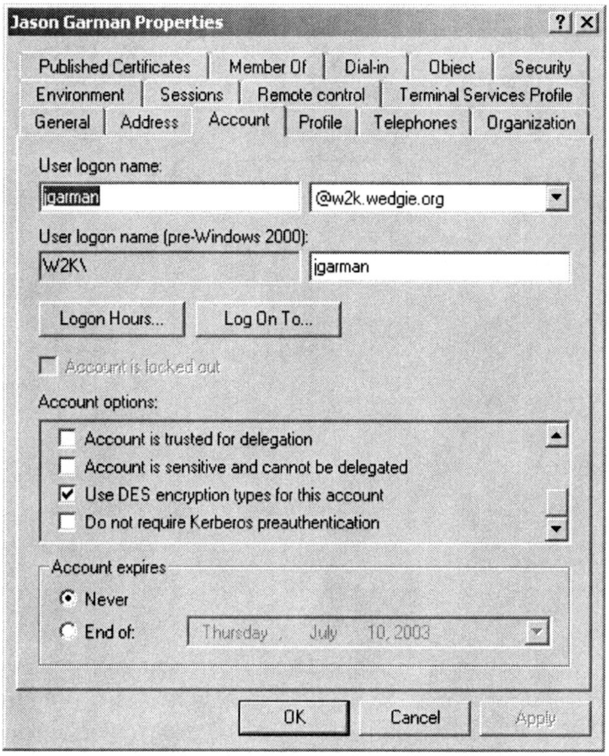

Figure A-2. Active Directory user properties dialog box

confirmation, and clicking Finish will commit the changes back to the Active Directory server.

There is one peculiarity to be aware of when using a Windows domain controller for Unix clients. The default encryption type for Kerberos keys stored in a Windows domain controller is RC4. Before you can use these principals from most Unix clients or application servers, you must modify the principal to use DES encryption keys. The process to do this is documented in the next section.

Modifying principal attributes

To modify a principal's attributes, right-click on the principal's entry in the Active Directory Users and Computers window, and select Properties. The dialog box will appear (Figure A-2). Select the Account tab. Near the bottom is a list of checkboxes with the title "Account Options." There are two options in particular to pay attention to. These options are the "Use DES encryption types for this account" option and the "Do not require Kerberos preauthentication" option. Both of these options are important for interoperability with Unix clients and application servers.

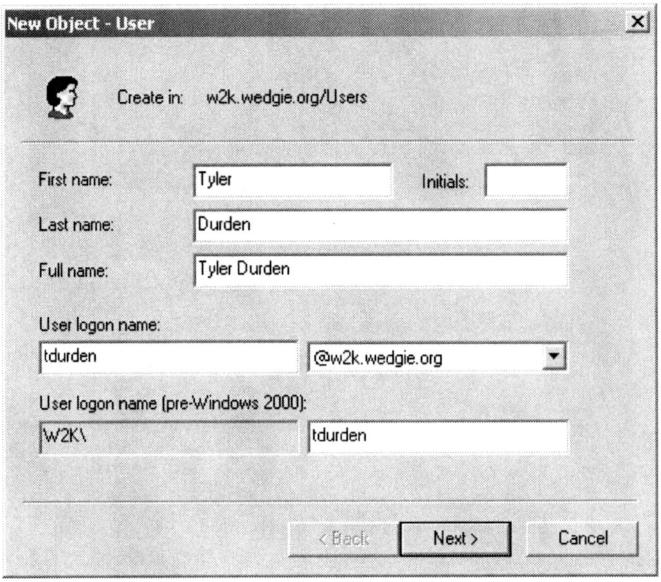

Figure A-3. Active Directory New User wizard

As discussed in the previous section, the default encryption type for new principals in Windows Active Directory is RC4. However, Unix clients only understand DES (and triple DES) keys. To successfully authenticate as a principal residing in a Windows domain controller from a Unix machine, you must check the "Use DES encryption types for this account" checkbox.

Windows domain controllers also differ from Unix KDCs in that they require clients to perform pre-authentication by default. Some older implementations of Kerberos 5 do not understand pre-authentication and so this option may have to be checked as well. More information on pre-authentication can be found in Chapter 6.

Here's one last snag that you'll run into if you're using a Windows domain controller with Unix-based application servers: you cannot directly create a principal that has an instance component. Therefore, service and host principals must be created with "fake" usernames, and a mapping established later between this username and the intended full principal. The process for performing this mapping is covered in Chapter 8, which discusses interoperability between Kerberos implementations.

Changing passwords

To change a principal's password through MMC, right-click on the principal's entry and choose Reset Password. A dialog box will appear asking for a new password and also gives an option to force the principal to change his password the next time he logs in.

Deleting principals

To delete a principal through MMC, right-click on the principal and click Delete.

Adding keys into keytabs

If you're adding service or host principals for Unix application servers, you'll need some way to extract a keytab from the Windows domain controller. Out of the box, Windows does not allow you to do this. However, Microsoft supplies a utility named ktpass in the Windows 2000 Resource Kit that creates a keytab for a given principal name and password. More information about ktpass and how to use it can be found in Chapter 8, which includes a discussion of interoperability scenarios between Windows- and Unix-based Kerberos implementations.

Configuration File Format

Both MIT and Heimdal use the same basic format for their text configuration file, *krb5.conf*. This file contains all of the information needed for the Kerberos libraries that are linked into Kerberos clients, servers, administrative utilities, and the KDC itself. Since this file is rather standardized between the major Kerberos implementations on Unix, a *krb5.conf* file generated for one can easily be used on another implementation, usually with no changes required.

While normally this configuration file is located in */etc*, an alternate location can be defined by setting the KRB5_CONFIG environment variable. Both MIT and Heimdal honor this environment variable. For example, in a Bourne shell, the following command would instruct further Kerberos applications to use the */etc/krb5.conf. backup* file as the Kerberos configuration file instead:

```
% export KRB5_CONFIG=/etc/krb5.conf.backup
```

The *krb5.conf* file is comprised of a number of key-value pairs, organized into groups, referred to as *stanzas*. Stanza names are enclosed in opening and closing brackets, and each key/value pair must belong to one stanza. Key/value pairs are separated by an equals sign, with the key name on the left and its associated value on the right of the equals sign. The value in a key/value pair can either be a single value, or it can be another set of key/value pairs, enclosed by braces. The most common example of this is in the realms stanza, where a key is defined for each realm, whose value is another set of key/value pairs defining the KDC and other important servers in that realm. That is, each key/value pair can take on of the two following forms:

```
key = value

keyWithSubkeys = {
    subkey1 = value
    subkey2 = value
};
```

A sample *krb5.conf* file is shown below:

```
[libdefaults]
        default_realm = SAMPLE.COM

[realms]
        SAMPLE.COM = {
                kdc = kerberos.sample.com:88
                kdc = kerberos-2.sample.com:88
                admin_server = kerberos.sample.com
        };

        W2K.SAMPLE.COM = {
                kdc = windows.sample.com:88
        };

[domain_realm]
        .sample.com = SAMPLE.COM
        sample.com = SAMPLE.COM
        testbox.sample.com = W2K.SAMPLE.COM
        windows.sample.com = W2K.SAMPLE.COM
```

This *krb5.conf* file defines three stanzas: libdefaults, realms, and domain_realm. These are the most common stanzas that are present in *krb5.conf* files and they represent the basic data that every Kerberos client and service needs to have in order to participate in the Kerberos protocol. The following six stanzas can be present in this file: libdefaults, appdefaults, realms, domain_realm, capaths, and logging. Additional stanzas may be defined by other implementations. We'll cover each of these stanzas in turn.

libdefaults

This stanza contains parameters relevant to the operation of the Kerberos library. The settings in this stanza apply globally to all of the Kerberos library functions for applications running on this host. Available settings in this stanza include:

default_realm

This is the most important setting in the *krb5.conf* file. The default_realm key defines the default realm that Kerberos clients and services will use. This should be set to the realm that this machine is a member of.

clockskew

The clockskew key defines the amount of time in seconds that the Kerberos library will allow two clocks to differ by and still consider the message valid. By default this setting is 300 seconds, or 5 minutes.

default_tkt_enctypes

This key defines the list of session key encryption types that the KDC will return to clients. This list can be separated by whitespace or commas. For example:

```
default_tkt_enctypes = des3-hmac-sha1 des-cbc-crc
```

default_tgs_enctypes

This key defines the list of session key encryption types requested by the Kerberos client libraries. This parameter takes the same type of options as the default_tkt_enctypes key above.

noaddresses

Setting this key to "yes" will cause the Kerberos library to request addressless tickets from the KDC. This option can be helpful when using NAT. More information on the affect of NAT on Kerberos can be found in the "Kerberos and NAT" section in Chapter 6.

appdefaults

The appdefaults stanza contains configuration parameters for individual Kerberized client and server applications. The Kerberos library includes functions to read parameters from this stanza, so some Kerberized applications may place Kerberos-specific configuration information into the *krb5.conf* file in the appdefaults stanza.

realms

The realms stanza contains parameters that are configurable on a per-realm basis. The most important configuration information contained in this stanza is the list of authoritative KDCs for each realm that this client will communicate with. Also, if settings in the global appdefaults stanza (described above) must be overridden for some Kerberos realms, key/value pairs that are valid for appdefaults may be placed in an appropriate realm entry in the realms stanza.

Each realm entry is comprised of a key whose name is a Kerberos realm. The value is a set of key/value pairs, which define the properties of that realm. The following settings can be found inside of a realm section:

kdc

Each kdc key defines one KDC in the realm. Multiple kdc directives can be listed when multiple KDCs are present in a realm. An optional port number can follow the domain name of the kdc in this directive, but as all Kerberos 5 implementations listen on the standardized Kerberos port, 88, this port number is not required.

admin_server

The admin_server key defines the Kerberos administrative server for this realm. This would typically be the master KDC for the realm, and is the server that clients will contact for services such as the kadmin service or password changing requests.

Note that the KDC configuration information may also be stored in DNS SRV records, as covered in Chapter 4.

domain_realm

This stanza defines the DNS domain name to Kerberos realm mappings used by the Kerberos libraries when performing service name canonicalization. When an application wishes to connect to a Kerberized server, it has to acquire a service ticket from the KDC. However, the client requires some method to determine what Kerberos realm, and consequently, what service principal, that it needs to request, and also what KDC to contact. Currently, the MIT and Heimdal distributions use the DNS domain name of the server, coupled with the domain_realm mapping, to determine what Kerberos realm that the server belongs to.

By default, if there is no domain_realm entry for a given hostname, a machine is assumed to be in the realm formed by the domain portion of the hostname, converted to all uppercase. For example, the server *bigserver.sample.com* would be assumed to be in the realm SAMPLE.COM. Note that this policy would place the server *sample.com* inside of a realm named COM, which probably isn't what you want.

The domain_realm stanza contains a list of key/value pairs, where the key is a DNS hostname or domain name, and the value is the associated Kerberos realm for that key. Domain-to-realm mappings for an entire DNS subdomain begin with a single dot (.) to signify that the realm mapping applies to any hosts inside of the given subdomain. Note that more specific entries override less specific ones. For example, given the domain_realm stanza given at the beginning of this section:

```
[domain_realm]
        .sample.com = SAMPLE.COM
        sample.com = SAMPLE.COM
        testbox.sample.com = W2K.SAMPLE.COM
        windows.sample.com = W2K.SAMPLE.COM
```

Two of the machines, *testbox.sample.com* and *windows.sample.com*, belong to the W2K.SAMPLE.COM Kerberos realm. All of the other hosts inside of the sample.com domain, including the host *sample.com* itself, are located in the SAMPLE.COM realm.

logging

This stanza defines the auditing parameters of both the Kerberos library and KDC. The contents of this stanza are covered in detail in Chapter 6.

capaths

The capaths stanza defines the certification paths that are used during cross-realm authentication to find the path authentication requests should take from one realm to another. Cross-realm authentication and the use of the capaths stanza are covered in Chapter 8.

Index

U

Unix
    KDCs, securing on, 117
    keytabs, creating from Windows domain
        controllers, 177
    partition table for hosts, 193
    security enhancement tools, 119
    security patches, sources of, 117
    Windows interoperability, 177–186
Unix clock synchronization, 52
user principal canonicalization, 215
usernames, 18
UTC (Universal Coordinated Time), 93

V

v5passwdd daemon, 61

W

Web Security, Privacy & Commerce
    book web site, xiv
Web services, 217
web-based authentication, 145–149
Windows
    Active Directory authorization field, 176
    cached login credentials, 175
        disabling, 176
    client authentication against
        non-Microsoft KDCs, 179–186
        standalone clients, 185
    clock synchronization, 52
    cross-realm trust, 180
    encryption algorithm support, 174
    Kerberos
        implementation issues, 173–177
        incompatibility, pre-Windows 2000
            systems, 180
        support in, 215

Kerberos implementations, 9
    ktpass program, 178
    supported salts, 174
    Unix interoperability, 177–186
    X11 Unix applications, accessing
        from, 160–164
Windows 2000 Hardening Guide, 121
Windows 2000, rotating logfile size,
    setting, 128
Windows domain controllers, 51, 73–77
    administration, 237–241
        adding keys into keytabs, 241
        adding principals, 238
        changing passwords, 240
        deleting principals, 241
        listing principals, 238
        modifying principal attributes, 239
    as KDCs for Unix clients, 177
    DNS service and, 76
    logging, 128
        interpretation of data, 134
    password lifetimes, setting, 116
    password strength-checking, 114
    pre-authentication, 110
    realms, creating, 73
    restricting login privileges, 120
    security concerns, 119
    Unix keytabs, creating from, 177
wkt command (MIT ktutil), 228
WRQ, Inc., 160
WS-Security specification, 217

X

Xerox Palo Alto Research Center, 24

Y

Young, Eric, 7
Yu, Tom, 54

About the Author

Jason Garman is currently working with computer forensics for the national defense and intelligence communities at Aegis Research Corporation. Previously, he worked at several biotech firms in the Washington, D.C. area, where he helped clients design and implement secure yet easy-to-use research networks. Jason enjoys working with the practical application of tools and techniques to solve computer and network security problems.

Colophon

Our look is the result of reader comments, our own experimentation, and feedback from distribution channels. Distinctive covers complement our distinctive approach to technical topics, breathing personality and life into potentially dry subjects.

The animal on the cover of *Kerberos: The Definitive Guide* is a barred owl (*Strix varia*). It is distinguished by the brown bar markings on its chest and the distinctive dark rings around its eyes. The barred owl generally resides in the woodlands of North America, making its nest in the cavity of trees. The female owl lays between two to four eggs, and the parents often remain with the young for more than four months, making them an exception among other types of owls. Barred owls stay with their chosen mate for life and tend to live about 20 years.

The barred owl eats mainly small mammals, such as mice, shrews, and squirrels. The barred owl will also eat birds, fish, frogs, and insects. These owls can grow to approximately 17 inches, with a wingspan of 44 inches. They are territorial in spring and fall, hooting at other owls to warn them against intruding. The barred owl's only natural predator is the Great Horned owl, but many deaths are attributed to human influence, such as shooting, car accident, or loss of habitat.

Colleen Gorman was the production editor and the copyeditor for *Kerberos: The Definitive Guide*. Mary Brady, Marlowe Shaeffer, Jane Ellin, and Mary Anne Weeks Mayo provided quality control. John Bickelhaupt wrote the index.

Ellie Volckhausen designed the cover of this book, based on a series design by Edie Freedman. The cover image is an engraving from *Heck's Pictorial Archive of Nature and Science*. Jessamyn Read produced the cover layout with QuarkXPress 4.1 using Adobe's ITC Garamond font.

David Futato designed the interior layout. This book was converted by Julie Hawks to FrameMaker 5.5.6 with a format conversion tool created by Erik Ray, Jason McIntosh, Neil Walls, and Mike Sierra that uses Perl and XML technologies. The text font is Linotype Birka; the heading font is Adobe Myriad Condensed; and the code font is LucasFont's TheSans Mono Condensed. The illustrations that appear in the book were produced by Robert Romano and Jessamyn Read using Macromedia FreeHand 9 and Adobe Photoshop 6. The tip and warning icons were drawn by Christopher Bing. This colophon was written by Colleen Gorman.

LaVergne, TN USA
10 February 2011
215976LV00003B/169/P

9 780596 004033